The Coach Trip

Jo Lyons

Happy Reading

Jo Lyons

Gekko Press

Copyright © 2023 by Jo Lyons

All rights reserved.

No portion of this book may be reproduced in any form without written permission from the publisher or author, except as permitted by U.K. copyright law.

ISBN: 978-1-7392220-2-4

Also by this author

Benidorm, actually

Your Place or Mine?

For Wez and Rob
"True Love Never Dies"

Chapter 1

Most people in this line of work like to start the day with an espresso, a growth in followers and a catty argument, not a full-scale, emergency team meeting. Today will be particularly hostile because I've been put in charge. It's a trial run for the promotion I have worked incredibly hard for all year. My team are fully aware, but as I sweep an apprehensive gaze around the boardroom, the air is thick with no one caring.

'Your sister is trolling you again, Nell,' Pippa announces, bustling in late while reading from her phone. 'She's tweeting about tragic on-again-slash-*mostly*-off-again relationships.'

Heebie-jeebies crawl up my spine because knowledge is power in the PR industry. Pippa pauses dramatically before taking her place beside me at the head of the table. 'She says waiting around for a man until your ovaries shrivel is not hashtag living your own truth.'

Suddenly, everyone is interested in Pippa's casual reference to my personal life and the state of my fallopian tubes.

'That doesn't mean she's talking about me,' I say.

Oh, but she is.
'And it's not a tragic relationship,' I add defensively.
I haven't seen him for three days. I have no idea where he is or what he's doing.
'You need to stand up to them both if you ask me,' she says loudly.
Pippa is right, but it's not that simple. My boyfriend, Dan, is focussing on work right now. We both are. The company is about to restructure, and we are determined to rise through the ranks. Whereas my younger sister, Ava, has a penchant for beginning the day with a mind game and I suspect today's *drama du jour* will have an unexpected twist because she knows, as well as hurtling towards thirty, today is the most important break of my career. And while I appreciate that she is one of these carefree, influencer types, who has thousands of followers hanging off her every word, it's the fact that she's also bat-shit crazy, wildly unpredictable and clearly out to ruin my life that is of considerable concern to me. She joined the company barely a year ago on a fast-track internship programme, and she's made sure we all know about it. Before I can explain, the boardroom door flies open.

'Nell, is it me, or does my vagina look a bit too *pronounced* in these trousers?'

I am aghast. Sometimes my sister forgets that we are at our place of work. Besides, she means her vulva. She'd be packing a bag for prison if she was flashing her vagina at us. Trust her to pick this moment. She clearly thinks nothing of bursting through the door while me and my team of highly trained social media strategists are all hard at it, discussing corporate affairs and the epic publicity disaster that has landed at our feet. The higher-ups have ordered us to fix it immediately. IMMEDIATELY!

Snapping to attention, I give Ava a withering glare and apologise to my team. I mean, they must be horrified. And while they are often mean and highly despicable creatures, they are extremely professional. I have never known them to entertain anything that is not work-related.

Alarmingly, they are now eyeing Ava's pubic bone with interest. I watch as she takes them all in and without batting an eyelid, she shifts her weight this way and that, their eyes following her hips, entranced. She even points to her vaginal area in case of any geographical doubt, encouraging them confidently, 'Tell me the truth now.'

She's deliberately not making eye contact with me. One of her many power plays to make me feel inferior. Well, not today she won't, not while I'm in command. We haven't a moment to lose, and the team will be looking for me to get rid of her quickly.

The loud, booming voice of our Creative Director, Lance, cuts through the pondering. 'You've a lovely pelvic girdle. Lovely.'

My jaw is about to hit the floor but apparently, he is not alone in his thinking.

'Not a hint of camel toe.'

'You're so blessed.'

'Very rotund nethers. Impressively so.'

Like I said, they are all highly professional.

'Ahem. If I could just focus our attention on the order of business,' I say.

We may work for the same company, but Ava is seven years younger than me, so she should be a bit more respectful. She rolls her eyes at me and tuts loudly. 'Okay, carry on, Nelly-Belly,' she barks as if she's in charge.

I receive a few pitiful stares from my team. They know full well what she is like. They've seen her prancing about. I'm relieved to see her twirl round and make for the door. I won't make a fuss. It'll be easier to let her *think* she's in charge. Then we can get on with running the company's PR Department and save a major embarrassment from happening. Just as Ava reaches out to take the door handle, she turns slowly.

'Oh yes,' she giggles, sweeping her gaze across us all in turn. 'I almost forgot.' She points to her brain and twirls her finger around. 'I'm your new boss! Hashtag effective immediately.' She spins on her delicate high heels, and as the door slams shut behind her, all eyes swoop towards me.

'She didn't tell you, did she?' says a delighted Lance. 'Ouch. How embarrasing for you.'

Shitting, shitting hell.

I spring up and cross the sprawling open-plan office. Who in their right mind would put my bonkers, selfish, thoughtless sister in charge of actual humans? This can't be right. I chase after her sashaying hips. Surely, it won't be true. She hasn't been at the company long enough for starters. I've been with the company *much* longer, and I've got an *actual* Business degree that I *actually* finished, unlike Ava who dropped out to go find herself in Thailand. No, this can't be right. She would have told me if she was going for the same job.

'Ava!' I hiss loudly. She picks up her pace while I scurry behind. 'Ava!' I say more forcefully, trying to keep my voice down. She comes to an abrupt halt right next to a group of handsome buggers who somehow gravitated towards each other like an area in a zoo dedicated to fine-looking, well-proportioned male species. Most of us find this section of the office too imposing to visit. Not so, my sister. She swirls dramatically round, her glorious blonde hair swishing like a theatre curtain, luring the eye of every single one of these striking men-specimens.

'Oh Nelly-Belly! I didn't see you there,' she lies smoothly.

'Can I have a word?' I say. 'And I've asked you *several* times not to call me that.' It's not even a nickname. She just made it up when she started working here to make out that we're close, which we aren't. She clearly does it to humiliate me. I feel my cheeks burn from just the thought of these menfellas watching.

Ava eventually lets out a tiresome sigh. 'Listen. I'm like managing over two hundred people across ten regional offices now.' She rolls her eyes as though this is the last bothersome thing she wants to do. 'So, I don't have time to stand about all day gossiping.' She sweeps her gaze flirtatiously across the menfellas, before raising a stern eyebrow.

'It's not gossip!' I declare with afront, although I hope to Christ that it *is* gossip. I really don't understand why Karen, our boss, would choose to promote Ava over literally anyone else, never mind me.

'Whatever!' she sighs, making me seem childish. 'Be quick, or else.'

I ignore this lightly veiled threat. 'Ava, I just wanted to ask if... how you... did you go for my promotion without telling me?'

'*Your* promotion?'

'But you knew I... I manifested it... I wrote it down on a...'

I watch open-mouthed as my sister cuts me off mid-sentence, turning sharply to teeter away down the office.

I race back to my team, who are all furiously tapping away on their phones and showing each other their screens.

'Yep, it's official,' Pippa confirms. 'Ava is the new Senior Buzz and Brand Warrior. It's all over the intranet and she's already posted it on her socials.'

I check Ava's Instagram. She's posted a selfie on her story. She's perched provocatively on her new desk, holding a bottle of prosecco to her lips and is about to suck it like a cucumber, with the caption #powerfulwomen #alwaysrecycle.

Oh Christ.

I wipe my forehead with the back of my hand as casually as I can with seven pairs of delighted eyes boring into me. The temperature in this room has suddenly increased by a thousand degrees. I can feel the heat prickling my face, my heartbeat thumping and a familiar twisting in my stomach. Did Ava just steal my promotion from under me? After all the favours I've done for her! But more gut-wrenching than that, why didn't Dan warn me? He's the assistant to the deputy CEO of the entire fecking company, and okay, we've kept our on/off relationship under wraps for almost two years but still... *what the fuck?*

'Okay, team, it is essential that we do *not* get distracted. We have only two hours to turn this PR disaster around,' I say, trying to keep the panic from my voice. 'So, if you could all please put your phones down. And focus.'

'Are you okay?' Lance asks. 'You're sweating like a heroin addict.'

Oh for eff's sake, why can't this god-awful team of toxic scavengers be nice to me just this once?

'I'm fine, thank you.' I take in his abnormally wide face and jutting, froggy eyes. He will undermine me at the first opportunity. I've never heard him say one nice thing in all the years I've known him.

'I don't have to remind you that Milly-May is the face of our biggest client and their bestselling men's grooming range ManUp,' I say, ignoring him. 'We *also* need to make it clear that *women* are better than this,' I remind them, our eyes fixed on the screen showing a photo of an angry but gorgeous, mammoth-haired woman pouting back at us.

Although they keep straight faces, I see doubt reflected in the men's eyes. We've all seen the footage of Milly-May, very recently single, celebrity lifestyle influencer and now staunch man-hater, Pornstar Martini in one hand, giving the finger with the other, while fuming about what considerable tosspot wankers men are. Smiling blandly to mask my discomfort, I clear my throat anxiously. 'We need to turn her views into positives.'

All those not in possession of a penis nod their heads understandingly. All those in possession, raise their eyebrows accusingly at me.

'OMG look what Ava's just posted!' yells Pippa, breaking the tension. She swipes up her phone to reveal a pic of Ava looking up into the camera with sad, sexy eyes and pouting lips. 'Why can't women be happy for other women? Sisterhood is power.' #saltysister #womensupportwomen #girlongirl #dontbeahater and she's tagged in Milly-May!

Animosity balloons from my team. Even Pippa, my trusted ally, is looking at me woefully. Probably because even though my baby sister is now my boss (because she has stolen my promotion from right under my nose and I am apparently the last to know), she has made me look like a right jealous cow.

'You've let Ava walk all over you, again. And on your birthday too. Yikes. Lunch is still on you though, yeah?' Pippa says to break the tension.

My eyes bulge with panic as a thick silence swallows the room. Even though I'm more than qualified, *over*qualified if anything, to handle a situation like this, my mind is a complete, terrifying blank.

'It wasn't like that,' I say weakly in my defence, to a group of disbelieving faces. 'You know what Ava is like. I'm sure it's just a joke. I'm happy for her. I am. I really am. I hope she does well.'

On reflection this sort of behaviour would be very typical, but I just can't quite believe that she would do this to me. It's brutal.

'Nell, you're too nice to be in charge of people. No one respects that. You need to stop people pleasing,' Pippa interrupts. 'You're not chocolate.' She is nodding to the team, and they are nodding back.

Oh my God. When was that ever a crime?

The atmosphere has turned rapidly uncomfortable. They need some strong leadership and guidance and unfortunately, I, the human equivalent of a soft-centred cherry cream, am still in charge until noon. So, they'll just have to wait.

Chapter 2

'So, any ideas on how to backtrack on these Milly-May tweets?' I say tensely, my lips shrivelling into a cat's bum. I mean if my sister is now our new boss, what hope have we got? What is the point in working late every evening and coming in early to show you really, really want to do well in the company if they go and throw a perfectly good promotion away on one's crackpot sister who never arrives early and spends the day hashtagging nonsense?

After a minute of torturous silence, watching my team rudely swipe away on their phones, the weight of these home truths makes something in me crumble. I think my one and only life goal may have rested on that promotion. I put all my eggs in one basket, and now they're being cracked open to make someone else a fluffy omelette.

'Ahem, what we need is some... some low-hanging fruit. If we... if we could just lift the bonnet on the engine,' I ramble. I've now got multiple sets of unimpressed eyes boring into me, ready to pounce and take me down. None of them have an ounce of respect for me, even after all of these years. The suggestion of getting all of our ducks in a row disintegrates on my tongue. 'No, what we need is a helicopter view of the situation. That's right, a helicopter view in order to square the circle... which is obviously the problem in this metaphor.'

My sister has well and truly shafted me and I didn't even see it coming. It hit me like a high-speed train.

The Creative Director drums his fingers on the table, snapping me back to attention. 'This is an awfully long run up. Even for you, Nell. What next? Getting our ducks in a row?'

He's right. I need to stop focussing on my sister and get my head in the game. I still have a job to do and a reputation to salvage.

I fire questions around the table. 'We have two reputations at stake. How can we turn this situation to an advantage, so that ManUp profit from this?'

Silence.

'How about we turn Milly-May's situation into a tale of resilience? Of a woman buying her own flowers and holding her own hand? Learning to love yourself is the greatest love of all vibes.'

It's as though I have turned on a switch. The whole team start talking at once.

Finally, we have managed to salvage the PR disaster with only minutes to spare. I am relieved to see they all look grudgingly respectful. It has been a veritable triumph in terms of teamwork, but the higher-up boss, Karen, doesn't exactly seem thrilled as she sweeps in and walks right up to me. 'Can I have a word?'

'Will it take long?' Pippa asks her.

Karen glares at me as though I'm somehow to blame for other employees talking to her.

'It's my birthday lunch,' I explain. 'They're expecting me to buy them drinks.'

'Can't the team manage without you for five minutes?' Karen says, turning to face them. 'Off you go. Nell can catch you up.'

The team watch me follow Karen to the lifts. When we reach her office, Karen says, 'Nell, darling.' Because apparently when you've reached this high a rung in the chain of command it's okay to be intimate and also because she's a woman it's not seen as patronising or over-familiar in any way. 'I hear you had a rough morning?'

'No. Everything went fine,' I explain. 'It wasn't easy, but we got Milly-May to post that perhaps if her boyfriend had worn her sponsors' ManUp products then he'd have manned-up enough to do the right thing in the first place. We reminded men that women don't really need them for much because we can do everything ourselves these days.'

Karen's lip curls encouragingly at one side, so I continue. 'She got four hundred thousand likes across all her social media platforms and the company got a spike in online pay per click sales by 200%. It was a good rescue.'

She looks at me quizzically. 'Listen, I'll get to the point. Ava said the rescue was all *her* idea. She reached out first to Milly-May. I saw the tweet myself.'

Feck! It's true, she did! 'No but, well, yes but...'

'It does put your team into question. What is the point

of it, if you can't do the one function you are paid to do?' Karen shifts her eyes from side to side then back to mine. 'And of course, one employee barely out of internship is much cheaper than a whole team. You understand.'

My jaw falls open as I take in what Karen is saying.

'I hear daily tales from Ava of bickering and hours wasted answering emails from your department, such as "Where is my elastic band?", "Have you seen my cup?" and my own personal favourite, "No, the other cup".' Karen makes a crazy face, laughing to herself as she pulls out reams of printed-out email messages, plonking them with a heavy thud in front of me. She allows me to cast a quick glance over them.

Shite.

An uncomfortable silence envelops the room as I scan page after page of evidence clearly pointing to mindless timewasting from our team. Ava must have hacked into my computer.

'And these updates from you to Pippa about Ryan Reynolds. I mean we all know how important celebrities are in times of global crisis and huge economic turbulence, but are these strictly necessary?' Karen slides me a printout of Ryan in the shower, soaping himself extravagantly. 'Well perhaps this one is, but you get my point.'

I hang my head in shame. 'So, you gave my promotion to Ava because she illegally copied private emails, took the credit for our big win today and because she will basically stop at nothing to get you more Instagram likes?'

'No. Of course not,' Karen reprimands, making me feel

very small for even thinking it. 'Well, yes, that *is* exactly why, but Eleanor, darling, we need people in charge who are charismatic and, you know...' Karen stops to look me rudely up and down. '... she'll be managing over two hundred people across ten regional offices. She's more assertive than you. She tells nearly a million followers exactly what to buy and how to live. Whereas you... now, what can you tell me about these emails?' she says, sitting back on her throne when I make no attempt to refute the evidence before me.

I push Ava's treachery to one side of my mind along with the insults and the conclusion that everyone thinks I'm dull as shit. Karen might have a tiny point. My team do tend to bicker a lot. This proof is very incriminating.

Karen continues in a serious tone, 'There's more. We've brought in a transformation expert. We're headed for a humungous shake-up. Only those keen to succeed will be kept on. It's what's best for the company that matters.'

I'm confused. I've sacrificed my entire social life *and* most weekends *and* most of my crappy relationships ALL so that I can be the one to manage over two hundred people across ten regional fecking offices.

'Anyway, must get on!' she chuckles, shaking her head as if this is all a huge joke and not the end of my career, before picking up her desk phone to indicate that our meeting is over. She waves me off. 'I'll leave you to update the team.'

'You want me... *me* to tell the team? Tell them we're potentially going to lose our jobs?'

Surely, she wouldn't do that to me. I'm too nice.

Karen frowns. 'No. That's not what I said.'

I let out a gusty sigh of relief.

'I need you to tell them that they are *definitely* going to lose their jobs.'

I leave the office in a confused daze. Not only will I NOT be getting a promotion, but I NEVER will. I zig-zag my way across to Ava's section, full of fury, only to find she isn't there.

'Ava's out celebrating with everyone,' comes a tired voice from behind a computer screen.

'Everyone?' I ask.

'You didn't get an invite either? Literally *everyone* got invited.'

As I sit staring at the empty desks around me, beads of sweat running down my back, I wonder how I'll break the news to the team. They'll be devastated. I message Dan, to see if his shoulder is available. I need it for a bit of a cry, some advice on how to confront my sister and to commiserate over an 'after work' gin cocktail or ten.

No reply.

Like me, he's probably working through lunch. I make my way up to the next floor to see him. I'm in search of reassurance. In fact, maybe it is time Dan and I moved in together. Maybe, we need to take our relationship to the next level and commit to each other. I'm twenty-nine years old. I should have my own sofa and matching curtains by now, instead of living with my parents and sister. I find his chair empty.

'He's gone out to lunch already.' I turn around to face Dan's assistant, reddening as he gives me a look that suggests something is up.

Oh Christ.

I'm determined not to become paranoid, but I'd be a fool not to even think that Dan might be out celebrating with my sister. 'Any idea *who* he went out to lunch with? On *my* birthday?'

He mumbles to his keyboard that he has no idea about that either. I check his Instagram to see that he is currently out enjoying gin cocktails on *MY* birthday. How nice for him. I peer closely at the selfie he has taken of his drink. His silhouette is reflected off the glass table. He looks like he has his arm around a woman, pulling her in close. Whoever it is, she has long hair just like my sister.

Men. Lying, cheating, good-for-nothing feckers.

An hour later, I hear the boisterous approach of my team piling out of the lift. Apparently, I have missed 'one hell of a birthday lunch'.

'How did it go with Karen?' Pippa asks.

The whole team look thrilled with themselves.

'The meeting was...' I pause as they all gather round me for the good news.

A disastrous minefield of professional failure on my part.

'It was... '

I need to tell them the truth.

'Was she over the moon?' asks Lance, the Creative Director. 'Are we all getting promoted?'

'Not quite,' I say, wondering how on Earth to explain that we could all lose our jobs and it may be Ryan Reynolds' fault.

'Look at this!' gasps Pippa, looking up from her computer. 'Everyone, check the intranet.'

The team disperses back to their desks as we are treated to a rundown of all the rumours flying around the company about people losing their jobs. If the atmosphere wasn't bad enough, then the URGENT AND CONFIDENTIAL email we all receive a few minutes later seals the deal. HR announce that the company has a new partner, the ICF, which is short for International Corporate Finance, and will be carrying out a transformation. There is a stampede towards me as soon as everyone has read the email. It would seem that because I missed the team lunch and am related to management, they assume I must be in on it. They snarl angrily at me and demand to know what is going on.

'Look, I'm sure everything will be fine. Let's not panic. Karen did say something about a shake-up but... it's probably just a precaution.'

I have suddenly gone to pieces in the face of conflict and pray that what I'm saying is true. No company would replace an entire team with one intern.

'Is this to do with Ava?' Pippa says angrily, looking about at the team.

Like a fish on a hook, I wonder how to get round the fact

that Ava has thrown us all under the bus. No matter what she's done or how I feel about it, she's my sister. I can't do it.

I am saved from telling them the whole truth as, a short while later, Karen emerges from the lift. 'I'm sure Nell has already told you, so this shouldn't be a surprise...' she says to us and ten minutes later, myself and the entire team, are out of work. We are all on Garden Leave hashtag effective immediately.

Chapter 3

I ring Dan to see what is going on, both on the work front and the cocktail front but I get no answer. Then I send him a message. He pings one straight back to say he's too busy to talk but he'll call me later. I tell him it's urgent and ask him to pick up, but he doesn't reply. I try to ring Ava, but her phone keeps going straight to voicemail.

How can this be happening? What on earth am I supposed to do now?

My own sister has plotted and schemed to put me out of work, alienated my work colleagues, for all I know is in cahoots with my boyfriend and has made it impossible for me to continue living at home under the same roof as her.

I am cast immediately into a pit of despair. The looks on the faces of my colleagues as we all packed up our desks at lightning speed; confused, upset, frightened, angry. Even if they are complete wankers, most of them have families to feed, mortgages and bills to pay. They all refused to look me in the eye or even say goodbye. I literally have no one to turn to. My phone pings with a message. It's from Ava.

'Nelly-Belly, don't take it personally, okay? I've posted up some inspirational quotes so retweet them, yeah?' Hashtag silver lining, hashtag look on the bright side.

Don't take it frigging personally? I mean WTF?

My phone pings again. Another message from Ava to remind me that as one door closes another door...

I immediately block her number from my phone. I need a plan. I need to get away from this house. I cannot bear the thought of Ava trying to act like she has done no wrong. In fact, she will act as though she has done me the mother of all favours and our parents will believe every word of it because she is perfect in their eyes and can do no wrong. I glance at the clock. She'll be walking through the doors in a few hours. My heart is thumping out of my chest and there's a ringing in my ears as blood rushes to my head. I massage away the tingle of sweat forming at the base of my neck. I need to act quickly.

Think, think.
Where can I go?
Who do I know?

I've spent the last six years being a workaholic so my very few friends are work colleagues and none of them want to speak to me. I put my head in my hands and search my brain for a quick fix that does not involve travelling to the Far East to find myself in some elephant sanctuary, although elephants seem such majestic creatures and could be a nice distraction. I did do my gap year in an animal rescue centre but it was bloody hard work. Perhaps a nice relaxing retreat is in order. I could stay there for twenty to thirty years until this embarrassing catastrophe has blown over.

I quickly flick to Milly-May's Instagram to see how she handles a good crisis. There's a picture of her looking radiant in what looks like a steaming hot spring, saying she has just arrived at the Centre for Massage in Iceland, and it's sorting her right out, hashtag new beginnings, hashtag over it, hashtag spiritual awakening. A thought occurs. There is a way out of this. A way that I can escape, just for a while, until I come up with a plan. I quickly ring my dad. He is enduring a day out at Ikea.

'Dad?' I say urgently.

'Yes, my love? Is everything alright? I'll put your mother on.'

'No, don't!'

I am the daughter of two very poor listeners. My mother is a controlling meddler, and my father favours weak parenting to keep the peace. I promptly burst into noisy sobs (his kryptonite) and blurt out what has happened. I can hear my mother trying to grapple the phone off him in the background.

In an unusual move, my father, sounding rather like he is defending a pro-wrestling title, confirms that I'm not to worry and that everything will turn out for the best. Then I run around the house searching for keys, my passport and some money. There is a flight leaving in two hours and come hell or high water, I am going to be on it. I yank my centuries-old, tatty suitcase out from under the bed, the handle coming easily away. Fortunately, I know where I can get a far newer one. She'll never miss it, and besides, if it weren't for her treachery, I wouldn't be packing my whole life up like this in the first place.

Somehow, and I'm truly not proud of myself – not by a long stretch – within minutes, I'm lugging a bitterly-full case back from my sister's room. I heave it up onto the bed and survey my new essentials; my sister's luxury face creams and her GHD Platinum straighteners. As I search for her Chanel sunglasses, I come across her collection of bikinis, flip flops and sarongs from her life-changing jaunt to Koh Phi Phi in search of her 'inner truth'. She'll not be needing them any time soon, not with her newly acquired, high-powered job of sacking people for a living. My phone pings to warn me that I have only five minutes before the taxi comes. Just enough time to fling in all of my bits and pieces; the sum total of my life so far and everything I'll ever need to start a new one, far from here and more importantly, far from Ava.

A minute and a half later and I am done. I survey the open case, satisfied that, in the interests of restoring balance, the passport and the handful of assorted knickers at least, are mine. And I'm confident that by the time I land in Spain, I will no longer be quite so livid... or light-fingered. One thing I know for certain, is that I AM NO LONGER A PEOPLE PLEASER. No matter what you do for them, they will only disappoint you and let you down. I've not even had so much as a single 'happy birthday' from any member of my family.

· ♥ · ♥ · ♥ · ♥ · ♥ ·

A whirlwind two-hour flight later, and everything suddenly feels real. As the cabin crew wave me off the plane and wish me good luck, I give them a brave smile. Apparently, the noise of the engines does not drown out a person's heaving sobs in the rear toilet cubicle, as much as I had assumed it would. The gentle knock on the toilet door was followed by a warm smile and four miniature bottles of vodka and doll-sized cans of Diet Coke for me to take back to my seat. I am now officially going to be living in Spain until I can come up with a plan. A plan that involves more than just running away, that is. I have booked myself into a spa retreat (the stress buster package) for three days before heading over to my family's holiday villa. Not only is it my favourite place in the whole world, but crucially, it is Ava and mother-free. We've hardly used it over the last few years due to my parents discovering booze cruises.

I can feel my heart hammering in my chest as I follow the crowd of passengers through to the terminal.

Deep breaths. What am I doing?

Deep breaths. Have I gone completely insane?

I am approaching thirty years old. I have no friends, no command of the language, no job. But I am not going to panic. I will stay at our family getaway and figure things out, right after this mini panic attack I appear to be having. My lungs are billowing from my chest like bagpipes.

'Are you okay?' asks a tall man with a strong Scottish

accent in the passport queue next to me.

Where to bloody start? My life is in a catastrophic mess of exponential proportions.

'Yes, of course,' I snap at him.

Some people are so incredibly nosy.

Deep breaths.

Deep breaths.

A wave of exhaustion envelops me as I struggle for air in the heat. My hand flies instinctively to my chest. I'm definitely going to have a heart attack and it will be all Ava's fault.

'I just thought you looked a bit –'

'No, I'm fine.' I say defensively, turning to see who this intrusive person is that's towering over me, and offering unsolicited opinions. 'If anything, you're the one who looks "*a bit*".'

I watch him physically regret ever having made the enquiry as he hastily turns to gaze in the opposite direction. Why do people think they have the right to interfere? He's seems about my age. He should put his airpods in and block out the world like normal people, but instead we are stuck awkwardly with each other in this, the world's slowest queue. He rakes a hand slowly through his dark hair, letting it fall messily back into place. He looks very tanned and is wearing a cool T-shirt that hugs his biceps, and shorts that fit him perfectly given his height. Maybe he is a paramedic. He certainly has the well-toned arms for it. And the long legs. And the stubbled chin. And the kind eyes.

'I just thought you looked a bit upset,' he says, catching

me eyeing him up and down. I stare blankly back.

Upset? Upset? Of course, I'm bloody upset, who wouldn't be with the day I've had?

His eyes are brimming with sympathy. He tilts his head to one side, inviting me to share my heavy burden. Suddenly, the pent-up fury of this afternoon explodes out of me in loud, gurgling, uncontrollable sobs. 'WHAAAA!' I howl, grabbing tightly onto him for balance. 'It's my sister. My back-stabbing, AWFUL BLOODY SIST... ER... ERRRR... EERRR.'

My wailing is attracting the attention of everyone in the vicinity while he stands rigid, taking a moment to process, scanning my face.

Christ but it's hot. I wheeze, unable to catch my breath.

We lock eyes for a fraction too long, and before I have a chance to explain that I've just endured an extremely harrowing day, he swivels his eyes past my head, across the arrivals lounge to bellow with the lungs of a drill sergeant, 'OVER HERE! BLOODY CYSTS! HELP! EMERGENCIA!'

Bloody cysts?

The crowd seem horrified that I'm about to explode all over their hand luggage and brand-new holiday espadrilles. It's enough to snap me out of it.

'I don't have bloody cysts! Who said anything about cysts?' I say, stepping away from him.

'*You* did. You said you had a bloody cyst. Has it burst? Where's the stabbing pain? In your back, did you say?'

The crowd cautiously move further away from us.

How humiliating.

'I said *sister*,' I tell him firmly, as though I'm consulting with my GP. 'Back-stabbing sister not CYST!'

He looks confused.

I'm going to have to spell it out. 'It's my bloody sister, she's the reason I'm so upset!'

'Oh.'

He sounds almost deflated at the lack of emergency. Unfortunately, the combination of embarrassing myself in front of this heroic man-mountain and the confusion on the faces surrounding us, acts as a tipping point.

I develop what I can only describe as sudden-onset 'persecution complex'.

I take a ginormous breath in, filling my lungs. 'SHE'S RUINED MY WHOLE FECKIN LIFE!' And although that feels good, I can tell that it'll be a very, very temporary release.

My nosy companion looks like he is about to have a triple heart attack as we hear heavy footfall.

Armed guards charge in our direction and immediately manhandle us out of the queue and over to a small, very official-looking room, to face a very severe, moustached police officer. He is not happy.

I look at my Good Samaritan. He is not happy either.

I burst into noisy tears.

Chapter 4

'Sorry!' I say repeatedly, wiping my tears with the back of my hand and blowing my nose with the box of tissues pushed in front of me. 'It's my birthday. I'm supposed to be hap... hap... happy.'

'Names!' the police officer shouts.

'Oliver,' blurts the nosy guy immediately.

They turn to look at me. 'Nell,' I sniff. 'As in short for Eleanor.'

Say what you like about the Spanish, but they take crying damsels in distress very seriously. He turns sharply to Oliver, 'Why have you upset your lady-woman? On her birthday?'

'I didn't know it was her birthday,' he explains, as the policeman offers me more tissues.

The policeman glares at him as though he's a prolific womaniser. He picks up a pen and reaches for a form to fill in.

'She's not my lady-woman, I mean my... I mean we're not together. Tell him I was just being polite. Tell him it's not me who upset you,' he says, turning to me horror-struck.

I stare blankly for a second while I experience an out-of-body encounter. I see myself hunched over the box of tissues, all damsel in distress, while these two men regard me as some suspicious package about to explode at any minute.

I shake my head sadly.

'He's right. He was just being nosy.'

Somehow, the police officer misconstrues this and tuts, causing Oliver to beg me to be a little clearer on the matter. I have a quick think about giving them the full lecture on my family politics. It might be good to get a military perspective.

'You see, it's my sister's fault. She takes everything that is mine.' I watch their jaws slacken as I sniff loudly a few more times, and settle back in the chair. 'She's always been the favourite child. A menopausal 'surprise' according to my parents.'

The word menopause has deeply unsettled them both but I continue with my harrowing narrative.

'She exploded into our lives like a pink, fluffy grenade and grew up expecting the world to be at her beck and call.' Childhood memories come flooding back of a mini despot wearing spotted wellies, a frown and a tutu, terrorising my every move. 'She gets everything she wants, even though it's me who is the nice one and runs around after them all. She's selfish and controlling and vain. Unbelievably vain. She has nearly a million followers. Look, I'll show you...' I dig around for my phone.

·♥·♥·♥·♥·♥·

Half an hour later and the Spanish have decided that they no longer think I am a threat to national security or well-intentioned males, and even though I've come clean about my deep disappointment in my family and of people in the workplace, they have seen fit to release me into the wild. Oliver could not get away from me fast enough. From the way he kept rudely sighing and checking his phone every two minutes, I'm not convinced he was paying full attention to my upsetting autobiography anyway.

I have a sharp word with myself as the heatwave encompasses me on leaving the cool airconditioned security office. I pick up my heavy case and lug it over to the bus stop to check when the next bus to Albir is due. I must get a grip. This is not the time to be having a colossal breakdown. I must stay positive, but the more I think about returning back home, facing my family and the endless scrolling for jobs, the longer it makes me want to stay away. The sun is shining, the early evening sky is an amazing cobalt blue. I feel calmer just looking at it. Maybe I should stay here. Permanently. Everyone is too busy to visit our holiday villa these days, so it seems a waste not to use it properly. Besides, what have I got to lose? There's literally nothing and no one to go back for.

I sit down at the bus stop and get straight onto Facebook to check what local groups there are and what jobs are going. If this is going to work, then the first thing I need is to replace the job I've just lost with a much better one. One that doesn't involve people this time.

Say what you like about Millennials, we may all still live at home with our parents but if there's one thing we are bloody brilliant at, it is stalking people on the internet and turning our hands to any, and I mean ANY, job going that will pay cash. Anything. Anything at all. I flick through the adverts. Unfortunately, it's very slim pickings jobs-wise. I could teach English for 2 hours a week. I could work in a restaurant or bar for 96 hours a week. I could sell mojitos on the beach for 140 hours a week. All involving too much people-contact for my liking. I see an urgent vacancy for a naked cleaner.

Stay positive. Think positive thoughts. Send positive vibes out into the universe.

Within minutes, I find the only thing remotely doable that seems like a step up. It's an advert for someone to join a coaching company. They are looking for a life coach who can help expand the business by guiding people to be the best versions of themselves, flexible hours. If there's one thing I'm an expert in, especially after today, it is not living your best life. I'd totally understand people who feel that life is passing them by. That they are only ever living their second best life. It might even be quite nice to listen to people moan about not achieving their goals. I might meet others who feel like a complete failure. I can tell them they are not alone and that people do hit rock bottom at times. I quickly search 'Life Coach' and get reading.

'Hello again.'

It's Oliver, looking awkwardly down at me. I scootch up the bench so he can sit down. Typical. I would never have told him intimate details of my personal goings-on if I'd thought I'd ever see him again.

'Feeling any better?'

'Yes, thanks,' I say politely, wondering why he's still bothering. 'Yourself?'

'Well, I could have done without getting detained for an hour and missing my lift, but you know,' he says, seeming a bit annoyed.

I immediately bristle. 'You'll have to take that up with the Spanish authorities.'

He shakes his head, looking away.

Once I'm on the bus and settled into my seat, which is only one row down from Oliver, I bring up the job advert on my phone. From what I've found out, I'd be perfect for it. You have to be a kind, compassionate and caring person. You have to be well-organised, have good listening skills and have lots of life experience. The downside is that I'm not quite ready to face people yet. But I'm sure after a few days at the retreat my anger towards the human race will have subsided enough to ensure I can function in the workplace.

I ring the number and ask to speak to someone called Nidi about this life coaching job.

'Hello, I mean hola,' I say, trying to sound friendly.

The receptionist speaks to me in rapid Spanish. *Gaaah!*

'I'm sorry. I was just saying 'hola' to be polite,' I say. 'I can't actually speak that much Spanish. Do you speak English?'

The receptionist starts hissing down the phone. 'Yes, of course,' she replies.

'Can I speak to Nidi about the job advert, please?'

'If you want,' she says abruptly. 'But she is busy saging the office. The moon is not quite right. She can feel it in her kidneys.'

I must have misheard. Maybe she is cooking dinner. 'What do you mean the moon isn't right?'

While the receptionist presses lots of buttons and mistakenly puts me on hold several times before hissing into the phone and mumbling something in Spanish that I can't understand, I take a quick look around to make sure no one is listening in. I'm surprised to make eye contact with several passengers dotted around me.

Everyone is listening in! Everyone. I glare at them as I swivel my eyes round the bus.

Oliver is the first to drop his gaze. He clears his throat and looks quickly away, out of the window. The others follow suit but I can feel their ears pricking up.

How embarrassing.

I slump down in my seat hoping that they can't hear. When I'm eventually put through to Nidi she asks me lots of pertinent questions and within minutes I feel as though I'm chatting to a friend.

'Nice to talk to you, Nell. How are you?' she asks.

A seething hot mess, fresh from being detained by the

armed police at the airport and trapped on a bus full of curtain twitchers.

'How long have you been in Spain for?'

Less than five minutes.

I hope she can't hear the beeping and rumble of buses around me as we leave the airport. She asks where I would be based, and it turns out our family villa is only a short twenty-minute walk from her office, down near the beach, so I cling to this as a clear sign it's meant to be.

'Do you have family here?' she asks.

You mean the people I grew up with who stabbed me in the back?

'No. No, I have no family. Just me. All... gone. Thank God,' I say.

I have no idea why that slipped out but they may as well be dead to me at this present moment in time.

There's an understandable hesitation while she makes soothing noises and offers commiserations.

I am a terrible person. Terrible.

I take the opportunity to check that no one is still listening in.

Gaaah! They are ALL fecking listening. They are craning their necks and their eyes are out on stalks. Except Oliver. He is staring hard out of the window. I shake my head disapprovingly at them.

'Would you say you were a people person?' Nidi asks.

'Yes,' I say forcefully. 'I'd say I was a people person, yes. I love people. Love them.' I scowl at the passengers still looking at me before crouching right down in my seat.

I need to get through this interview as quickly as I can.

Nidi continues with the Spanish Inquisition and, reeling from the humiliation of the redundancy, my meltdown at the airport, this bus load of nosy parkers, before I know it, out of desperation, I'm telling her everything she wants to hear.

'Fluent in Spanish? Yes, almost. Me llamo Nell,' I say letting out a nervous horsey laugh. 'Me gusta jugar al padel y me gusta hacer salchichas.'

Mystifying. I've never once played paddle tennis or made my own sausage.

'Am I qualified? Yes, yes, plenty of experience in events and PR, yes. Social media expert. Managing a team, no problemo.' I panic.

It all feels a bit surreal. Technically speaking, I *am* qualified; just not in life coaching. But I NEED this job. I NEED it so badly.

Thankfully, Nidi agrees to giving me a trial run and ends the call.

With shaking hands I switch off my phone and let out a sigh of relief. I desperately need something positive to cling to and this opportunity seems to be it. So what, if it is partly based on a lie? Loads of people 'embellish' the truth on their CVs. Actors saying they can horse ride. People saying they have done charity work and they like going to art galleries. It's almost expected these days. I'll just push it to the back of my mind and focus on reinventing myself. I can't go back and live at home anymore because my sister has stabbed me in the back. I can't throw myself into work because I no longer have a job, and I can't turn to my boyfriend for support because he's a complete wanker and is ghosting me.

Nonetheless, I am determined *not* to have a meltdown over any of it.

While the mountains and the twinkling Mediterranean give way to the sprawling, high-rise towers that signal Benidorm in the distance, I begin to plan my new life in Spain. As the bus pulls into the station, I am still trying to convince myself that I can totally do this. I will simply spend the next few days at the relaxing retreat, frantically studying the language and qualifying to be a life coach online.

'Good luck with the new job.'

I turn to see Oliver getting up out of his seat. 'Um, thanks,' I say, managing to raise a half smile for him.

'So, you're a life coach, are you?'

'Um, yes.'

'What kind of life coach exactly?' he asks casually as he takes his rucksack down from the overhead storage. *What did I say about him being unbelievably nosy? He must have some sort of condition.*

'The kind who likes to be left alone,' I snap, tiredness getting the better of me.

'Understood,' he says. 'I'm sure you'll be great at it.'

'Yeah, right. You literally just heard me lie my way through the interview.'

His eyes balloon at my confession.

'I had no choice if you must know. I've just been made redundant, remember? Stabbed in the back by my sister?

Who will now be managing over two hundred people across ten regional offices instead of me, which you'd know if you'd been listening properly.'

Silence. Plenty of it.

'Right-o. Right. Right. The redundancy. Yes. Terrible. Anyway, so... good luck again,' he says, sounding eager to escape. 'At least your new office is right near the beach, so that's something.'

He must have listened to the whole conversation; the nosy, nosy bastard.

I tut rudely at him. 'I have to say you do sound a bit stalkery,' I say unkindly. 'And not in a good way.'

His eyes nearly shoot out of his face. 'I'm so sorry. That wasn't my intention at all. I just meant... well, good luck again. I won't bother you any further,' he says, his cheeks blossoming a deep shade of pink.

We get off the bus, heave our cases out from underneath the hold, and take a moment to stare at each other, digesting the weirdness of our situation. I feel bad for being so incredibly mean to him. It's not like me. It's the day I've had. It's made me clinically bitchy.

'Sorry. That was rude. I'm just not in a good place right now. Good luck with whatever you will be doing.' *AKA minding your own business.* 'As long as it's not anywhere near me, obviously.' I meant it as a joke, but even to my ears it has come out wrong.

'You have my word,' he says stiffly, turning away to busy himself with his bags.

A hippy campervan pulls up and beeps rudely in our

faces. 'TAXI FOR WELLNESS SPA AND RETREAT!' screeches the driver from his window at everyone in the crowd jostling to retrieve their cases. Thank goodness, my escape vehicle has arrived.

'Here!' We both yell in unison before looking startled at each other.

The driver leaps out of his car, waving his piece of paper.

'Oleevair, yes? And Eeeleay... elly-nelly-ay-nor? Yes?'

'Eleanor. Nell, yes.'

I can't effing believe it. Oliver looks as rattled as me as we climb into the van. We sit next to each other as the driver throws our bags in after us, plonks himself down and yells over his shoulder, 'You late!'

We just have time to belt ourselves in, before we are thrown backwards as the van speeds off.

'What are the chances?' Oliver jokes to break the awkward silence. He is gripping the door handle tightly to avoid being thrown on top of me, as we take a bend at breakneck speed. 'How long are you staying at the retreat?'

'Three days,' I say, clinging onto the seat for dear life as the van hurtles through the town taking every corner at a 45° angle. 'You?'

'Same. I've booked The Happy Bunny package,' he says trying to straighten up. 'You?'

'The stress buster. The Platinum Triple Worry Plus package.'

'Ah, yes,' he says understandingly. 'Good choice.'

Patronising.

So, so patronising.

Chapter 5

Finally, the built-up surroundings melt away to reveal glorious mountain views and rustic landscapes, and the van slows to thirty miles above the speed limit. It would be lovely, mindful even, but I have to listen to Oliver bleating on for 30 minutes, thinking he is helping me with his persistent warnings about webs of lies getting out of hand and consequences and so on.

There's no need for this level of conversation. I am already embarrassed to my core about it all, the Olympic gold medal standard of rudeness I have displayed, and my overall panicky hot-mess exterior. Plus, he's taking up most of the back seat with his hugeness. Plus, the more I look at him, the more handsome he gets.

'Some say it's better to think with your eyes closed. It really focuses the mind. Otherwise, there's a tendency to drift,' he says.

The only things drifting are my eyes, from the trees that line the road to his incredibly good-looking face.

I am suddenly aware of how attracted I am to him. It causes a heat to rise from my neck.

'Being out of work can have a big impact on your self-esteem and sense of identity. If your job has always been a big part of your life, it can make you wonder who you are without it,' he says, tapping his hand on his knee. He has incredibly muscular legs. 'I'd say be kind to yourself during this difficult time. Use it as a chance to reflect on what makes you feel happy and fulfilled. To plot a course to the future. In fact–'

Of course, he'd have all the answers. The good-looking ones always do.

'Thanks, but that's kind of why I've booked this retreat. Time to think things through? By myself?' I glance down to see his beefy biceps are touching me, causing an unnecessary fluttering in my stomach. I shift away from him slightly.

He stares at me with a bemused expression. I take no notice of his slightly raised eyebrows and sit silently, staring out of the window, pretending to think things through instead of wondering whether he can sense the effect he is having on me.

I bolt out of the van as soon as we arrive at our destination.

'Here, I'll help you with your bags,' Oliver offers.

'No thanks.'

'Suit yourself,' he says, marching off slightly ahead of me to the reception. With any luck this place will be big enough to avoid bumping into him, while I am here figuring out how to become a convincing life coach, while also contemplating the rest of my life, while also getting to grips with the language, while also trying NOT to have a massive bloody stroke with the stress.

A serene-looking elderly gentleman in a white kaftan floats towards us, gently flicking his long grey hair over his shoulder. 'Velcome, velcome, velcome. Vee heff bin expecting you. Pleez follow me.'

We walk into the 1970's style orange and brown reception, drop our bags and bask in the cool waft of air from the huge ceiling fan as Gandalf The Grey (real name Starbeam Night Sky) pushes two shot glasses of green sludge into our hands. Oliver is deliberately not looking my way. Hopefully, our rooms will be at opposite ends of the complex.

'Leave begs. Begs vee take to vooms 10 und 11,' he instructs before he misconstrues my disappointed expression, and his eyes widen. 'Ah, I no realise you couple! You vant same voom?' He looks Oliver appreciatively up and down. 'Big, big bed, yah?'

'NO!' I blurt out at the same time Oliver says, 'Absolutely not!'

Which to me is a fraction too forceful and rude sounding, if entirely honest. It causes me to childishly glare at him and add, 'Never in a million years!'

After a moment's hesitation, Gandalf chooses to ignore our vehement outburst. 'Drink these. Vee start in ten minoots. You refresh in vooms. Then you come to Serenity Fountain for evening induction,' he says, swinging his arm towards the hotel gardens before floating off. 'Come. I show you fountain.'

I slide my eyes over to Oliver. 'Well,' I say, raising the shot glass, 'Up yours?' and knock it back.

Oliver stares at me, runs his hand through his thick, glossy hair and suddenly bursts out laughing. It transforms his face. His eyes are twinkling, his teeth are perfect and somehow he's even better looking. The first thing I'll insist on is a room change as far away as possible from this distracting beefy-armed giant.

We follow Gandalf out through some patio doors to a delightful terrace, dotted with tables and chairs, white parasols and twinkling lights perfect for fine dining and sipping cocktails under the starry sky. A vision pops immediately into my head of what needs to happen tonight. A luxurious bath. An exquisite, celebratory five-course meal for my birthday. And a crate of delicious wine. Perfect.

While Oliver follows Gandalf to the gardens, I dash back to reception to make sure they change my room. I'm dismayed to see Gandalf has teleported himself, via dark arcane magics, back to behind the reception desk.

'It's very important that I am not anywhere near the man I came in with,' I stress as quietly as I can.

Gandalf smiles serenely at me and hands me an old-fashioned, heavy, brass key from the 1800's. There's a tag hanging from it. It has the number 10 written on it.

'No, you don't understand,' I say out of the side of my mouth. 'I need to be away from...'

'Problem?' Oliver asks, coming up behind me.

Typical. I let out an exasperated sigh, 'No. No problem.'

I watch Gandalf hand him a similar key with the number 11 on it. He smiles at Oliver, saying, 'Vee place good energies in your vooms.'

He turns to me and declares that they have placed many, many calming crystals in mine. 'To combat your frazzled mind und... how you say? Your difficult nature, yah?'

Difficult? This morning I was *too* nice. Now, apparently, I'm *too* difficult.

Oliver is visibly trying not to smirk. 'Don't worry, I will keep a respectful distance.'

'Good. Make sure that you do.'

Why? Why am I being so rude?

· ♥ · ♥ · ♥ · ♥ · ♥ ·

'Velcome, velcome,' says Gandalf ten minutes later, sweeping his arm over the grass to encourage Oliver and I to sit on it.

Oliver walks to the furthest point away from me and settles himself down. He's still got an annoyingly bemused look on his face. It gives me a chance to study him a bit further. He seems very relaxed and sure of himself. His long, tanned legs are sprawled on the grass, while he leans back on his toned biceps. They're like small watermelons bursting to be free.

I run my eyes the length of him and take in the whole effect. He has an incredibly taut stomach. I linger over it a while wondering how on Earth a person gets a body like that. I rake my eyes up towards his profile, just in time to see him watching me with a perplexed expression.

Shite.

I tear my eyes from his to concentrate on the horrors that Gandalf is telling us. I'm appalled to discover we will be wifi and phones free – apparently this is a thing at retreats.

What thing? Why?

How the hell am I going to qualify as a Life Coach in the next 72 hours without the internet? How am I to miraculously wake up speaking Spanish like a native without the aid of one of those learn while you sleep dua-lingua apps? I feel my heart rate almost explode. I begin arguing bitterly with Gandalf, but he fails to see the emergency.

'Fine,' I say, masking how upset I am. I battle as to how honest to be with him. This is an emergency situation after all. 'But I'll need to use it in my room because... there's something that... I'll pay extra. I *need* wifi in my room, okay?'

Gandalf looks sceptical.

'Surely we get some downtime? To do what we want? Alone?' I plead.

Some luxury bloody retreat this is turning out to be.

There is a brief questioning silence hanging in the air while the entire group turn, too interested as to what I'm about to say next, but I'm beaten to it by Gandalf.

'Vee encourage self-love, of course vee do,' he says, 'but without the intervebs, yah?'

Self love? This barmy oddball thinks that while I'm in the middle of a substantial breakdown, the thing I'd focus on would be rubbing myself raw to whatever I can find on the dark web?

'No. No. No. You've got it all wrong,' I say forcefully. I've just about had enough of people for one day. 'I don't need the internet for… ' The entire group is staring at me. *Why am I bothering?* 'I've got better things to do than… look, I need the wifi for something really urgent. It's work-related.'

'Vee are one heart. One tribe. One Earth,' he says doing a heart shape with his hands as though it is somehow relevant.

Before I can clarify, Gandalf hands over to a similarly dressed white warlock with flowing Jesus waves, a pointed grey goatee and a handlebar moustache, called Endless Cloud. I stare mesmerised at his multi-coloured rubber foot gloves. He smiles beatifically and gives us a little bow as he says, 'Namaste', before putting a shushing finger gently to his lips (to halt the childish sniggers from the group) and turns to give me a waggle of his woolly eyebrows.

Dear God Almighty.

There are a dozen or so of us in the group. Endless Cloud gathers us around him so that we are sitting in a shamanican circle. We are told that we each have an individual itinerary for our stay as he hands round an information pack to each of us, plus some mandatory group activities that we all must do; spirit dance, tribal drums, third eye healing techniques, New Moon incantations, gong therapy, throat singing, charcoal nibbling and so on.

'Your wibe is your tribe,' he repeats to each of us in turn.

'Vibe,' I say as he bends low to hand me the itinerary. I'm still annoyed over the lack of wifi and feeling petty. 'It's vibe, not wibe.'

He smiles and floats away as though I hadn't said a word.

I scan the leaflet only to be dealt a further devastating blow – no sugar, no wheat, no dairy, NO ALCOHOL. Even Oliver appears alarmed at this. No meat, no caffeine, no gluten, NO SPEAKING for certain periods of time. We have slots when we are allowed to speak. SLOTS!!!

What the feck have I done? This is cruel torture. And I'll be far, far worse off for not having a drink tonight after the day of shit I've had. There's no way I'm putting up with that. What about the fine dining and the excessive wine intake? It's my birthday for God's sakes.

'Excuse me again,' I say, interrupting Endless Cloud. 'It says here no alcohol? That doesn't include wine, does it? I assume you mean no liqueurs or spirits?' I ask, my voice almost a whimper. This time the whole group is nodding hopefully along with me. Oliver gives me an enthusiastic thumbs up.

Gandalf jumps in to answer. 'Elly-nellyeor, alcohol no eez necessary for your alone activity.'

Jesus Christ, he still thinks I've only come here to get pissed and flick myself off.

'It's not for that. I just...' I say, tailing off. I feel the fight draining from me. I'm exhausted.

What to say? I need an industrial-sized glass of wine to combat the fact that I have critical levels of toxic bitterness seeping through my veins? I feel out-of-control anger towards my sister and ex-boyfriend whenever I think of them? And I just told a multitude of fibs to get a job that I desperately need and now won't be able to do because there's no bloody wifi?

I can feel my lip wobble. 'It's my birthday today.'

Gandalf closes his eyes and arranges his fingers to make a peace sign. After a few moments it is clear that he may stay frozen this way for some time.

Pointless. Utterly pointless.

I receive a few half-hearted birthday congratulations, but the alcohol-free bombshell has sapped the joy from us all.

'I'll see if they can organise a birthday cake for you,' Oliver says quietly to me. The sudden kindness brings a lump to my throat.

'When is dinner?' Oliver asks Gandalf.

Gandalf's eyes spring open, quick to answer. 'Hunger is a state of mind.'

'Well, no, it clearly isn't,' Oliver says impatiently. 'We missed the evening meal because we were delayed by...' He looks over his shoulder at me and I wait for him to blame me for the airport mix-up with the police. '... by an incident at the airport. We'll both need to eat.'

Thank God, I'm starving.

'Eez good you fast. No food. Just sleep. Autophagy will reset entire immune system,' Gandalf says with a smile as though this is good news.

Oliver's jaw drops open. I look him up and down again. He probably needs to eat his body weight in protein every day to maintain that kind of physique.

Endless Cloud sweeps forward to wish everyone a good night. He throws what looks like crushed lavender pot pouri at us from a small basket in his hand. Most of it seems to land in my hair. 'May your spirits be at one with your souls. Rest and be at peace.'

This day keeps on getting worse and worse. I march away from him towards my room. I poke the heavy key into the lock and push open the large ornate door with a loud creak. As promised, the room is so ablaze with the glare of crystals reflecting from every surface that I hardly know where to look.

I'm so ridiculously tired and hungry, I fall face first into the big soft bed, relieved it's not a straw mattress on the floor.

'Happy birthday,' I whisper to myself, and within seconds I am out like a light.

Chapter 6

What seems like a few hours later, I'm woken by a God-awful clanging. My eyes spring open, trying to make sense of the pitch black. I hear a scurrying noise outside and fly to my balcony.

'Fire! Where's the fire?' I hear someone yelling to my right. I can just about make out a huge shape on the balcony next to mine.

'Oliver? Is that you?'

'Nell?' he yells back, sounding panicked. 'What's the ringing? I smell smoke. Is there a forest fire?'

Like I should know?

'Would I be standing talking to you if the whole place was burning down?' I say. I can hear the stroppy tone, and I'm not loving it, but before Oliver can say anything, we hear a wailing sound.

Oliver gasps, I can just make out his hands flying to his face like that painting The Scream. 'It must have spread to the retreat. Quick, Nell, grab your essentials and get out of there. We need to evacuate. NOW!'

He really isn't great in a crisis situation but he is thought-

ful, I'll give him that.

'Now?' All I can think of is that apart from Ava's GHDs and Chanel sunglasses, I haven't anything worth saving.

'Yes. Over there, look!' He points to the source of light being thrown across the retreat towards us. He's right, there is a strange orange glow rising from the far side of the retreat.

I turn to Oliver. He's standing on the balcony next to mine, a few feet away but there's something not quite right about this situation. In the panic, my eyes adjust to the darkness. No, that can't be right.

'Are you naked?' I squeak.

What is wrong with him?

'I didn't have time to find my robe,' he says. 'Besides, I hardly think it matters when it's a life or death situation.'

'Well, could you at least cover up before we run screaming for our lives?'

He gives me a disbelieving look.

'Well, could you at least stop staring at my genitals while you talk to me?' he says sharply.

Gaaaah!

'Well.... erm, could you stop... being so sensitive?'

This tit-for-tat sounds incredibly infantile when so many people are burning to death around us. Suddenly, the clanging stops and the wailing increases.

Oliver shushes me.

He's so rude. And still incredibly naked.

'Listen, do you hear that?'

I'm not sure I want to hear people dying of smoke inhalation and horrific burns. 'Shouldn't we be running for our lives?' I say, baffled as to why I can't seem to drag my eyes away from his magnificent torso. 'I mean... trying to save them. Shouldn't we be trying to save them?'

'Wait... the smoke on the wind, it's no wild fire.' He sniffs the air and lets out a huge, exasperated sigh. 'It smells of patchouli.'

He's right it does. I'm getting a distinct whiff of wild garlic too.

'Look.' Oliver points to the orange glow. 'It looks like some sort of bonfire.'

I stare at the distant shimmer. 'But what's that awful sound? Why are people in pain?'

We listen to the wailing.

'For fuck's sake,' he swears furiously. 'Of course. It was on the itinerary. It's some sort of pagan ritual involving a cauldron. Oh, and the wearing of owl masks.'

'Masks?' Now it just sounds creepy.

'An optional extra for the Happy Bunny Deluxe package,' Oliver explains. 'Jesus. What have they sent me to?'

My heartbeat slows down at the news there will be no imminent burning to death. I half laugh to myself. 'What sort of bonkers... wait, you were *sent* here? Why? Are you being punished?'

Oliver cups his hands over his bollocks to hide his very large penis. 'Really? You want to chit-chat about work right now?' he says rudely, stomping back into his room.

Interesting.

·♥·♥·♥·♥·♥·

I change into the robe hanging on the back of my door and survey myself in the ridiculously large mirror dominating the bedroom. I glare at the loose smock and unflattering drawstring baggy pants and hope I haven't just joined a cult by mistake. I grab the induction pack and remove my itinerary. Thankfully, the first morning activity after breakfast for me is a detox massage, which sounds relaxing and exactly what I need.

Just then, there's a knock at my door and a muffled sound. Oliver and I open our doors at the same time and lock eyes. I see his gaze travel the length of my body before he stares angrily at my feet.

Oh Christ, he's not looking at my toes.

'What's this?' I ask, bending to retrieve the stick and tiny pile of nuts from the napkin on the floor.

'Breakfast,' he says glumly before scooping it up and slamming his door shut. I take the stick inside and stuff the nuts down my throat. I scour the itinerary. Breakfast day one: liquorice root, chew slowly to lower blood pressure and to eliminate angry toxins.

I. AM. FECKING. FURIOUS.

There's movement outside my room. Someone is going to get it. I am boiling with rage. I yank open the door to see Gandalf standing outside Oliver's door with a huge platter of fruit and a mouth-watering array of bite-sized, baked goods. Oliver answers the door in much the same way I did. He looks down at the platter, back up to Gandalf and breaks into a huge grin.

'For me?'

'Yes. Apologies. Zee Heppy Bunny Peckage. Eez for you.'

I watch them bow to each other before Gandalf turns to me, smiling. 'Enjoy your stick.'

· ♥ · ♥ · ♥ · ♥ · ♥ ·

'You have a lot of resentment in your lower abdomen,' my bossy masseuse accuses, twenty minutes later, prodding my stomach forcefully. 'It's causing a gassy build-up. Let me see if I can release the pressure.'

How can this be true? How? All I've eaten is a stick.

'NO! Do not release any –' but it's too late. I am mortified. Thank God we are in a hut type of place that is mainly open to the elements and nestled on the edge of the forest, far from the main camp. There's a roof, two beds and an awful lot of bowls containing foul-smelling oils.

Time seems to stand still while she bends me this way and that, releasing flumes of trapped gas from places you'd never guess held any. She cracks bones as she goes, tut-tutting about how tight and inflexible I am.

'You are the shape of a chair. Your bones are literally welded into the shape of a seat. When will you people realise there's more to life than working? You must bend each day or you will break. Motion is lotion.'

As if it isn't quite humiliating enough, ten minutes later Oliver comes in and lies down on the table next to me. This can't be right. I very definitely told him NOT to follow me around. He half-smiles at me and signals to a sign in his hand. It says, 'I am observing a spiritual silence'.

Thank goodness for small mercies I suppose.

I turn my head away from him and pray that my masseuse won't be trying to locate any stubborn pockets of gassy build up in front of him.

I listen to Oliver's masseuse making soothing noises, practically cooing at him. It's such an obvious attempt at seduction, I'm almost embarrassed for her. Oliver is having a very limiting effect on her vocabulary.

'Amazing. What amazing energy you have. Do you work out? You're in amazing shape. Simply amazing.'

By stark contrast, my masseuse sighs loudly. 'See? The bloating has massively gone down, but I have to say you're as hard as rock. And you have such terrible energies.'

I find myself apologising more than once as she digs around in my internal organs. Then with unexpected force, she flips me over and gets to work, pummelling the life out of my back.

Pummel, pummel, grind, grind.

Pointy knuckles are stabbing into my knotty back. I'm writhing in agony against the backdrop of gentle yoga music and Oliver's contented sighs, and repeated thumbs up for his masseuse, who we learn is called Charmagne because her mother was such a great lover.

Really, this is too much. Why don't they get a room?

'A lover of fine wines!' she giggles. 'Chardonnay and champagne! So I'm Charmagne!'

Oliver catches my eye and is trying not to snigger. He looks pretty content to me. *I mean who wouldn't?* He's having his head cradled by Charmagne, her breasts are all but in his face, and she's flirting up a storm. While I'm over here, being battered like a fish.

· ♥ · ♥ · ♥ · ♥ · ♥ ·

When the whole ordeal is over, I am shepherded over to an enthusiastic-looking group of people who tell me that we are going to be spending the next five hours staring at a pebble. Maybe it is because I am weak with hunger, filled with despair, and every bone in my body now aches, that when faced with this news, my entire soul splinters. I drop to the ground, head in hands like a professional footballer missing the winning penalty of the World Cup.

How long have I been here? What am I doing? What is the point of it all? When did my life choices take me down such a bewildering path?

Endless Cloud comes over to wave a crystal in my face. I watch mesmerised as he swishes it this way and that, an inch from my nose.

'Shanti, shanti, shanti,' he coos. His hand lands with a heavy thump on my shoulder jolting me from the hypnotic trance. 'Feeling better, yah?'

I look from the crystal up to his woolly eyebrows and burst into tears. He is quick to envelop me in a bony cuddle that is so uncomfortable my tears immediately stop.

· ♥ · ♥ · ♥ · ♥ · ♥ ·

When, what seems like the four years we have spent pebble gazing, finally comes to an end, we learn dinner is to be orthodox, earth-friendly and vegan. It is to be cooked as a group with whatever we can collect from the next activity, which is 'Forest Bathing'.

'Vee will experience Shinrin-yoku. Our tree friends are waiting for us, yah?'

I let out a disappointed sigh. 'Christ, why can't we eat here and go to bed? I'm shattered,' I say to equally tired faces around me. Who knew that staring at a pebble would be so utterly draining?

Gandalf smiles at us and floats away.

Essentially, we are embarking on a moonlit hike into the forest and up a great bloody mountain to enjoy hugging thousand-year old trees and the like, and to forage for nuts, fruits and wild mushrooms. This simply isn't on. I'm starving hungry and clearly not a squirrel. I look around for Gandalf to voice my many complaints. He glides over as if anticipating my grievance and thrusts a sign into my hands just as we are about to set off.

Oh great. It's my turn for silence.

I hear Oliver chatting animatedly with the other group members as we set off. He is asking them questions about themselves and they are keen to tell him their whole life stories. He really is a nosy bugger. He looks the picture of good health and immensely relaxed. His skin is glowing whereas I feel like a shrivelled crone in comparison.

· ♥ · ♥ · ♥ · ♥ · ♥ ·

A surprisingly short while later, we have feasted on a BBQ of dried, shrivelled forest floor remnants that even a starving hamster would turn its nose up at, and we've thanked the trees by way of dry humping them. My stomach is so empty that I feel light-headed and as I look around the group and the natural surroundings, it all feels other-worldly. Bizarrely, as we make our way back to the retreat, I realise, due to the sheer physical exhaustion of it, I haven't thought about Dan or my sister or their betrayal once.

Gandalf takes the sign back from me with a knowing flick of his long locks. I have no words to say to him. I wouldn't know where to begin anyway.

'Shanti,' he whispers.

Fuck off, I want to whisper back.

But I don't. I'm too well-mannered and tired. I dig out the huge metal key from my pocket and return abruptly to my room. After a relaxing candle-lit bath, scented with calm-inducing aromatherapy oils, I wrap myself in Spain's tiniest towel and wander out on to the balcony to gaze at the starry night, glistening up in the sky. I contemplate what I'm going to do with my life and whether a Lottery win is my only credible option at this juncture, when a movement to my right causes me to jump. It's Oliver, doing the same, stretching almost naked thanks to his own tiny towel, on the next balcony along. At least he's covering up this time.

His lean torso does something funny to my pelvis, there's a definite twanging sensation, and as he rakes a hand sensually through his hair and turns in slow motion towards me, we experience an awkward moment as he catches me peeking at him. Blatantly sexualising him if you will. I watch a smile spread over his face.

Shitting hell.

I scamper back inside and leap into bed. I hear him sliding his balcony door closed and let out a breath I didn't realise I was holding.

Think about sleep.
Think about breathing.
Do not think about that thigh.
That solid thigh poking out from the gap in the towel.
Clear your mind, Nell. You can do this.

A feeling of calm and quiet that I haven't felt for quite some time, possibly even years, washes over me. I breathe in the scent of the huge bunches of lavender arranged around the bed next to the crystals and drift off into a deep sleep.

Chapter 7

The next day before sunrise, we are all woken for some Vinyasa Flow yoga by the familiar wailing and dinging of a gong. According to our notes, when we hear this, we must silently rise, don our robes and make our way along to the Serenity Fountain for some 'Dawn Bathing'. We will become one with our bodies before we present ourselves to the day.

'Deep breaths. Hold for three... four, five and... gently release into Lion's breath,' Endless Cloud is whispering to the already assembled group who appear to be standing on one leg, the other bent at the knee, arms above their heads. I slip into the group unnoticed under the cover of darkness. Or I would have done if it wasn't for my terrible balance. As the group embark on a series of stretches, legs akimbo leaning forward to grab the toes, Endless Cloud wafts over to lean on my back with a pointy elbow to get me closer to my feet. Unfortunately, it is starting to get light, and it feels like I'm being mounted by a ghost with cobwebby hair and saucepan eyes.

Next, a Cow Pose on all fours. This time I'm left to my

own devices but I'm acutely aware that my bottom is within sniffing distance of Oliver who, the dawn light reveals, is immediately behind me.

Typical.

I can't help feeling self-conscious and after a series of embarrassing positions, with me far too stiff to do them, I slide my eyes over to see Oliver very comfortably assuming the Half Moon. Endless Cloud is keen to administer praise and openly flirts with him. Whereas I am impatiently sighed at every two minutes for getting everything catastrophically wrong. Endless Cloud pairs me with Oliver to see if I can fare any better.

Mortifying.

He instructs Oliver to put his knees into my back, pulling at my arms to open up my chest. He warns the group against the evils of pent-up bitterness and points directly at me.

Thankfully the group are all trying to avoid looking at me to spare me any further embarrassment.

Then there's something that seems very like we're in the missionary position, so Oliver and I both feel the need to keep mouthing apologies as we look awkwardly at each other amid the eerie silence. A gentle ding rings out to indicate a change of position. Endless Cloud comes over to shove his shoulder into the back of my thigh, and then tells Oliver to do the same. With his big, firm hands round my waist, me on all fours, him pulling me back, me stretching out my hands to reach an unknown mystical force, then him flipping me over. I get the distinct impression that this is not yoga, this is definitely tantric sex.

'Shanti, shanti, shanti,' croons Endless Cloud melodiously as he drifts from couple to couple. The sweat is literally pouring off me but everyone else is gliding serenely about, this way and that. Next, we take turns lying down, Oliver between my legs an inch from my crotch, face up thankfully, his head cradled in my hands as I knead him like a loaf of bread. I keep getting wafts of his man scent which is very woody, clean-smelling and quite intoxicating.

Just as I think I've probably bathed in enough Dawn, we find ourselves flat on our backs buzzing gently to ourselves during Bees Breath, gradually getting louder until we are instructed to take our thumbs out of our ears and, just to rid the group of any last vestiges of dignity, we get back into our couples. Oliver and I find ourselves shyly reuniting to engage in what very much feels like doggy style, Reverse Cowgirl, and to finish off, the Butter Churner.

Never again. This is the last retreat I'll ever go on. I really feel I've been mis-sold the experience.

Finally, we sit back in our circle to take the opportunity to be in the moment, listening to our breath, our bodies limp, all the tension in our shoulders and lives draining away.

It's an enormous relief when it's all over. Like me, Oliver seems mega-embarrassed.

'Peace out,' whispers Endless cloud loudly enough for us all to hear. He bows, hands in prayer.

'Peace out,' we all say in response, mirroring his action.

Everyone turns to look at me with shocked expressions. Endless Cloud gives me a sad, disappointed look and floats off. Oliver leans over to me. 'Seriously?'

I have no idea what he means.

He shakes his head. 'You just told him to peace off.'

Oh God. I can't do this. I simply can't do it.

Thankfully, I'm pulled away to pursue no one's favourite activity of Tear Seeking which, I'm appalled to find out, is some form of communal crying.

The small group sit crossed-legged and before I can turn to leave, Gandalf gently puts his hands on my shoulders and pushes me down to join them. Thank God Oliver is off elsewhere doing some Whispering Fingers thing as part of his Happy Bunny experience. Tear Seeking is the most hideous thing I've ever encountered, yet within minutes, I'm sobbing along with the rest of them, and Gandalf is rubbing light circles on my back to encourage me to let it all out.

'What are you afraid of?' Gandalf asks me, taking my palm and running his bony finger down the lines as though the answer is hidden somewhere in my veins.

'Nothing.'

I'm a warrior. I fear nothing.

'Look deeper. Into your soul.'

Christ Almighty.

'I don't know. Sharks?'

He looks annoyed. 'What are you afraid of?'

You repeating this question over and over until we die.

'I'm not sure what you mean.'

'I can't read you. You are very closed off. You are surrounded by purple. It's no use... it will take hours,' he sighs, making a bridge with his fingers. 'Probably seven or eight hours before you open.'

He smiles unexpectedly. 'And when you do. It will be beautiful. You will shine and you will know yourself.'

We do a polite bow before he moves through the group, reading palms and stroking the air above people's heads.

· ♥ · ♥ · ♥ · ♥ · ♥ ·

Our detox breakfast – a bowl of straw basically - is deeply unsatisfying and dry as sticks. So is the midday salad of leaves and celery. And the silent dinner is such a disappointment that I am close to tears. The coffee we were promised turned out to be a caffeine enema.

The miserable faces around me dig around their plates to see if there's any actual food hidden under the mossy lumps. Then Endless Cloud appears holding a large sign, 'Surprise!' and gets our hopes up only to reveal the decanter he is carrying is full of hot water with lemon slices. It is clearly not the neat gin that it should be. It's too much. I would kill for a glass of chilled Sauvignon right now.

A wave of resentment washes over me as I excuse myself from the table using mime.

Gandalf intercepts. His soft smile just makes me feel worse.

'I've forgotten what it feels like to be happy,' I blurt out before I know what I'm saying.

He looks down at his wrist. 'Seven and a half hours. Very good.'

He's as mad as a box of frogs.

'You are open at last. Be free, Nell. Be free of your anger.'
Like it is that easy.

· ♥ · ♥ · ♥ · ♥ · ♥ ·

I'm bitterly regretting my decision to come here. Instead of heading straight to my room, I take myself off for an unscheduled walk, and within minutes I am pounding along a forest track, the fresh, mountain air whipping through my hair, invigorating my soul. I can feel my mind clearing with each step. I allow myself to wander into the past, back when Ava and I were children. Back through bright green Irish smocks (Riverdance), Lycra leotards (jazzfunk), glitter tutus (disco ballet) and Turkish veils (exotic belly dancing). Isn't Ava gorgeous? Have you thought about sending her to the Bolshoi Academy - like it's just at the end of the street. How about Britain's Got Talent? Do you think she'll make the Olympics? The more the jealousy between the other mothers grew, the more my own mother would puff out her chest and exaggerate my sister's capabilities, treating Ava like a diva. 'We have dancing tonight so we MUST keep a light tummy.'

Me and my father would frequently share an eye roll between us, and I'd get a knowing wink. Eventually, it must have taken its toll on the family budget.

'SHOES! MORE SHOES!' I'd hear my mother yelling and 'NEW COSTUMES! FABULOUS NEW COSTUMES! MUST HAVE! MUST! MUST! NEED! NEED!'

Cupboards were stuffed to the brim, colourful plumes, chiffon veils and sparkling dresses spilling out everywhere upstairs and then soon even the dining room couldn't hold them all. The hallway from the front door to the kitchen all-but-disappeared behind racks of theatrical costumes and when one day, my father couldn't find his golf clubs. He lost his temper with my mother calling her ridiculous and accusing her of getting far too carried away. And this bit I think I'll remember for the rest of my life, my father yelled, 'Nell has just as much talent as Ava has. If only you would stop to take notice!'

My mother never did stop to take notice, but I did balloon with love for my father for sticking up for me. And of course, neither parent knew that Ava and I had been hiding at the top of the stairs listening to their argument unfold. We looked silently at each other and scarpered to bed. We never spoke of it again.

As I reach the end of the track, I slow my pace and turn around. I have a new life now, away from it all. I shall leave all of that baggage behind me.

Just as I'm wondering if there's any way I could fake an emergency to get a taxi out of here, I stumble across a small stone barn hidden at the back of the property. I peer in through the small open window and can't believe my eyes. A lake's worth of wine and mountains of food.

I stare blindly at it, my taste buds salivating while my inner moral compass whizzes back and forth. These must be confiscated goodies that innocent customers, like me, have brought in thinking that this place would be more of a relaxing getaway than the terrifying boot camp it actually is.

I really shouldn't.

Ah fuck it.

Within seconds, I've opened the door and I'm helping myself. I rip open a bag of crisps and stuff them in my mouth. I swipe up a bottle of pop and glug it straight down while I'm yanking off the lid to some cheese. As I'm frantically rifling through the shelves for chocolate biscuits, a rustling noise behind me causes me to freeze.

Oh dear.

I spin round to see Oliver staring at the stolen goods in my arms.

Chapter 8

I stiffen, bracing myself for a sanctimonious lecture. I tilt my chin, hug my ill-gotten stash tightly to me and glare at him.

He lifts an eyebrow.

Here it comes. Any second now. He's taking it all in. His eyes are darting back and forth over the heavily laden shelves before coming to rest sharply on mine. The corners of his eyes crinkle as he squints disappointedly, but I simply do not care. I straighten to my full height of not much above the national average.

He shakes his head slowly.

'That won't be anywhere near enough,' he says, swiftly launching at the dusty bottles of wine on the shelves and scooping up armfuls of fatty produce. 'Here, take this. And these. I'll grab those and... aha, they will do nicely thank you very much. How are you with gluten?'

And before I know it, we are scampering through the woods with bottles of wine, a box of multi-flavoured crisps, a wedge of Manchego cheese, cartons of olives swimming in herby oil and two freshly baked baguettes between us. We are giggling hysterically and shushing each other for fear of getting caught.

We find a small clearing hidden behind the trees, have the same thought and whip off our baggy tunics to make a picnic blanket. We plonk ourselves down. Fortunately, I'd had the foresight to wear a very flimsy little vest top with no bra underneath, but Oliver apparently didn't. I rummage around the food pile to stop my eyes from wandering over to his naked six-pack.

I hope this isn't going to be awkward. Him giving off catalogue-model vibes and me, in an ironic twist of fate, giving off pervert-stalker vibes.

'Christ, I need this,' says Oliver, tearing off some bread and a lump of cheese and handing them to me. Surprisingly, once we've had a few bites to eat we relax easily into each other's company.

'What sort of utter horseshit are they feeding us?' I ask. 'This beats those dry sticks that's for sure.'

'I know,' agrees Oliver. 'And those two warlocks? What's their game?'

'I'll be leaving worse off than when I arrived! I've never been so frigging stressed. Did you have to do any Tear Seeking? I mean, what the actual fuck is going on? I think I picked the wrong package.'

'Hmmm,' Oliver says, cramming more cheese and half a baguette into his mouth. 'I got forced to come here from work. The bastards.'

He doesn't seem the type to be ordered about by anybody.

'Who do you work for?'

He yanks the cork out of the wine bottle with his teeth and blows it onto the ground, holding it out to me before picking up another and doing the same thing again. He glugs it down wiping his mouth with the back of his hand.

'A company of morons.'

'Ah, now I am a veritable expert in that field. I bet you any money I have far worse tales to tell than you,' I say downing half of the bottle almost in one go.

Oliver's face lights up unexpectedly. 'Ah yes, the whole sister making you redundant saga.'

'Wait until I tell you about Karen the boss.'

'Let me guess. She's a sexually confident woman in her forties and everyone needs to know about it.'

We spend the next hour trying to suppress our laughter while swapping workplace horror stories. Oliver is having trouble breaking away from the company. He has not enjoyed working for them for a number of years, but can't quite bring himself to leave the generous pay and conditions.

'Your sister sounds like a nightmare,' he says, deflecting attention away from himself.

'She is.'

'Why do you let her walk all over you like that?'

I freeze mid-slug and realise I have no proper answer. 'Well, I... don't let her walk all over me for a start, and for your information... I... erm, I'm very assertive with her. I've made it sound worse than it is. You know, for comedic effect.'

Oliver breaks off more cheese, handing it over to me. 'Here, you simply haven't lived until you've tried Tree Tickling,' he says, quickly changing the subject. I force a smile while he demonstrates what he got up to all afternoon, which was tickling each other on the arms and neck with leaves.

'I'll show you,' he says, which feels like a deliberate tactic to distract me and pull me out of the mood that seems to be grabbing hold of me. I stuff the cheese in my mouth and savour the strong flavour. It is delicious.

'Okay then. Do your worst,' I say, reluctantly holding out my arm.

Oliver takes my wrist gently and turns it palm up. He plucks a leaf from a nearby branch and trails it round my hand and along my arm. It is a very slow and sensual act, far from the harrowing sobs that my group were treated to. I take a deep breath in and feel my whole body relax.

'Close your eyes,' he whispers. The sensation is unbelievably enhanced by not being able to see him or the world around. The tension drains away from me.

Now, I'm not entirely sure how this comes about (possibly due to us both having downed at least a bottle of wine each), but one minute I'm sitting with my back to Oliver as he runs a leaf lightly down my neck and over my bare shoulder, tantalisingly slowly down my arm, skirmishing the side of my boob and the next, I've turned towards him, and I'm offering him my neck to kiss. Which he does, expertly. Then before I know it, we are making out under the stars like frisky teenagers.

'You have incredible lips,' he says, trailing a line of kisses down to my neck. 'And you have unbelievably soft skin.'

My whole body is covered in goosebumps at the surge of electricity crackling between us. We are kissing like explorers navigating unchartered seas. We kiss for hours and hours, only stopping to glug more wine. Soon, we are grinding leisurely against each other, my hands tangled in his hair. It's like a pressure valve has been released, hissing pent-up energy into the atmosphere. Oliver's hands spread out over my taut stomach, reaching up to cup a breast in each of his paws. I hear his breath quicken as he massages them lightly, sweeping his thumbs expertly over my nipples.

'Christ, these are magnificent,' he groans against my lips as our kiss grows ever hungrier. My hands slide down to his buttocks. They are rock hard as I grab him and pull him towards me. I am having a huge effect on him, and I like it.

Eventually, we break free when we both realise we are at the point of no return; Oliver's erection about to burst from his baggy pants and my nipples poking through the vest top like a couple of large Greek olives. We stare at each other in wonder before a distant clanging of gongs breaks the spell and reminds us that we need to be in bed before the chimes finish.

'If we get caught, Endless Cloud will be very disappointed in us,' I whisper, suddenly aware of our rule breaking and wrong-doings.

Sitting bolt upright, Oliver apologises. 'Yes, you're right. Sorry. I hope I haven't overstepped.'

I may have scarred him for life at the airport.

'No. No, of course not,' I say all breathy, shaking my mussed-up hair from my face and adjusting my vest. 'It was a most highly...'

Even though my thoughts are full of lust, I suddenly sound very formal, like I'm giving feedback at a job appraisal. I clear my throat. 'It was a most highly enjoyable... encounter. Fully consensual and, erm, above board. Top marks.'

Top marks? My emotions have been all over the place since the redundancy shock. I can feel the endorphins plummetting.

'Likewise. I also enjoyed our *encounter*,' Oliver says, avoiding eye contact as he pulls me up and hurriedly gathers together the rest of the stash. 'I didn't mean to... erm... go quite so far with the Tree Tickling.'

I think he is terrified of being accused of coming on too strong.

Ding. Ding.

Now that I've managed to turn the atmosphere weird, we race back to our rooms in a rather awkward silence, with Oliver yanking at his pants to hide his massive boner.

When we arrive at my door, he leans forward to kiss me goodnight with a polite peck to my cheek just as I stick out my hand to shake his, as though his job interview is at an end and I'll be in touch forthwith.

Disappointingly, the result is me rather forcefully jabbing him in the solar plexus. He instinctively leaps away from me with a confused look before dashing into his room, just as the last dong rings out across the hot, sticky night.

· ♥ · ♥ · ♥ · ♥ · ♥ ·

The next day I awake embarrassed to my core at having made out with Oliver so enthusiastically, only to spoil it at the end. He couldn't get away from me fast enough. Memories of me drunkenly pouring my heart out to him about all my petty grievances, Ava and work and how bitter I feel, come back to haunt me. What must he think? And OH MY GOD he knows I've told a pack of lies to get this life coaching job too.

The irony. Me, a life coach when I'm a seething hot mess and now enjoy the company of others like a kick in the tits.

I can't bear to face him, so to avoid further humiliation, I skip the dawn spirit dance in favour of lying in bed with a hangover. I'm going to give the tribal drums a miss too. My head can't take it. I will simply lie here and think my headache away.

Huge mistake. I. AM. RAVENOUS AND SEVERELY DEHYDRATED.

I could really do with some bread and cheese and salty crisps. I weigh up my options. Break into the barn again or break into Oliver's room for the leftover stash while he's out Dawn Bathing with his happy bunnies. I poke my head outside the door, only to make out Gandalf ghoulishly floating down the corridor away from me. He has left a pile of rabbit droppings, half an apple and another stick for me to chew, on a little wooden platter outside my room. I close the door gently. Oliver's room it is then.

I clamber over the narrow gap between our balconies in my baggy robe rather clumsily. Thankfully, he's left the balcony door open.

Christ, what a mess. In the darkness, I can just about make out his robe lying on the floor. Bottles, bags of crisps, something long and hard. I poke a toe at it. A baguette. And what looks like a…

A light snaps on, scaring me half to death.

Oliver lets out a piercing scream. It seems to last forever. He is lying spread-eagled on the bed and stark-bollock naked like Vitruvian man. *Glorious* would be the first word that springs to mind.

He grasps for suitable vocabulary befitting this humiliating scenario, while I watch helpless from my position, frozen in front of him at the foot of the bed. I've got a bird's eye view right up the length of him. It's positively outstanding. I blink rapidly.

Snap out of it.

Not glorious. Magnificent. That's it.

Snap out of it before he thinks you are some kind of sexual deviant.

'WHAT THE FUCK ARE YOU DOING?' Oliver eventually roars.

Instinctively, I fling the bag of crisps I'm holding onto his crotch. He holds it in place and sits bolt upright. He's annoyed. Very annoyed.

'Well?'

Chapter 9

Oliver's question hangs in the air.

I gulp. 'Well, indeed.'

'Is that all you have to say?' Oliver asks, his face softening. He seems relieved and then, after a moment of catching his breath, slightly amused.

He is so overwhelmingly attractive that it has turned me mute. I chew my bottom lip. It's all I can do in the face of such beauty. Even his bed-hair is perfect.

'I wake to find you've broken into my room and you're staring at me from the foot of my bed. I think you should at least tell me what you're doing here, and how long you've been watching me.' He sounds like a barrister for the prosecution. He's also making me sound like an awful pervert.

I reach down for the baguette and hold it up as though I'm producing evidence.

'What's that? Exhibit A?'

I find his sarcasm quite endearing.

'Sorry. I was just so hungry. I really didn't think you'd be in here.'

Oliver breaks into a smile. 'I couldn't face the spirit dancing either.' He indicates for me to turn around. 'Give me a second.'

I spin round to face the wall as I hear the bed creak under his weight. I reach out with my toe and hook his robe, flinging it expertly behind me.

'Thanks,' he says. A few seconds later, I hear him open the door. 'Here. This is what we need.'

Oliver is carrying his Happy Bunny tray of fruit and pastries over to the bed. He pats the space beside him. 'Want some?'

My eyes are on stalks. 'Love some. It's very kind of you to share.'

'It's very kind of you to join me,' he says formally. 'I don't usually make time for breakfast.'

'Tell me about yourself,' I say.

'What do you want to know?' he says, grinning.

How do men not know what girls want to know about them? *How?* It's obvious. We want to know how many girls they've been out with. Were they in love with any of them? If so, how many times? How deeply in love? Was there recently a special someone? Is she pretty? Is she still around? Is she still in love with you?

'Erm, where do you live?' *Oh my God. Could I have picked a more boring question?*

'I have a base here in Altea, one of the whitewashed townhouses up near the church in the old town.'

'A base?'

'Yeah. I travel a lot. I'm thinking of leaving the company I work for and starting a new business from scratch.'

Now, that should be a very interesting line of enquiry to pursue, shouldn't it? But my brain has other ideas.

'Do you live... alone?'

His eyes light up. 'If you're asking me if I'm in a relationship then, no. I'm single,' he says. 'By choice. My work is very demanding. Anything else?'

'No,' I say, embarrassed at being caught out. 'That will be all, for now.'

Now, I sound like the one in court.

Oliver plays along. 'Thank you, Your Honour. Let the case for the defendant rest.' He flicks his gaze to the food and bottles lying around on the floor. 'We're partners in crime now. Which reminds me, I better get rid of the evidence.'

'Shame to let it all go to waste,' I say through a mouthful of croissant. 'All I got this morning was another stick and half an apple.'

'Why don't you take it?' Oliver suggests. 'In case you get hungry later. After you've enjoyed your stick.' He starts grinning. It lights up his entire face. A giggle escapes from his lips. 'Sorry. I'm sure there's a perfectly good reason they are feeding you twigs.'

His laughter is infectious and before I know it, I am chuckling along. 'They must have taken one look at me and asked themselves the only question that matters. Which stress buster package would suit a girl who carries within her the potential to suck out joy from everyone and everything around her?'

Oliver is nodding. 'How do we stop her reaching into

your soul like a Nosferatu, leaving you an undead husk of a being, resentful of all around you and seething with anger? Perhaps they're expecting you to combust into flames during one of the rituals.'

He's taking it a bit far now, but at least I get to see his eyes sparkle and his hair shine in the glow of the lamp. We stifle our giggles when we hear a noise that sounds like footsteps outside in the hallway. Oliver is ramming a whole pain aux raisin in his mouth, indicating we need to get a move on.

'We'll be late for the Healing Waters. They're taking us to Algar Falls today.'

I scamper off the bed and over to the door. I open it a fraction and peep out to make sure the coast is clear. Oliver comes up behind me with an armful of cheese, crisps and a full wine bottle.

'To stop you breaking and entering,' he says. Thoughts of his extreme nakedness flood my mind causing me to become immediately flustered.

He hands me the wine. 'Maybe I'll break into your room this time.'

Oh my.

I take the stash from him and sneak back into my room.

· ♥ · ♥ · ♥ · ♥ · ♥ ·

If I thought Oliver was hot this morning, then that's nothing compared to the show he is putting on at the waterfall. After we have piled out of the camper van, Oliver joins his Happy Bunnies in a cooling dip. I am forced to watch from afar as my group engage in no one's favourite activity of drawing symbols on pieces of stone and 'gifting' them back to the water.

'These symbols are your burdens,' Gandalf is telling us. 'They represent the heavy rocks we place in our hearts. Be free of them. Let them go.' He makes a huge show of picking up a rock, chalking on a scribble that looks like a shoe and dunking it in the water with a splash.

'Was that a shoe?' I ask.

He nods and stares down to his Jesus-sandled toes. He wiggles them for us. 'Now they are free.'

Nonsense. Utter nonsense.

Once we have finished, we are told that our reward is to float face-up in the ice-cold waters of the fall for at least an hour. *Oh goody. Can't wait.* Everyone begins to strip off and I notice that they are wearing appropriately modest bathing suits, whereas I am wearing a flimsy, neon-pink 'over here, look at me' string bikini that I stole from my sister. As I self-consciously peel away my robe under the unbearable heat of the midday sun, I can feel Oliver's gaze on me, even though when I look over, he seems to be making a huge effort to look in the opposite direction. I gingerly step into the water. It is instantly soothing and exhilarating at the same time. I gasp at the icy temperature and plunge straight in. Oliver swims up to me.

'You'll feel great after a few minutes,' he promises. He's referring to our hangovers and he's not wrong. As I lie back and allow the water to freeze my brain, I can feel the blood gush to my head, sweeping it clean. The sound of the waterfall lulls me into a trance. I'm aware of Oliver floating beside me and try my best not to look at him. Each time I so much as lift my head from the water to see where he is, Gandalf and Endless Cloud fix me a questioning look.

When the billion years of floating is up and I can no longer feel my body, a dinging chime indicates that it is time to get out. I stand up, waist high in the fresh mountain pool and squeeze the water from my long plait. I catch Oliver staring at me. He instantly looks away and places his hands on two rocks, expertly hauling himself out of the water in one fluid movement. The droplets of water run over his rippling muscles, highlighting how well-defined his back is. They drip slowly down his spine, dispersing at the line of his shorts, which are clinging to him like a second skin, revealing a fine outline of perfectly shaped...

'ELLY-NELLY-NOR! This way please.' Endless Cloud is watching me like a hawk, beckoning me to the opposite side of the waterfall.

I climb out and dry off with one of the rags that Endless Cloud is handing out to my group. A quick glance over to the Happy Bunnies reveals that they are being handed fluffy white towels.

Oliver gives me a sheepish look.

'Let's go!' Endless Cloud waves to my group. 'Follow me. We heff lunch, standing on one leg.'

Jesus Christ.

As I stuff the wet rag into my bag, a loud barking distracts me. It is coming from behind a clump of rocks. It's not just any type of barking, it's a distressed sound. If my gap year at the animal rescue centre taught me anything, it was to recognise pain in other creatures. I take a step towards where the sound is coming from.

'Hurry please,' Endless Cloud is yelling.

As a group, we summon up the bare modicum of enthusiasm, don our robes and follow him along the narrow ledge, away from the waterfall. The barking becomes more distressed and a sixth sense flows through me. I turn back towards the rocks and hurry to see what the poor creature is worried about. Maybe it is injured.

As soon as I clamber round to see what is happening, I let out a piercing scream.

Chapter 10

There's a man's body floating face down in the water, trapped between two rocks. His dog is jumping at the water's edge, frantically barking and spinning round. Eyes wild and terrified. Without thinking, I jump straight in and pull the body away from the rocks. I turn him over and cradle his head in my arm. He's unconscious. I drag him to the edge but he's too heavy for me to lift.

Out of nowhere, Oliver is heaving him up and lying him flat. He then reaches in to pull me out of the water as though I weigh nothing at all. If it wasn't for the medical need to act urgently, I'd say it was immensely romantic.

I throw myself down to administer the sort of first aid that you see on Baywatch. Checking for breathing. No signs. Feeling for a pulse. Zilch. Pumping his chest, 'One elephant, two elephant, three elephant... '

Oliver is staring at me with an alarmed expression. He's gripped with fear. 'Go get help!' I yell at him.

He snaps out of it and runs off yelling, 'Emergencia! EMERGENCIA GRANDE!'

The dog is frantically licking his owner's face and making

a whining sound like he's crying. My heart lurches for it. This man looks as though he's in his sixties or seventies. I'd bet the freezing cold water brought on a heart attack. I cover his cold, lifeless lips with my own and breathe some air into his lungs. I feel them expand beneath his ribcage. I do the same again and go back to pumping ferociously on his chest.

'Come on,' I pray, making eye contact with the dog. He stops barking as though he knows what's going on and doesn't want to distract me. His eyes are full of intelligence.

I turn back to the man and repeat the breathing. It seems to last forever, and just as I begin to lose hope of saving him, his eyes spring open and he gasps for breath.

Thank God.

The dog smothers his face, his mouth, his ears with licks of joy until the man makes sense of where he is and what happened.

'Lie still,' I tell him, popping my backpack under his head for comfort. 'Help is on the way.'

A few minutes later, Oliver returns with a frightened-looking twelve-year-old boy holding a first aid kit. There's a huge crowd behind him. He takes one look at me holding the old man's hand and breathes a sigh of relief. Oliver is staring at me as though I have single-handedly saved the planet.

·♥·♥·♥·♥·♥·

I try very hard not to act like I make a habit of saving lives, but it is very difficult. The group are making such a fuss, especially Oliver.

'The way you took charge. You're incredible,' he says, respect shining from his eyes.

I nod modestly. After all, the entire campervan of Bunnies and Stress-heads are listening to his praise.

'And the way you trusted your gut, followed your instinct. If you'd listened to Endless Cloud the man would be dead,' he observes. We hear an embarrassed cough from the front of the van. 'And the way you handled the crowd afterwards and organised us all into a human stretcher. It was like a military operation. So focussed. So efficient.'

I roll my eyes. Really, this adoration is too much.

'Go on,' I say, smiling cheekily at him. I'm hoping he repeats the part about me being an epic goddess.

Oliver catches my look and moves in close. He whispers in my ear, 'I am hugely attracted to your strong sense of humility. It's very endearing.'

'And I am hugely attracted to your hero-worshipping.'

Oliver, looks at me intensely and allows his gaze to fall to my lips. He looks for all intents and purposes like a man desperate to kiss me.

At that moment, we are thrown forward by the campervan screeching to a halt and Gandalf ordering everyone to get changed out of our swimming things and to gather at the fountain in 'twenty minoots for a surprise'.

Oliver and I scamper back to our rooms. I am as high as a kite with excitement. I feel bursting with joy at the levels of hashtag respect hashtag boss lady vibes that Oliver is giving off. He lingers at his door, turning the big iron key slowly. While his eyes wander the length of my body hungrily, a nod of his head towards the open door invites me to join him. I get a flashback to my sister and her pronounced pelvic girdle and before I can help it, my hips are shifting into a slightly more flattering angle.

'We have twenty minutes,' he says.

My heart is racing. I know what goes on under that big sack of a robe. I have seen his magnificence for myself and I want it.

I want it real bad. All twenty minutes of it.

'Give me a second,' I say, trying to keep from panting with lust. 'I'll be with you in just a moment.'

Jesus, I sound like a doctor doing her rounds.

'I'll be waiting.' Oliver winks at me. 'Without the packet of crisps this time.'

Oh my God. It's me who is about to have a heart attack.

I race into my room and over to the bathroom to do my teeth and freshen up.

When I emerge, one glance around my bedroom stops me in my tracks. The newly-made bed, the neatly folded clothes, the spotless floor and the distinct lack of stolen baked goods tells me I'm in big trouble.

A quiet knock on my door, and Gandalf standing with a raised eyebrow and a bottle of wine in his hand, confirms it.

'Would that be a reward for my heroic behaviour today, by any chance?' I gulp.

He shakes his head sadly.

'I need to ask you to come viz me. Bring your begs, pleez.'
Oh dear.

· ♥ · ♥ · ♥ · ♥ · ♥ ·

While the group are gathered at the fountain, I hurriedly say goodbye to Endless Cloud who is giving me a look of pity as I thrust the heavy metal key at him a day early.

'You heff acted alone or you heff accomplice?'

'Alone,' I say. 'Totally alone.'

No point in Oliver getting thrown out too. Apparently, that delicious wine we drank was from Gandalf's special reserve. He was keeping it to mark the end of his year-long 'abstemiousness of all nice things'. No wonder he looked so tearful. They have every right to ask me to leave.

'You hef broken all of the rules.'

My mind flies to the theft, the excessive dry humping of one of their guests and the breaking and entering. I suppose I have.

'Vizout rules, vere vould vee be?' Endless Cload is asking me.

'Columbia?'

He shakes his head.

I drag my case outside. I am mortified. Fancy being asked to leave under such disgraceful conditions. I've gone from hero to zero in under sixty seconds. The whole retreat must have heard about my rule-breaking by now. Plus, I'm not given a chance to say goodbye to Oliver who, for all I know, is still sprawled naked on his bed, waiting for me to administer some sexual favours.

I blink rapidly to expel the vivid images of him and try to concentrate on what Endless Cloud is saying.

'Your path is golden. Your time is now. Rise to the challenge.'

I have no idea what he means so I apologise once again, only for him to waft a bunch of sage at me, smiling as though he knows what the future has in store for me.

The campervan pulls up. It's the same awful driver who brought me here, so I arrive at my family villa in double quick time, shaken and disoriented.

·♥·♥·♥·♥·♥·

Our white-washed, single-storey villa, is nestled in a walled garden of palm trees. Wrought iron gates lead to a gravel courtyard exposing a wide driveway which leads to a large oak wooden door.

A wave of sadness envelops me as I remember the last time I was here. I was with my family and having a lovely time. How far apart we have all grown since then.

I fish out the keys and let myself in. I'm hit by the musty smell that comes with the place not being used for a couple of summers. I hurry round and lift up all of the shutters and throw open the glass patio doors to the back garden and pool area. The place is instantly flooded with light, the smell of the sea in the near distance and earthy palm trees warming in the rising sun. I cross the living room to locate the router for the wifi, switch everything on and with a huge sigh of relief, I connect to the world wide web.

It takes only a few minutes to find a website providing online training for people wanting to become life coaches. There's even one doing 'quick qualifications' including certificates and proof of 'accreditation' within a week. It'll take what I have left on my credit card until my redundancy pay out comes through, and leave me with barely any money to eat, but at least I'll have my self-respect. I sign up immediately.

I briefly wonder what Pippa is up to and whether she is still angry with me. I check my phone to see if she has messaged. Nothing. I check my DMs to see if Dan has been in touch. Nothing. He hasn't posted anything since the gin cocktail lunch. I stare at the outline of his reflection and the woman next to him and feel the heavy weight of disappointment.

Letting out a long, slow breath, I text Dad to tell him that I have settled in and that I have already got myself a new job (probably) and not to worry. I tell him I just need some space to get myself sorted and some time to put all of this distress behind me, but that it is definitely all, I repeat, ALL, Ava's fault. One hundred percent all her fault. I press send, sit back and promptly burst into tears.

Deep breaths.

Deep breaths.

I can do this. I'll get a new job, new life and new friends. I'll forget all about Dan ghosting me after two years together and Oliver and the intimate time we shared. I have no idea what he will make of me disappearing like that without so much as a goodbye.

Instead, I will concentrate on work and becoming super successful. I will show my sister and my judgemental mother exactly how brilliant I can be. My life is going to be fabulous, starting first thing tomorrow.

Chapter 11
One long and harrowing week or so later...

'I can't believe that we've been working together for over a week already!' Nidi, my new boss, says excitedly. 'It's flown by so quickly, hasn't it?'

I stare back, nodding. 'It certainly has.'

It certainly hasn't.

'You've taken to this like a duck to water, haven't you?' she says, smiling at me.

I certainly have not.

'I think we will make a great team. Everything happens for a reason, as they say. And by they...' Nidi pauses to stare into the middle distance. 'I mean the universe. Our very life force, you know?'

I nod back in agreement.

No, I do not know.

She has been like this all week. She's a young, pregnant Indian version of Gandalf with her *moonstones* this and her *stars aligning with our auras* that. Then she'd surprise me with some in-depth insights into neurolinguistic programming, changing mindsets and tales of transforming people's lives through sage and turmeric, as though it's very scientific and real.

Managing your finances via breathwork took some persuading at first, but she's taught me to tap my third eye and rub my chakras with assorted crystals to cure various issues like lack of ambition and kidney function. It's all been terribly confusing, but she insists that bringing all aspects of a client into the therapy and mental health space will work more effectively.

The *Quick Qualify* website mentioned none of this.

'It's all in here, my life coaching bible,' she says, turning her huge, dark eyes on me while pushing the mighty great tome my way. 'You've really embraced the whole ethos and holistic style of life coaching, Nell. There's a rawness, an honesty about you that people will connect with.'

I have no words. I haven't been honest since the moment I arrived. It has been a real test of my moral compass, which I am convinced must be broken.

Working with Nidi in Spain makes my old life in England seem years and years ago, instead of only two weeks. With every moment that passes, I am sure she will find out that I am a fraud and send me packing, and I'd hate to upset her in such a heavily pregnant state. I have a continual, dull sensation of anxiety clouding my every move. I am amazed she has not seen past my fake smile and long silences while I pretend I'm *active* listening when really I'm a hot panicky mess of confusion.

'Don't forget we need to schedule in time to do a performance review tomorrow with a new client who booked with us yesterday. I'll observe the first session before you start life coaching on your own. I've informed the ICF that I'm your official mentor.'

What new client? 'ICF?' I say, keeping the panic from my voice. *Should I know who that is?*

'International Coaching Federation,' she explains. 'Didn't you have to register with them when you first qualified?'

I pretend it rings a bell. 'Ah, *that* ICF. Yes... yes. Good, good.'

'And you also have that interview with the Costa Blanca Radio. Don't forget to mention the business singles event, will you? That could pull in a lot of interest.'

Oh God. While she was talking about the business singles event earlier, I had been daydreaming about Oliver, wondering where he is and what he is doing. How long he lay there waiting for me.

'Self-employed people and micro-businesses often lack networking opportunities.' Nidi tells me. 'We'll match them with complementary businesses, and you never know, love might blossom too.'

Sweet baby Jesus, I'd rather stick pins in my eyes.

Lots of clients are the absolute last thing I need right now, until I have a clue about what I'm doing.

Nidi insists her new assistant, with the world's longest name, Maria-José-Inmaculada-Carmen, helps me with the interview. 'It will give her some much-needed experience,' Nidi says, ushering her into my office, 'and hopefully help with her people skills.' Which, I'm pleased to see, are even worse than mine. I've barely said more than two words to her since I started because she has such a moody and unapproachable demeanour. And she keeps hissing at people down the phone.

As well as the Life Coach Handbook, the *Quick Qualify* online course has provided me with lists upon lists of phrases that life coaches might come out with such as *living your purpose, owning your truth* and *plotting a course to the future*. I've been up until 3am every night cramming to pass the modules so that they can send me an accreditation certificate to show Nidi. I've told another white lie and said that I lost it in transit and have asked for a replacement to be sent out. Thank God I have a brain like a sponge when it comes to learning new skills and remembering things. It used to come in very handy in the workplace, especially for important meetings, thinking on my feet and holding professional grudges. I've also been observing Nidi's habits, such as placing mood crystals in corners and hanging up pictures of pebbles and raindrops on a pond. But I must draw the line at spraying the psychic protection mist and rearranging the office before a full moon.

· ♥ · ♥ · ♥ · ♥ · ♥ ·

I drive Maria-José-Inmaculada-Carmen into Benidorm and we locate the radio station headquarters with barely a word between us because she is on her phone, and it feels rude to interrupt. We are ushered into the recording studio and fitted with headphones. It looks very professional, and there are more staff here than I imagined for a local radio station. My stress levels are beginning to rise. I place my lists and handbook discreetly beside me with a shaking hand as the presenter comes in and settles herself on the chair opposite. Hopefully, she will have no idea about life coaching.

She smiles at us and then barks at a man at the mixing desk, 'Play something long while I finish this fag!' A Spanish instrumental immediately blasts out across the studio.

Maria-José-Inmaculada-Carmen and I watch mesmerised as she rummages around in her bag, not once pausing for breath as she takes three back-to-back calls, offers us a ciggie, tuts as we decline (although I'm sure Maria-José-Inmaculada-Carmen was about to reach for one) and then proceeds to scribble away on her notepad declaring that she is writing her shopping list before she forgets what she needs to pick up from the Mercadona after the show. 'Brain fog!'

'How old is she?' Maria-José-Inmaculada-Carmen whispers to me. 'It is so difficult to tell these days, especially when you Breets have lived out here in Spain for decades and not once thought to apply sun cream to your leathery, wrinkled faces.'

See? Zero people skills.

I point to the microphone poking between us as the presenter pushes her sunglasses up onto the top of her head. 'I'm seventy-three,' she says, screwing her eyes at us.

This is not going well at all.

'BEETROOT!' she suddenly yells.

'YES PLEASE!' I yell back instinctively.

Christ alive. My nerves are in shreds as it is. Maria-José-Inmaculada-Carmen turns to give me a strange look.

Juniper is quick to react. 'No. I forgot the beetroot. I swear by a good beetroot cleanse, don't you?' she says, cackling. 'Especially when you get to my age.'

She then launches into an unnecessarily detailed account of her alimentary tract.

'Can I just stop you there, Juniper?' I say firmly but politely to her. 'I'm sure we could talk all day about how your bowel activity has shown considerable improvement since you went gluten-free. I mean whose hasn't? But could we start the interview, please? I am extremely busy.'

By busy, I mean, of course, desperate for this to be over with. She's told us all we need to know about herself and the trouble she has processing wheat.

Suddenly the Spanish guitar solo is ripped from the airwaves. Juniper flicks some switches and stubs out her cigarette.

'Welcome back, and thank you for keeping me company today. We have two very interesting guests coming up for you now. They are SO desperate to talk to you because they claim to have the answers to ALL of life's problems.'

Shitting hell.

'The first question I have, Eleanor, is why do you think engaging the services of a life coach are vital to today's generation of lost and hopeless underachievers?'

Fuck.

'Call me Nell,' I say, turning to bring Maria-José-Inmaculada-Carmen into the conversation. 'And it's not just underachievers, is it? We cater for all sorts of sad and desperate people, don't we? Life coaching is vital to them. Vital. Isn't it?'

'Yes, but *vital* in what way?' Juniper asks.

I've been so busy studying all week - literally every night - my brain is completely frazzled and unfortunately for me, when faced with a set of headphones, a microphone and a beady-eyed old crone, I've momentarily forgotten what a life coach does and why anyone would need them. My mind is a complete blank. Plus, I've had the terrible fears of people finding out that I'm an inexcusable charlatan.

'Would you like to answer this one?' I say to Maria-José-Inmaculada-Carmen. She nods back, a vacant look in her eye. It is about time I checked to make sure she knows what a life coach is.

The presenter leans in excited to hear what my assistant has to say about my valuable and life-changing services as a life coach.

Maria-José-Inmaculada-Carmen swivels her wide eyes from me to the presenter and back again. I can see she is unnerved at this question, opening and closing her mouth. From the little I know of her, Maria-José-Inmaculada-Carmen rarely shows enthusiasm for anything other than her *Hola!* magazine. It doesn't take me or the presenter long to realise that this very basic question has stumped her. It's almost as if Maria-José-Inmaculada-Carmen has not even *heard* of a life coach never mind read the handbook. I quickly glance down at my notes and jump in to rescue her from the embarrassment of not knowing what her employer does for a living.

'We prevent people, no we *help* people with boring jobs and boring lives,' I glance down at the notes. My brain is a congealed lump of hummus. 'I help them find purpose and... erm... truth to... their... erm... so they can really own their truth, you know?'

I can see the presenter is amused at this vaguer than vague answer. She dips her head and scribbles some notes on her pad. I roll my eyes at Maria-José-Inmaculada-Carmen. Maybe this was not such a great idea after all.

'You help people like a counsellor would?' Maria-José-Inmaculada-Carmen says, trying to be helpful.

'No, nothing like a counsellor,' I reply, trying to keep the annoyance from my voice. Nidi specifically told us both last week that a coach is nothing like a counsellor.

'Like a therapist?' Maria-José-Inmaculada-Carmen asks me hesitantly.

'No, nothing like a therapist.'

That too was on the list of what it's not.

'Like career guidance?' she asks, furrowing her brow.

'What? No, nothing like that.'

This bickering is just embarrassing us both. The presenter stifles a giggle. I open up the handbook and turn to Juniper. I better spell it out for all of our sakes. 'It says here that being a life coach is about *helping* and *supporting* people through life's challenging moments.' I say through tight lips, snapping it shut with a loud thwack. Let's hope that's the end of it.

Shitting hell.

'And SINGLE people!' I blurt out, suddenly remembering the whole point of this unbearable interview. 'SINGLE people from local businesses, especially.'

Juniper perks up. 'Oh?'

'They just naturally want to stay in their comfort zones, you see?' I explain, adlibbing from a scrap of paper with the details on. 'And that can lead to fear of attachment. Marriage or self-employment is like hurling yourself off the roof, figuratively speaking. They often know what to do but don't want to do it. They need a push. Life coaches provide that push. And we are inviting people to our event, our SINGLES business event, I mean our BUSINESS singles event in three weeks' time. We will reveal our top coaching tips to help singles become… not so…?'

I literally have no idea what I'm saying.

'Single?' Juniper says.

'Yes. We will help them open the door to more business and love and… whatnot,' I mumble, looking away. I'm hardly what you'd call the poster girl for a successful romance, never mind a successful career. And besides, I haven't even started to look into it, even though it was the first thing Nidi asked me to do. I can only assume bitterness is preventing me wanting to see other people happy, successful in business or finding love.

'I see,' the presenter says. 'So, to sum up, what you are saying is that your job, being a *life coach*,' I watch her do air quotation marks before checking back through her notes, 'is to take literally anybody willing to pay, especially SINGLES and tell them what they already know so that they can find love and happiness... before they hurl themselves off the roof?' She doubles over laughing, wiping tears away from her eyes. 'I've been self-employed and single for years. Who knew we were all in such danger?'

Good grief. I wipe my sweaty palms on my thighs. I can't take much more.

'Yes,' Maria-José-Inmaculada-Carmen says, relaxing back into her chair, eyeing the packet of cigarettes on the table in front of us. 'Exactly correct.'

Why am I even bothering? Why?

'I'm definitely coming along to that event. Book me four places. No five. I'll bring my mum. She's about to turn ninety-seven and wants to get back on the horse. Will the place be wheelchair accessible? And for all you single listeners out there, we'll see you in three weeks at the...'

Fuck me.

'At the erm, venue and times to be announced shortly on the website.'

'Si,' nods Maria-José-Inmaculada-Carmen like she has any fucking clue about it.

I take a beat. This whole interview has been an utter disaster. We need to do it again. Who knows how many people will listen to it. I'd die if anyone I know in England was listening in.

'Actually, Juniper, I'm so sorry. Can we record all of this again, please? We've come across sounding like a pair of idiots who couldn't life coach their way out of a paper bag.'

Juniper smiles reassuringly back at me and tilts her head. She takes a long drag on her cigarette and sighs. 'Oh, honey, I would... but we're recording *live* to over four-hundred thousand loyal listeners worldwide.' She studies the monitor in front of her. 'Actually, we're just over the half-million mark today. But we're used to hearing all kinds of idiots on this show, aren't we listeners?'

Juniper clucks huskily into the microphone and after a few more awkward questions, the interview draws to a close. 'Thanks again for your company today and thanks to our rather... entertaining guests, Nell Weston and Maria-José-Inma... our two life coach experts.'

Deep breaths.
Deep breaths.

Chapter 12

We return to the office in stunned silence. I feel my insides wind tight, accompanied by the familiar sinking of my mood. I owe it to myself and Nidi to stop carrying on like a bellend and to come clean, otherwise, I'll end up bursting a main artery or hurling *myself* off a roof at this rate. But if I do confess, she's bound to sack me straight away and I'll be reduced to giving back massages to hairy men or selling mojitos on the beach for one euro an hour. Besides, it's too late. The interview has reached hundreds of thousands of listeners. They are all expecting to come and hear me share the secret to romantic and business success.

Maria-José-Inmaculada-Carmen flees to her desk and grabs the phone to speak animatedly with whoever is on the other end. Her mother, judging by the numerous times she says the word 'madre'. I flop down onto the sofa in the office Nidi has generously given me to work from. She pops her head around the door.

'How was the interview?' she asks, tilting her head to the right. She's even cocking her left eyebrow, which I'm pretty certain she said means, 'I'm genuinely interested'.

Now I'm in trouble.

'How do *you* think it went?' I say tightly, mirroring her actions. After a solid week of observing her, I know some of her tricks.

'I didn't manage to catch any of it.' She tilts her head back upright. 'But I'm sure you were great, and we'll have plenty of interest.'

I daren't tell her that there's fuck all chance of that happening. And even worse, I'm feeling quite relieved about it.

'Ready for the performance review tomorrow?' she asks. 'I can't wait to see you in action. I've booked a new client for 11am to give you time to prep.'

Shitting hell.

'See you tomorrow!' Nidi waves, skipping off down the corridor, leaving Maria-José-Inmaculada-Carmen and me to lock up the office.

· ♥ · ♥ · ♥ · ♥ · ♥ ·

When I reach the villa, I flick open the manual Nidi gave me and search the contents. There's nothing to cover being caught in one's own web of lies but there is a section called Emergency Quick Fixes. I scan the pages to see heavy panting will get rid of negative toxins and hopefully take the clients mind off their immediate problems, in my case, the need for wine and a certificate saying I'm a qualified life coach. And I could always use this time wisely to do some *proper* marketing and advertising. After I check Twitter to see what's going on in the world, and what Ryan Reynolds' opinions are on it all.

As my head hits the pillow, I vow to get up the following morning and go for a jog. And maybe drink some green tea with a shot of cleansing apple cider vinegar containing The Mother like Nidi does. These goals, to lead a super healthy, meaningful life, are extremely important to me. EXTREMELY.

·♥·♥·♥·♥·♥·

After what seems the blink of an eye, my alarm goes off. I'll have a mere two minutes to lie with my eyes closed and visualise exactly which jogging route I will take, before I get up and run like a cheetah along the promenade. Visualising the action gives me a ninety percent chance of actually doing it.

'Decide what you want to do. VISUALISE it. Do it!' Nidi often chants to motivate and spur the clients into action. I imagine myself powering along, arms and legs like pistons, pumping me full of adrenalin. Brain cells multiplying. Fat simply melting away with each stride. Visions of me floating serenely through the office, smiling and helping people as I go. Social media saying wonderful things about me. Selfies of me looking fabulous. Hair shining. Cheeks glowing with joy. Clients queuing round the block for me to sort their lives out for them.

Shitting hell.

I must have dropped off! *Gaaaah!* I am seriously late for work now. How did three hours just disappear? Just like that. *How? How?*

I yank on yesterday's clothes, dash to my car and fly through reception to my office, without so much as a good morning, yelling at Maria-José-Inmaculada-Carmen.

'I'M LATE! LATE! GET ME THE NOTES! QUICK THE NOTES!'

I slam my door shut. Within minutes, any chance to take a moment of calm evaporates, as my phone rings loudly interrupting the silence, and along with it the chance to remind myself that I am happy in my own skin and have everything, and by that, I mean NOTHING to look bloody forward to except faking at being a bloody Life Coach today with my first ever client, *poor sod*, while being WATCHED like a hawk by Nidi who has said she will be popping in to do a performance review. I need a few minutes to compose myself. I will ignore it.

I am looking forward to my first client like you'd look forward to a smear test.

When it rings again thirty seconds later, my whole body clenches. I grab the phone and draw a huge breath in. 'Maria-José-Inmaculada-Carmen, I'm right in the middle of an early-morning meditation about me having an affair with Ryan Reynolds.'

'So sorry Miss Weston but your eleven o'clock, he has arrived too early.'

'Well, tell him he can wait until I'm finished,' I sigh impatiently, unable to help myself. I am in no hurry to do this session knowing that Nidi is going to observe me. 'Unless he actually *is* Ryan Reynolds. And I can tell by your tone that he's not. If Mr eleven o'clock was even MILDLY attractive, you'd be using your fake I-can-barely-speak-the-language Spanish accent.'

I hear her flounder. She knows I'm right. I picked up on this very quickly last week.

'Um... Miss Weston, you're on loudspeaker and I think it is very possible the client can hear you, yes, he is nodding his head, so let me just press....'

I hear the distinct sound of a man coughing with embarrassment in the background, while I wait a split second to give her time to find the massive button with the unmistakable loudspeaker icon on it. Honestly, a blind child of two could operate the telephone system.

'For God's sake, why would you do that? Just don't press that button. DO NOT press it.'

'Sorry, Miss Weston, I will definitely remember the next time.'

'But that's the fourth time this week you've said that! Never-bloody-mind, check his breath for garlic, no actually, just give him one of those extra-large mints, in case, and send him in. And by the way, I DID NOT appreciate you telling anybody and everybody who rang up yesterday, that I was out getting vaginal cream with Nidi.'

'Um Miss Weston,' she tries to interrupt, but I've got her over a barrel. We've had numerous bizarre emails corroborating the facts. Why Nidi also posted it on the Facebook page will forever be a mystery to me. She is a little like my over-sharing sister in that respect. I didn't even want to go for the bloody thing, but she insisted because she is thinking of doing a deal where if we recommend them to clients, they will get a discount. And something about vaginal steams being very detoxifying and spiritual.

'You know I clearly said STEAM, not CREAM. I was out getting a vaginal STEAM with Nidi. Huge difference,' I spit crossly, my patience with her wearing thin. I know I shouldn't snipe at her, but it's difficult not to, especially since she's quite useless, and I'm borderline psychotic at the present moment.

'And for your information, it is highly UNPROFESSIONAL to disclose what a person, especially your EMPLOYERS, do with their vaginas. Is that CLEAR?'

A thought suddenly occurs to me, 'Unless you are Gwyneth Paltrow. She seems to make a good living out of it but still... you are NOT to mention my vagina to anyone.'

I must stop panic-talking. Verbal diarrhoea is a delaying tactic. I must stop it at once.

At least Maria-José-Inmaculada-Carmen sounds contrite. 'No, Miss Weston... I will no longer mention your new and fresh vagina... so, which button to turn off the loud speaker did you say?'

Oh Christ.

Slamming the phone down, I take a few rapid breaths and tap my wrists in equal bursts, as per the Emergency Quick Fix instructions and stare frantically at the door handle, waiting for it to turn. I'm a disgrace. An absolute fucking disgrace. I can feel my colossal meltdown bubbling dangerously close to the surface as I break into a torrential sweat.

Deep breaths.

Deep breaths.

I tear at my itchy scalp and scratch until it is sore. If only I'd come clean and confessed to Nidi. None of this would be happening. But then I'd be out of a job, desperate and a laughingstock. My eyes flick to a brightly coloured feather duster lying on the coffee table. It's a constant reminder that I'd have to take that naked cleaning job. I am not sure if there are rules against openly discussing the health of your vagina, commenting on a client's looks and questioning the freshness of his breath, but if there was, I have broken quite a few.

Nidi will be mortified if she finds out. I need to calm down and act professionally.

Hopefully, I think to myself, my first-ever client will have some sort of fatal heart attack between Maria-José-Inmaculada-Carmen's reception desk and the three feet to my door.

No such luck.

There is a gentle knock on my door. Instinctively, I rush over. I am going to have serious words with our assistant after this. I take a deep calming breath in and swing open the door, a wide, manic smile plastered onto my face.

As soon as he smiles back, mine instantly withers.

Christ almighty, my heart leaps to my throat.

It is Oliver, and he has a questioning look on his face.

Chapter 13

We take a beat to stare at one another as Oliver unwraps an extra-large mint and pops it casually into his mouth, without breaking eye contact.

'I heard the radio interview yesterday and was passing by,' he says, chewing the mint and swallowing it. 'I thought I'd check to see how things were going.'

Badly of course.

I continue to stare at him. Even perplexed, he is managing to have quite the effect on me.

His dark brown eyes bore holes into mine. 'Especially after the last time we saw each other. We kind of left things a bit *awkwardly.*'

Akwardly? Which awkward situation could he be referring to? The one where I whined on like a broken record before rubbing myself against his manhood as though I had a bad case of the clap? Or me breaking into his room and screaming at him while he frantically tried to hide his one-eyed snake with a bag of Monster Munch? Or the one where he invited me in to bounce up and down on him and I disappeared without trace?

I yank him by the arm into my office, slamming the door firmly behind me before Maria-José-Inmaculada-Carmen can hear any more.

'What are you doing here?' I say, fear gripping me like a vice. 'Are you my eleven o'clock appointment?' I quickly make a mental list of all the lies that he overheard me tell last week.

I am a qualified life coach.

I am an orphan.

I speak Spanish like a native.

And the worst one; I am a people person.

I take in his giant physique. There's a whole chapter in the Life Coach Handbook on body language and physical attributes. He is extremely tall. With a thick head of short dark brown hair. He has one of those Roman noses that could mean he's very authoritative. A square jawline which could mean he's decisive, a good forehead meaning he's intelligent and not easily fobbed off. With kind, honest eyes. And a nice, friendly smile with a row of filmstar teeth.

He could ruin everything.

'No. I didn't book an appointment, but I see that you didn't take any of my advice,' he says. 'How is it going?'

'Things are going well, actually.'

I'm fresh out of a three-day panic attack and I have a steam-cleaned vagina.

I clear my throat. 'Yes. Things are going very well.'

He doesn't believe me for a second. He looks amused, if anything.

'I wanted to thank you, for taking the fall at the retreat.

Gandalf told me you were asked to leave. He didn't say why but I figured it out when you didn't... come back.' He gives me a shy look. 'Anyway, I'm sorry. I would have taken the blame. I hope you're not taking this job because you didn't have enough time at the retreat to think things through. Grasping at the first thing to come along.'

I shake my head.

He couldn't be more spot on.

'Because you might only create new problems for yourself,' he says, sounding like the Dalai Lama.

'I'm not creating new ones.'

I'm very much creating new ones.

He ignores me. 'Who's the miserable vampire on reception?' he says, walking casually over to the window.

He's also very astute.

'The new assistant. She's job averse. And she hates me.'

Oliver seems amused. 'And you're people averse. How's that going to work?'

I shake my head disapprovingly at his childish joke until a sudden thought occurs to me. 'What are you doing right now?' I ask, inviting him to sit down.

'Why? Is there something I can help you with?'

He listens as I outline my current predicament. He does owe me one after all.

'So, you want me to *pretend* to be your client so that you can *pretend* to be a life coach in front of your new boss and new assistant who hates you?'

I nod.

'And you want *me* to pay for this *pretence*, so that your

boss pays you for doing something that you *aren't* even qualified to do?'

I keep nodding. He's definitely coming round to the idea and I'm running out of time.

'In other words, a complete breach of trust, not to mention the legalities of breaking contractual agreements?'

Oh, my word. I do hope he isn't going to go on and on. I haven't got all day.

'Yes,' I say impatiently. 'You're making it all sound much worse than it is.'

He raises an eyebrow.

'Will you do it, or not?' I ask in a desperate tone.

He takes a million years to mull it over.

'Sure, why not?' Then he throws his head back and laughs like a drain as I manhandle him across the office onto the good sofa.

'Sit there and think up some reason why you're here,' I instruct. 'You know like erm, you're desperately unhappy about something in your life.'

'I do actually have an issue with the people at work I was telling you about.'

Who cares? Don't we all?

I stare at him. Bingo!

'I know! You hate your brother. He's selfish and spoilt. Everything in life is so easy for him. And he's handsome, he's rich, he's popular. Everything you're not. Okay?' I spring up. 'I'll get us some coffee.'

'Okay. So, do you still want me to think of a reason to be here, or did you just give me one?' He has an annoying sparkle in his eye. It is enormously sexy.

'Oliver. I hope you're not going to be like this during the session,' I say. 'Keep up. You have an awful brother. He's ruined your life. It's very simple. Just play along. I'll ring through for Nidi.'

'What's he called?'

'Who?'

'My imaginary brother, the one I hate.'

He's such a time-waster! Who cares what his brother is called?

'Eduardo?' I suggest.

'So, he's Italian? We're stepbrothers perhaps? He's older? His gold-digging mother is after my family fortune?' Oliver's eyes light up. 'And I suspect she's having an affair and is plotting to kill my father and run off with the money. Eduardo is her accomplice. No!' he yells animatedly. 'Eduardo is her LOVER. He's only pretending to be the son, my stepbrother. Right. Right. But the joke's on him because I'm a secret undercover agent. I've got it,' he says triumphantly, slightly out of breath with all the excitement. 'What do you think?'

'Jesus Christ, Oliver, it's life coaching not an episode of *Dallas*. Try not to be difficult.' I say firmly. 'Let's practise first and then I'll let Nidi know I'm ready for her to observe me with my first client.'

Oliver's face falls. 'So, I can't be CIA?'

'I hardly think she'll believe you're American, even if she can see past your thick Scottish accent. And how many newly-weds get poisoned by their adulterous bride-to-be?'

Deep breaths.
Deep breaths.

'Fair enough,' he says, grinning. 'Look, I should tell you that honesty is one of my cornerstones. I'm really not comfortable with lying to…'

'Not this again,' I cut in. 'Look, we have no choice, do we?'

'Well, we do have a choice. We could tell the truth.'

He's so difficult. I hope all my clients aren't going to be like this when I tell them what to do.

'What good would that do?' I say patiently. 'We all tell lies. Christ, you only have to look on Instagram to see that. You should see the shit that I've posted. No one expects it to be completely true. We all want to believe life is better than it really is. Or at least, we all hope that it will get better.'

I'll stop there. He doesn't need to know that I may or may not have posted that I'm living my best life, I go out every night, and I'm running my own business as a life coach here in Spain. Where I speak Spanish like a native.

'Why do we do that?' he asks, suddenly serious. 'Why are we never happy with what we have? Why do we always focus on what we haven't got? Living our second best lives.'

'And that,' I say, smiling as it all comes flooding back to me. The hours of study. The weeklong observations of Nidi in action with all manner of clients. 'Is a great way to open a conversation with a life coach.'

Oliver edges closer. 'Go on.'

'In order to answer those questions, you need a clear understanding of who you are and what makes life meaningful for you. What gives you a sense of purpose.'

Oh God. Oliver is looking at me strangely.

My voice drops a full octave. 'A good life coach can help you figure out where you want to go in life and how to get there.'

Oliver looks thoughtful and seems mesmerised by what I'm saying. We are both startled by a rapping on the door. Nidi pokes her face through.

'So sorry to interrupt, Nell.' Nidi glances at Oliver and acknowledges him with a nod. 'I'll have to postpone the observation. Devin's called. I need to go home.'

'That's okay,' I say, relief flooding through me. 'Is there anything you need me to do?'

'No, thank you. I should be back later. Session going well?'

She smiles encouragingly at Oliver, who dutifully gives her a thumbs up. Nidi gives me a reassuring look before quietly closing the door.

'Thank fuck for that,' I say, blowing out my cheeks.

'She seems nice,' Oliver says.

'She is. She's a white witch version of Gandalf. You'd bloody love her.'

'Which mystical wiccan does she belong to?' He points around the room to the various crystals and mantras hanging on the walls, the bunches of lilacs, sage and rosemary. 'At least you could stuff a chicken at a moment's notice.'

He's quite funny really.

He picks up a bottle of psychic mist. 'Should I be worried?'

He gets it. He totally gets it.

'No, but it might be the only option when this life coaching doesn't work out.'

'How do you know you'll not be any good at it?'

'Hello? Didn't you hear me on the radio? No one in their right mind will want to come and do a session with me.'

'I would,' he says kindly. 'I mean, how many sessions will it take to get to the bottom of my issues with Eduardo and my murderous stepmother?'

I start laughing. I'm very attracted to his face. He has very kind eyes that sparkle with life and energy.

'That's the first time I've laughed since...' I stop mid-sentence. Since we were rolling about, engaged in wanton fornication. His mind appears to have gone to the same place.

'Can I see you again?' he asks softly.

Oh.

It's taking me a few seconds to gather my thoughts. He waits patiently while I blink at him and think of something sophisticated to say. There's definitely a spark there. A sort of sizzling sexual undercurrent. He must feel it too, remnants from our dalliance last week at the spa retreat.

'Obviously, there's a certain client confidentiality to maintain.'

'Obviously,' he agrees.

My cheeks are burning. I try to stop myself, but for some inexplicable reason, I rise slowly from the sofa, pick up the feather duster and begin to busy myself dusting crystals and shelves. 'And a certain professionalism to uphold.'

Dust, dust.

'And considering our...'

Flit, float.

'Our, you know, romantic history,' I smile shyly at him from over my shoulder, dithering like a girlie fool. I'm really teasing the moment out. I wonder, if like me, he is imagining me cleaning naked. 'I suppose we could... you know. If Nidi has no objections.'

I reach out and trail the feather duster down his arm, just like he did to me with the leaf last week. Even the mere memory of it makes me tingle all over.

He seems conflicted. Or confused. It is something of a moral dilemma I suppose. I take a seat beside him, wondering who should make the first move. My lips feel drawn to him like magnets. But even though I'm leaning in, an inch from his nose, my eyes willing him to rip my bra off with his teeth, as the superior authority in the room, I should leave the first move to him.

'I mean,' he says, looking down at the awful line of dust that I've left on his sleeve, before impatiently wiping it off. 'Can I see you again for another session? An actual life coaching session.'

Chapter 14

I throw the feather duster across the room with more force than I mean to and cringe when it lands with a loud thwack against one of the larger crystals. 'Yes. No. Sorry. No. Of course, you meant that.'

Feck! Feck! Feck!

Oliver shifts away from me. 'I need to offer some sort of *proof* to my board of wankers, that I'm actively co-operating with their request for me to take some time off work to focus on my mental health. They are playing the *burnt out* card in the hopes that they can overrule my strategic decisions.' He shakes his head as he stares out of the window. 'Obviously, we wouldn't have to go through with actual sessions. Just book me in, I'll pay and you sign something at the end that says I've attended. It's a win-win for us both. I get to keep my job. You get to keep yours.'

How embarrassing.

'So much for honesty being one of your cornerstones. And I thought you hated your job and wanted out?' I'm pleased to see him blush.

'I do. I did. I just... I'm not sure I can just leave like that.

It's complicated. I've been there a long time.'

'Like I said, that's what life coaching is for. I can help you find the right path.'

He looks surprised. He must have a low-to-no opinion of what we do.

'I mean, I *could* but I'm fully booked,' I say, backtracking.

'Are you? I thought you had no clients yet, which is why you wanted me to pretend,' he says, before politely waiting for me to think up a quick way out of the fib.

'No, you're right. I'm not actually fully booked, but I don't think it's a good idea because we have,' I dare to look at him. 'We have *history*, you know? It would be very unprofessional, not to mention very dishonest.'

Pot. Kettle. Black.

My cheeks redden even more as I get a flashback to our rolling around on the forest floor and him skilfully teasing my nipples into a frenzy. How could he have forgotten our *history*? I was at my sensual peak, while he was caught up in a total and utter cyclone of female erotic pleasure-giving.

'But you just said, "if Nidi has no objections" it would be okay. And besides, I hardly think a bit of fooling around constitutes grounds for turning away legitimate business. We're all adults here.'

Fooling around?

I leap up, and he mirrors my actions. I push him out through the door into reception.

'Thanks for being a good sport, goodbye!' I say, hastily closing it behind me. I wait five whole minutes until I'm sure he's gone and march over to the reception desk. I need

Maria-José-Inmaculada-Carmen to *not* book him in should he ever try to, but she's too busy catching up with all of her relatives, including second cousins twice removed, on the phone. I'm furious with myself. *How could I think that Oliver would be asking me on a date? And fooling around? FOOLING AROUND?*

My fury is temporarily interrupted by Maria-José-Inmaculada-Carmen. She is tutting loudly, then shouting angrily, and now she is hissing weirdly. I will never understand this language. *Never*. I've told her, no personal calls at work. So far, she has smiled, nodded and carried on as if I simply did not say it. I am stood right in front of her, catching her red-handed in the act of not working and yet she is not bothered in the slightest.

I glare at her. 'Put that phone down!'

'But Miss West...'

'Now!'

I watch as she slams it back into the receiver, her eyes wide like a startled bunny rabbit.

'How many times have I told you no personal calls?'

'No fue personal. But Miss Weston...'

'Don't *but Miss Weston* me, Maria-José-Inmaculada-Carmen!' I squeal, just about getting to the end of her bloody name without passing out. That's another reason Nidi should have hired someone else. Someone with a much, much shorter name.

'Era tu hermana!' she yells back, full of fiery Spanish cheek that takes the wind right out of my sails.

'Oh,' I say shocked. My sister? We have not spoken for

over two weeks. Not since the day I left for Spain, in fact.

'What did she want?' I ask sharply. I stow the little nugget that Maria-José-Inmaculada-Carmen can only lie in Spanish away for now. 'And don't think for a second that I don't know you were talking to your mother afterwards. My sister speaks even worse Spanish than me,' I state triumphantly. *Shite.* I forgot I'm supposed to have a secure working grasp of the language.

Maria-José-Inmaculada-Carmen smiles insolently. 'Your *sister* Abba,' she says with a dramatic pause. 'As in the sister you say you NO have.'

Double shite.

'Ava,' I correct, glossing over the fact that I have told her and Nidi that I have no siblings. 'And I mean, I don't have a sister. She's just a...you must have misheard.'

'Miss Weston, your sister Abba,' she says insistently. I'm going to let it go. We could go around in endless circles with her pronunciation. 'Your sister, who NO exists, says to tell you...'

A loud banging from a cardoor downstairs interrupts our bickering.

'Must be the client at 11am. He arrives on time,' says Maria-José-Inmaculada-Carmen looking confused. 'So, who is this other client? The big one? He is new client?' She is looking confused at the diary and then at the computer screen and then at me.

My back is immediately up. An actual client is on his way up the feckin stairs, and I have no clue who it is.

'QUICK. NOTES! NOTES!'

'No notes,' she mutters at me without even looking up.
Gaaah!
'No notes? What do you mean no notes?'
'Ees off the website. Mr Max.'
Deep breaths.
Deep breaths.

She strolls to the window and looks down onto our little carpark. 'He arrive now. He is no Ryan Reynolds I must say,' Maria-José-Inmaculada-Carmen emits a familiar but strange hissing sound. I've never before heard her laugh, but I think this might be it.

I follow her over and peer down to see him getting out of his car. 'Maria-José-Inmaculada-Carmen, it doesn't matter how ugly the clients are as long as they pay us to help them,' I remind her. 'Besides Ryan Reynolds is an exceptionally good-looking man. Probably made in a lab. We shouldn't be comparing other human men to him. It wouldn't be fair.'

My new client looks up at us with a frown, almost as though he has heard every word we've just said.

Shitting hell.

· ♥ · ♥ · ♥ · ♥ · ♥ ·

'Please, take a seat Mr Max.' I smile sweetly at my new client as I usher him in and pretend to know what I'm doing. He nods politely, unable to talk for sucking on a colossal mint. I could hear Maria-José-Inmaculada-Carmen asking him if he had the breath of Satan, at least that's what it sounded like in Spanish. I can only imagine what he thought of that little exchange, but people in Spain chew raw garlic like the rest of the world chews gum. They'd put it in coffee if you let them.

I wait patiently for him to chew and swallow, before introducing myself.

'Mr Max, what are you hoping to achieve from our sessions together?' I ask, just as I've seen Nidi do many times last week. I flick my eyes over him to note he's dressed very much in the style of *no style*. He's a man in his thirties wearing that awful combo of torn jeans (designed for males under twenty) smartened up with a blazer (designed for those over forty) over a huge rugby shirt (designed for those who actually play rugby). A clear indication of indecision. And because I'm the sort to not judge and always look for the positives, I see immediately that he has well-kept nails and even though he has a jumpy manner about him, he is extremely polite and well-spoken. He is also very, very single-looking.

'It's just Max.'

'Of course, it is. Sorry about that.' I look down at my imaginary notes as though there's been an administrative error and not a Maria-José-Inmaculada-Carmen-related error.

Max shyly explains that he has only recently arrived in Spain and works for a UK-based company nearby. I've met his sort before. Back when I was a workaholic (just over a week ago) for an uncaring, gigantic corporation of selfish twats. I'm certain I can guess what his deal is.

'You devote long hard hours to the job and, while it pays

well,' I continue speedily, flicking my eyes to my pretend notes. '... you never seem to find the time to devote any of it to yourself, or your social life, because you are always under pressure to pursue a promotion.'

He tilts his head and crosses his legs.

'You probably can't remember the last time you hung out with friends or family, never mind went on a date, and this bit is *extremely* important,' I pause to take a breath and watch him lean in, 'you've never found yourself a good hairdresser or a sense of style that you can really *commit* to.' I watch his mouth fall open as I continue helpfully. 'You would like some coaching to bring balance to your life and help you perhaps open the door to love? You feel yourself yearning for someone to share a glass of wine and a take-away with, some romance and maybe a little drama?' I'll invite him to the SINGLES night. He'll love that.

I tilt my head slightly to the right like his and fix him my most professional look, 'Am I right?'

I feel like I'm nailing this. I wish Nidi was here observing.

He shakes his head. 'No, not really. No.'

Shite.

'I'd like to lose some weight and get fit,' he explains. 'Everything is centred around the beach here, and I'm having trouble meeting people. I feel too shy to join in.'

He looks absolutely fine to me. Some people wouldn't know a real problem if it came up and poked them in the eye.

'Have you tried a beetroot cleanse?' I take out the Wheel of Life diagram and we plough through the motions of life coaching. As I perceive them, aka from a charlatan's point of view.

· ♥ · ♥ · ♥ · ♥ · ♥ ·

Sixty excruciating minutes later, I escort him out with a deadline to join a walking group and visit an outdoor gym before the business singles night, even though he didn't express an interest in attending. I'm glad he didn't make a fuss over the misunderstanding with the extra-large mint. By the way he is self-consciously wiping his hand over his hair, I suspect he will also take my advice on board to get a decent haircut. I make a mental note to work on his eagerness to draw a veil over bizarre encounters.

As soon as he's out of the door, I turn to Maria-José-Inmaculada-Carmen. I watch her scurry to put down the *Hola!* magazine she has clearly been reading instead of working.

I take a deep calming breath. 'You mentioned earlier that a woman named Ava, called?'

Best not to fully commit to the lie until I know whether I can get away with it. I watch as she holds up her note pad and reads from it.

'Your sister? Yes. Abba called to say that she has been made redundant. That she is having... ' Maria-José-Inmaculada-Carmen waves a post-it at me, reading from it carefully. '... she is having a colossal quarter-life crisis and that she comes here to be life coach. She wants name of website for quick qualify. Same as you.'

Shitting hell.

I stare wide-eyed with disbelief at her, waiting for her to retract every evil word she has just articulately delivered. She stares boldly back and shows me her notepad.

'Ava is coming here?' I feel suddenly light-headed. 'To Spain? To be a life coach?'

'Yes. Same. As. You,' she repeats unnecessarily slowly as if English has become *my* second language not *hers*. I see she has even gone to the trouble of underlining the words. She points to them in case I simply can't make them out.

'And Google explained me that a quarter-life crisis involves anxiety over the direction and quality of one's life. Is very common. Especially in thee UK. Is very fashionable on Tweetair.' Maria-José-Inmaculada-Carmen is looking very, very pleased with herself. I rive again at my scalp while we stare at each other.

My scalp is on fire.

'Ava is coming here?'

Maybe she has misheard.

She nods solemnly. 'She says she has experience of managing more than two hundred people over ten regional offices. She is coming to help you run your business. This business that you own. This one. Where I am sitting.'

I think I'm having an actual stroke.

I can either act surprised as though these announcements of a sibling, a phoney baloney qualification and my new status as CEO are news to me, or I could come clean.

Or I could do neither.

Chapter 15

I dart back to my office for a sit-down, tapping wildly on my third eye and my temples, whilst breathing deeply in through my nostrils to encourage a solution to present itself.

Bollocks. Bollocks. Bollocks.

I quickly reach for my phone and dial my mother to find out what is going on. How can Ava just assume she can have the exact same quarter-life crisis as me and expect me to be happy about it? I need to put a quick spanner in the works and stop it from happening. My mother takes an age to pick up.

'Hello darling,' she answers smoothly. 'I wondered how long it would take you to ring.'

'Hello, Mother,' I say flatly. 'I'm guessing you have heard the news.'

'Of course, darling,' she says brightly, 'it was my idea.'

'What?' I explode.

'Well, you mentioned how great your job is going on Instagram and how brilliant it is to live out there, so I thought it would be perfect for your sister to come and do the same.

While she's looking for a proper job.'

Proper job? My mother ignores my silence and carries on.

'I mean, how hard can it be? Ava's a very clever girl. She's used to managing over two hundred people across ten regional offices, you know. I'm sure she can get the hang of being a life counsellor no problem.'

'Life coach.' I correct. And she has been in charge of two hundred poor souls for literally thirteen days, but I'd rather not sound petty.

'Well, whatever, darling. Just make sure you look after her. She's in quite the state. They really stitched her up.'

I perk up at this bit of information. Whilst it is great news to hear Ava is getting a taste of her own medicine, I'm now severely regretting my many exaggerated social media posts of me living my best life. Maybe it is time to be more truthful. I'm only ever living my second or even, third best life.

'But Mum,' I plead, 'the life coach business is a flooded market. Really, it is the WORST time to retrain and start a business. Literally EVERYONE is doing it these days. Life coaches are ten a penny.'

'Yes, your sister said the same thing. Anyway, she only has to do it as a kind of hobby to keep her busy until something better comes along.'

I am bloody seething inside, but I manage to stay civil.

'So, encourage her to do something else. Somewhere else,' I add tightly, but it is no use. Once my mother has made up her mind, it is very difficult to change it. She is in a different league altogether when it comes to stubbornness and thinking she is right all the time.

'Mother,' I say calmly in my professional voice. 'I can see why you would think that but, let's unpick your reasoning and explore the alternatives.'

'Don't bother trying any of that nonsense on me. She's booked on the early flight tomorrow morning.'

'TOMORROW? TOMORROW? ABSOLUTELY NOT. NO WAY.'

No way on this Earth will I allow it. No way. She can't come, and that's that.

My mother tuts. 'She arrives at ten-thirty into Alicante. Can you pick her up and use your *professional* skills to make sure she pulls herself together?'

My mother can be brutal sometimes. She makes the word *professional* sound like a made-up word to describe what I do.

'Surely, you can put her to work in your office. After all, you are the boss. And your father says that you both have to share the villa equally. It is her home as much as yours.'

'MOTHER!' I shout. I'm losing it now. 'Have you forgotten that Ava and I haven't spoken for almost two weeks? Not since, and I find it VERY difficult to believe that you and Dad have conveniently forgotten this little piece of information, SHE made ME redundant, remember? Or I wouldn't be in this bloody mess in the first place!'

'You're in a mess, are you?' she quickly latches on. 'Just as well she's coming then. You can help each other to sort your *lives* out. Honestly, we didn't have any of this in my day. We just got on with things. No fussing or emotional psycho-analysing, like your generation.'

'I'm not in a mess,' I backtrack, 'and if I were, she's the last bloody person I'd....'

I don't bother to finish because I can hear she's already hung up. Like a dark shadow hanging over me, I'm left choking in a toxic cloud.

Feck.

I'll have to pant extra hard to shift the toxins building up. I'm fighting a thunderous rage. First, Oliver flat-out rejects me, and now Ava is on her way to ruin things for me again. I check that my door is shut, and grab the Life Coach Handbook, leafing through until I reach emotional emergencies and scan the page.

With an angry slap, I shut the book. That's it. I've found just what I need. It's a bit extreme but needs must. I'm going to VISUALISE my anger as me on fire, and I need to put myself out. I check that my door is firmly shut one more time, before I fling myself to the ground in a foetal position.

I hate Ava for being so smug and superior and making me redundant and desperate. I know deep down this is a terrible way to feel about a family member, but I just can't help it. I just can't. Why couldn't she wait until I become an international bestselling lifestyle guru to Ryan Reynolds?

I quietly howl into my fist. All of my insides are wound so taut I feel about to snap. My eyes are squeezed shut so tight I can feel a searing headache coming on. The pain is slowly building inside my raging head. I hug my knees harder to my chest so it doesn't explode with anger before unfolding to turn over. My face is buried in the rough carpeting, scratching my cheek. I take a deep breath in and let out a thunderous low growl from deep within my very core.

I thump the carpet angrily. My face contorted against the rough pile. Yet somehow, the discomfort and pain are pleasing. The dizziness from rolling around is pleasantly numbing as I imagine the flames being put out. I relax into the movement, my body completely limp when suddenly, there's a shuffle of feet from outside of the office, a quiet knock and the click of my door gently opening.

Fuck no!!!!

A loud 'Ahem' jolts me from rolling around on the floor. I leap immediately up straightening my clothes, my hair and my face.

I lock eyes with a man.

A huge man.

My huge man.

'Jeez, and I thought *I* was supposed to be the one with the problems!' Oliver jokes to diffuse the situation while I yank down my skirt and untwist my top.

My lungs are billowing from my chest as his joke hangs in the air between us, me over by the window, and him standing rigidly by the door. His eyes are wide with shock.

It takes me only a split second more to regain my posture. A quick few taps on my wrists, three taps to my third eye and I'm composed, although my mind's a complete blank.

He continues to stare at me bog-eyed, his eyebrows up near his hairline. He takes a step forward before obviously thinking better of it. This is not going to go well. I see a myriad of emotions cross his face as he opens and closes his mouth, lost for words.

Hardly a great surprise.

I take in his rakish good looks and his fashionable shorts. Not too long. Not too short. And wait for further comments on my demonstrative display of mental collapse.

He shakes his head as he lazily takes in my insane, dishevelled appearance. He notices I am only wearing one shoe. The other having flung off during the rolling about. I can feel something stuck to my face. I slowly reach up and peel off a bright yellow post-it note from my cheek. It's a reminder from Maria-José-Inmaculada-Carmen that the International Coaching Federation called about my certificate. I look wild-eyed at him as I take in his bamboozled expression.

'Sorry, Nell' he says. 'Sorry to interrupt your... um... yoga?'

Yoga? Yoga? Like I'd have the fecking patience for yoga at a time like this!

'I was clearing a blockage. My erm... chakra. It's blocked.'

'Blockage. Right, right, of course.' He's making it sound like a plumbing issue.

'Well, it's more of a...'

How to describe it? Complete and utter breakdown? Monumental collapse of one's sanity?

'... an advanced form of throat singing.'

As our eyes meet, I detect a dangerous, playful, confidence.

'You have an air freshener sticking out of your hair.' He

has clamped his lips together. His shoulders are beginning to shake.

I remain unmoved. I'm not going to nurture his behaviour one little bit. I suppose he has had a bit of a shock catching me unawares like that. And shock can manifest itself in inappropriate ways, such as the need to giggle.

I wait two minutes.

And another two.

Finally, he composes himself, but his eyes are glassy. This is bloody ridiculous. I am a professional woman for goodness' sake. I let out an elaborate sigh. 'Why are you here?' I snap impatiently. 'I specifically said I didn't want to see you.'

Christ, but he's got me rattled.

'Why have you come back?' I repeat crossly.

'My phone. It must have dropped out of my pocket when you were strong-arming me out the door. I came straight back but you were with a client.'

I follow his gaze to the seat where he'd been sitting during the session just over an hour ago. There is a flat object on it.

'Anyway, I wanted to apologise for the misunderstanding earlier. I realise now, how what I said could've been misconstrued.' Oliver strides over to retrieve his phone. He turns it over to inspect it before tucking it in his pocket. I am entranced by how fluidly he moves for such a beefcake. 'I came to ask you out on a date.'

Oh.

Chapter 16

A date? We take a moment to stare at each other.

'Although, I'm not so sure now. I've literally been gone an hour. How has this,' he says, flapping his hand at me, 'happened in the meantime?'

It's a very fair question, but I'll keep the focus squarely on him. 'We all cope in different ways,' I say graciously.

I immediately see that he is thinking that's a bit rich coming from a woman of questionable sanity who has just been caught flailing about on the floor.

'Seriously, though,' he says, 'are you okay?'

I am pleased to see he has the decency to look me in the eye, but then to my absolute annoyance, he says, 'I feel like you're having a bit of a meltdown, and maybe *you* should see someone? Someone *qualified*?'

Of all the cheek.

'Okay, I'm sorry!' he yells, catching my thoughts. 'Honestly, I would not have come in if the vampire on reception hadn't told me to.'

I suppose it is her fault.

Oliver half-smiles at me. He looks genuinely concerned.

All of a sudden, the fight leaves me and I wilt down onto the sofa.

Oliver gingerly crosses the room to join me. 'Look. How can I help?'

His eyes are drawing me in. He slings an arm casually across the back of the sofa, settling in for the long haul. He is insanely good-looking and my stomach immediately flips at his close proximity.

'Tell me what's wrong.'

It feels like an invitation I can't refuse. I raise my eyes slowly in the most seductive way that any eyelids have ever risen before, weighed down with desire, and prepare to blow him away with just how fascinating my harrowing backstory can be.

'Well, as you know, it all started when my sister stole my promotion and made me redundant,' I snivel, glad to have someone to talk to. I tell him about how unfair it all was, whole departments done away with in the lean, austerity measures and how I had to run away from my great life and position of high authority (not strictly true, but makes for a more effective narrative) and start this lonely one, here in Spain, where no one knows me, but at least I don't have to face the everyday embarrassment of being unemployed while my sister steals my promotion and my boyfriend.

'It should have been me as Senior Buzz and Brand Warrior, managing over two hundred people across ten regional offices, not her.'

'Brand Warrior? Sounds important.'

He totally gets it.

I tell him of how I struggled to get the social media job in the first place, sending off thousands of applications, interview after interview and just when all my hard work paid off, my mother practically forced me to make sure my sister was able to slide into the same company having not had to lift a finger. 'Ava always has it so easy. She's always been the favourite. I could be drowning in the pool and my mother would step on my head to give Ava a gold medal for best wet hair.'

Oliver moves an inch closer, rivetted.

I'm trying not to sound like a whining five-year old. I tell him that I am in way over my head with Nidi's business because I exaggerated my way into the job. I have lied on my grid, making out that I run the company, which he could point out that he warned me against but doesn't, which earns him a multitude of brownie points.

Christ Almighty, I nearly forgot! 'And my sister is coming here tomorrow! To steal my job. Again.' I whimper pathetically, wishing he might comfort me and tell me that everything will be alright and that things will get better and that my sister will get everything that's coming to her.

Oliver remains quiet for a long time. He lets out a slow sigh. 'It seems I have met you at a very interesting time in your journey,' he says, sounding very, very emotionally aware. 'And just how long are you going to feel sorry for yourself? Sounds to me like you are wallowing in self-pity instead of dusting yourself off and getting on with your life. If you're not careful, it will pass you by.'

What??

'I mean,' he carries on quietly. 'Who lets a job title define them? You're still you with or without that job. Any decent friend would respect that. And yes, some of us have to work bloody hard for what we achieve, while others seem to get handed everything on a plate, but that's life.'

Excuse me?

'Seems to me that you need to take a long hard look at yourself, and appreciate everything you *have* got, instead of dwelling on the things you *haven't*.'

Two things happen at once that alarm me to my core. The main one being how terribly uninformed Oliver is – *how friggin dare he quote me back to me* - and secondly, he's googling one-handed and showing me a list of Emotional Freedom Techniques.

A prickly silence descends on us. A huge part of me wants to slap his face. It's almost as though *he* is trying to life coach *me*.

Cheeky, cheeky fecker.

'How can you say I'm wallowing in self-pity? You don't even know me.'

'I do know you. I know that you are kind and caring. You are compassionate and fun. You are clever and funny.'

I can feel my heart of ice instantly thaw at his lovely words. I'm outraged at him, but looking forward to hearing more.

'And you are an extremely good kisser,' he continues.

I have goosebumps on my arms.

'And yet, it's all hidden behind this… this…' He waves his palm around in a circle in front of me. '… this seething ball of bitterness and fury. It's such a shame.'

Huh? I sag back in my seat as the wind leaves my sails.

He's changed his tune quick enough!

'You are the rudest man I've ever met!'

I am a life coach. A certified (it should arrive any day now), highly experienced professional person. Eight years in the field as they'd say. And not just any field. The highly stressful field of online social media marketing. I'm the one who helps and advises NOT the other way round.

'Out,' I tell him. 'Out you get.'

He leaps up, trying to apologise but I don't give him a chance. I watch him dart across the room like he's fleeing a band of militia rebels.

'I'll call you,' he yells over his shoulder as he yanks open the door.

'Don't bother,' I fire back, watching him scurry through reception and down the stairs.

He's infuriating.

I turn to see an open-mouthed Maria-José-Inmaculada-Carmen taking in the show.

'Maria-José-Inmaculada-Carmen!' I screech and proceed to give her a piece of my mind. I mean, how could she let someone just walk in without me saying I was ready? *How? How?*

'But Miss Weston, I hear you screaming something. I thought it was signal to let gentleman enter,' she pleads, all wide innocent eyes. We lock eyes for a second. I'm not so sure. There's a touch of something demonic about her wilful misunderstanding.

'Well don't do it again,' I say. 'And make sure you charge him double for his session!'

'But Miss Weston,' she whispers, clearly pretending to be upset at me shouting at her. 'He is from the EEE-THAY-EFFF.'

'The what?' I demand. Surely, I heard that wrong.

'The EEE-THAY-EFFF,' she repeats carefully.

The ICF? Is she saying the ICF? Where have I heard that recently? It's sounds very familiar... *Shit*. My head is swimming. Nidi mentioned the ICF and something about notifying them that I'm about to begin coaching, and she would be my mentor. Could he be from the International Coach Federation, here in Alicante?

She speaks slowly as if testing me. 'I write it on the post-it note. Is very important for you.'

I stare wildly at her.

'Very, very important,' she repeats.

'Alright!' I snap at her. 'I get it!'

Oh my God. I can't breathe. I need to get this straight in my head. By some bizarre coincidence the nosy giant I shared a taxi with from the airport, got shit-faced with at the retreat where we made out like a pair of randy goats on heat, just happens to work at the Alicante branch of the ICF.

That's his company?

He works for a global training company?

Fuckedy fuck!!

I reach out to the reception desk for support and think back to whether he told me this, my brain scrambling about to join the dots. Did I ask him anything about himself?

No, why would I? At the retreat, I was far too busy hanging off his bulging biceps and dry humping him senseless. And during *his* life coaching session, I talked about myself.

Fancy him catching me rolling around screaming like a fucking crazy person. And me telling him to *pretend* to be a client while I *pretend* to be a qualified coach. I'm pretty certain there'll be a rule against that.

No wonder he agreed to it so easily. No wonder he's so nosy! It's his fucking job! Fucking hell, I'll get sacked, and I'll be unemployed again and desperate. I stamp back into my office. Within seconds, I have located my other shoe dangling from the lightshade as I remember his repeated warnings about webs of lies.

Cold realisation dawns.

I've successfully handed him my career on a plate. I stand the lamp back on the coffee table. I must have knocked it over while I was rolling about.

Nidi will be so disappointed that I've let her down. She'll possibly get struck off in the process too, causing unknown amounts of stress to her unborn child, and Ava is arriving just in time to enjoy the whole shit show. I can just picture my sister laughing when she hears the news. I need to stop him coming back so that he can't expose me as the complete lying fraud that I am.

Feckerty, feck, feck, feck!

'Maria-José-Inmaculada-Carmen,' I say from the doorway. 'Listen to me very, very carefully. Do not. I repeat. Do not...' I give her a chance to grasp the basics. 'DO NOT let that man book another appointment. Do you understand?'

Maria-José-Inmaculada-Carmen looks at me blankly. 'Si.'

Once back in my office, I let out a muffled cry, and for the billionth time, wish I was married to Ryan Reynolds. He'd know what to do. I'm sure I'd be a much happier person if I were Mrs Reynolds.

A huge searing headache pain rips me away from the fantasy, back to the huge hot mess I'm in. I race to the cooler to crack open the emergency bottle of Sauvignon Blanc. I pour a large glass and take a huge swig with one hand while I attempt to Google how Ryan handles a crisis.

On second thought, I should search for international job websites and flights out of here. I'm wondering if France still has those wine lakes, you hear about. I could move there and start again. Or I could escape to a secluded castle far away in Eastern Europe. Another few swigs and I'm wondering if the Greeks might be a friendlier race. And as I drain the last of the glass, I settle on the remote region of northern Peru. I'll go live with the randy mountain goats.

Chapter 17

'Hello Nell, have you got two minutes for a quick word?' Nidi asks politely, popping her head through the door a while later.

'Of course, I have,' I say, immediately clicking the job websites closed and swiftly sliding my empty wine glass into the desk drawer. I try to put aside my feeling of foreboding when I see Nidi making her way across to the window to take a seat on the good sofa. She pats the space next to her to indicate that I should go over.

Now I am significantly concerned. Nidi is a very experienced life coach. Which is why I can tell that she is about to life coach me right now. Maria-José-Inmaculada-Carmen must have told her about some of my truths; the existence of a sister and my not quite being qualified, my penchant for daytime drinking and the involvement of the ICF which might jeopardise her business. I really must put a stop to all of this lying.

'Nell, hun, don't look so worried,' she soothes. I pretend to laugh it off.

I'm absolutely shitting myself.

'Have you been drinking?' Nidi asks me, slightly alarmed.

'No, of course not,' I lie, reaching for a mint. It's barely 1pm. 'Oh, but I did spill some wine earlier, tidying up. Must be that, I think.'

It's true. I spilled at least 3 units straight down my throat.

'How are you?' she asks innocently, cutting across me. That is such a loaded question. Maybe she can sense I'm something approaching a complete disaster deep down. Which, apparently, for a Life Coach, is fairly embarrassing no matter how hard I've been working to hide it from the world.

I snap back to attention. 'Nidi,' I say, politely cutting to the chase. I tilt my head and reciprocate the eyebrow raise. I might as well brazen it out. 'What's this about? Hmm?'

I see her adjust the way she is sitting from a relaxed slouch to an upright position rubbing her hand gently over her neat bump. She turns to give me a warm smile. It's like the one that reeled me in the very first time we met. Here it comes.

'Well,' she says in her soothing way and reaches for my hands to cup them in hers. I feel my heartbeat quicken as I look into her soulful, all-seeing eyes.

She knows. She knows I'm a deceitful, horrible person.

In my defence, I am the product of very limp parenting. Of course I'm going to struggle.

'Devin's grandma died last night,' she says, taking a beat to let this land.

Oh. What a relief.

'Thank fuck for that.' I say, exhaling too loudly.

Nidi's eyebrows shoot up.

'Sorry... sorry. I meant it's such a shock.'

Now she is frowning.

'Not that I ever met her, I mean. I'm so sorry to hear that she died so tragically,' I say, unable to stop. 'Or however she went.'

'Thanks,' says Nidi, giving me an odd look. 'She died peacefully in her sleep.' She pulls me round to face her and gets straight to the point, 'I know you've only been here for five minutes, but...'

'I see,' I interrupt, my whole body sinking. This is familiar territory. I'm being let go. And this time, it's my own stupid fault. I can't even blame my sister. Well, I can, but... actually, yes, this all started with Ava. She's to blame for this whole web of lies in the first place. A ball of misery stirs deep within.

Nidi snaps me out of my bitter trance with a sharp click of her fingers. 'I need to ask a huge favour. We're going back to England to organise the funeral. Hindu funerals can be as big as the weddings. A couple of weeks long and Nani was very popular. It's terribly short notice, I know, but can you hold the fort here for a few weeks or so?'

Oh. I was not expecting this.

'When will you be going?' I say, relief flooding through me.

'We're hoping to leave today.'

Alcohol fumes are billowing out from my every pore in celebration.

'What about the day-to-day running of the business?' I

ask, trying not to sound too overjoyed.

Two weeks of sunbathing and scrolling through TikTok!

Nidi beams at me. 'It's such a relief to know that you've already had experience of running and growing a business like this already.'

I stare at her through a panicked haze, barely listening, as she talks me through her client to-do list and diary.

'Can you call each individual client and explain for me, please? It's a real shame that we didn't get your observation done or the mentoring, otherwise, you could have done my sessions while I'm away. That would have been so good for you.'

I nod my head politely. *I'd rather walk over burning hot coals.*

'Still, you and Maria-José-Inmaculada-Carmen can arrange the event between you and pre-assess any new clients ready for my return. That should keep you busy. Such a relief you used to be an events manager, isn't it?'

I gulp. *Another white lie.*

'Contact all the local businesses to come along and do as much PR through our socials as you can manage. I'll leave you details of the budget. Tell me the date as soon as you can so that I can be back in time.'

I am literally going to have a heart attack.

This is the best and worst possible timing. Both a blessing and a curse. Part of me is ecstatic at not having to tell her about Oliver being from the ICF and consequential exposure as a fraud. Nor do I need to reveal that the sister I said I didn't have, is arriving forthwith. The joy is immediately cancelled out by the sheer and horrific weight of being left in charge in my current state.

I take her hand in mine. 'Nidi, there's something I need to...'

'I can't tell you how grateful I am. Especially in my condition. Devin's so worried that the stress of running the business from the UK will harm the baby.' I watch her rub her belly and look at me with those glorious, warm, kind eyes. 'Thank you, Nell. It's a huge relief.'

Well, that's that then. I manage to keep a lid on the simmering meltdown until Nidi has finished telling me everything that she needs me to do in her absence, *to basically save the baby's life and increase our client portfolio exponentially* and has gone back to her office. Before I decide on how to silence Maria-José-Inmaculada-Carmen, it's crucial that nothing upsets Nidi or causes her to worry.

· ♥ · ♥ · ♥ · ♥ · ♥ ·

Maria-José-Inmaculada-Carmen is the only fly in the ointment. I figure after yesterday's disastrous interview, where she clearly let us both down, she owes me one. I've also caught her smoking and reading the *Hola!* magazine several times instead of working. Ditto chatting with her mother. She is going to have to severely up her game while Nidi is gone, otherwise we will run this business into the ground, which is precisely the opposite of what Nidi is expecting. She was very clear about this. We need to be at our most professional, treat clients with respect and keep them happy until she returns. We have to run the bookings, manage the website efficiently and keep track of the finances and payments. But above all, Nidi says, uphold the ethos of Life Coaching, which is to aim for where we want to be in the future and always be kind to ourselves and others.

That reminds me. I should let Maria-José-Inmaculada-Carmen know that *I* am in charge now and I will no longer put up with any of her unprofessional working practices. I march through to reception suddenly remembering a bee that I had in my bonnet yesterday but was too tired to do anything about. Oh yes, I need to teach her how to operate the three buttons on the telephone that even a cat could master in less time than it has taken her.

Me in actual charge. Compared to two hundred people across ten regional offices, this should not be as daunting as it feels.

Deep breaths.
Deep breaths.
I can do this.

I see Maria-José-Inmaculada-Carmen scuttling back to the reception desk. The window overlooking the street is wide open, and the place smells of smoke. She's been hanging out of the window, above our entrance, I should add, for all the clients and potential customers to see, smoking a cigarette and speaking to her mother on the phone. She knows this is strictly forbidden. She knows that we are to uphold the highest of professional standards at ALL times. I've even heard Nidi mention it to her more than once. I fly straight to the window to see, in the rush to pretend she's been doing nothing of the sort, she has left her *Hola!* magazine on the windowsill. I quickly grab it and whizz round accusingly.

'Did that ICF man ring to book an appointment while I was talking to Nidi?'

'Si.'

'And?'

Maria-José-Inmaculada-Carmen sulkily eyes the magazine rolled up in my hand, 'I say him you busy.'

'Busy? You mean fully booked?' I must check to see if she is up to something out of spite.

'Busy. Gone for intimate cleansing vaginal STEAM. I tell him it was URGENT. He says he will call back when you have finished steam cleaning yourself.'

How am I supposed to work like this? How?

Maria-José-Inmaculada-Carmen and I take a beat to eyeball each other. Her with her smoky breath and me with my stale wine fumes. All that's left of this god-forsaken business.

'Everything okay?' Nidi interrupts, coming into reception.

I plaster on a smile. 'Fine!' It comes out sounding the opposite.

'Devin's picking me up in half an hour and we're off to the airport. Thank you both so much. I know I'm leaving my business in good hands.'

Chapter 18

Right, no time to fester. We've waved Nidi off amid a blaze of instructions for me and Maria-José-Inmaculada-Carmen. It was a little overwhelming, so Maria-José-Inmaculada-Carmen is having some back-to-back ciggies out the window, and I have gone to my office to pretend I haven't noticed. I need to know exactly what Ryan Reynolds ate for breakfast this morning, then I need to crack on with finding out if Oliver is indeed from the ICF and whether I have a leg to stand on or not.

I told Maria-José-Inmaculada-Carmen that I am borrowing the appointments book for a little while and asked her to research any good online life coaching seminars in Spain that I can attend, especially if they are free, particularly to do with developing micro business, and anything at all on business SINGLES events and how to run them. I asked her to think about increasing traffic to the website and the possibility of how we could attract more clients.

Nidi has faith in me to keep this business going while she's away, and I am determined to do just that.

I fear that because I was so vague and inept on the radio,

we could have a whole manner of oddbods turning up. People who are single and looking for a romantic partner, people who are self-employed and looking for a business partner, people who are self-employed and are looking for a romantic partner who also owns their own business, or people who work for a business but just happen to be fucking single! And we are asking them to attend an event for no discernible reason that I can think of.

There's a knock on my door ten minutes later. Maria-José-Inmaculada-Carmen has a question. 'What you ask me to do?'

Oh my God. I spent twenty minutes explaining it all super slowly. I'll have to explain it all over again.

'What's trending?' I ask her. 'Is it increasing workplace productivity, people wanting career changes or better relationships? Dealing with stress? Pandemic weight gain? General malaise about work-life balance? Plastics? Cost of living crisis? Global warming?'

Oh dear. It appears this is too much for her to take in. She continues to stare at me open-mouthed. 'You know SEO? It's basic stuff Maria-José-Inmaculada-Carmen.'

'Si, si,' she nods, still looking at me like I just threatened to eat her Labradoodle. She's out of her comfort zone. I've noticed when put in situations where she is required to do what she is employed to do, she abruptly loses all command of the English language. As Nidi was firing important to do things at me, she suggested I take time to life coach Maria-José-Inmaculada-Carmen to help her achieve the goal of doing something useful at work, and for valuable learning experience for me. But regretfully, with her sulky face and sullen, downturned mouth, I haven't got the patience to even think about it.

'Maria-José-Inmaculada-Carmen,' I say looking her right in the eye. 'You *do* know what it is that we do, don't you? You were listening when I explained it to the presenter yesterday?'

Her wide-eyed blank stare is all the answer that I need.

Oh My Fucking God. Did she not even listen to a word I said during that crappy interview?

'What about everything Nidi just asked us to do while she's away? Did you understand any of that?'

Maria-José-Inmaculada-Carmen looks down at her nails. One of them is chipped. I can see her brain wandering as she inspects it from different angles. With a sigh, I'm tempted to ask her to Google 'How not to be a shit assistant', but I don't, instead I ask her to Google 'Reasons to hire a life coach' and tell her to start fucking reading.

'Maybe you should write it all down,' I suggest. 'On your many post-it notes.'

She looks at me as though I have delivered a major insult.

'You have client very soon.'

'No. I do not have a client very soon.'

'Yes,' she says.

'Cancel it.'

She heard Nidi tell me *not* to life coach her clients but to reschedule.

'Too late. He has left in car already. I tell him where to park. It takes him thirty minutes, he says.' Maria-José-Inmaculada-Carmen looks at me as though she's expecting a medal. 'You are the boss now, apparently.'

I have no words.

Thoughts fly through my brain, scrambling for attention. My first huge problem is that an actual, bone fide client is on his way to be life coached by Nidi, and it is too late to cancel.

My second huge problem is that my sister is coming tomorrow to make a fool of me, steal my job and ruin my life for the second time in as many weeks.

My third huge problem is that my walking-dead, chain-smoking assistant has far too long a name and far too terrible a work ethic to help me build my career into one that can provide a living for both of us. Nidi says we need to attract as many new clients from the business singles event as possible.

In addition, Oliver is potentially spying on me, which leads me to question what that heavy petting was all about and whether he was genuinely into me. I'll have to push that to one side for the moment.

I feel the panic rising.

Deep breaths.... one, two, three... in through the nostrils, out through the mouth... two, three.

'Who is it?

'Jiff.'

'Fine.' I say, keeping the terror from my voice. 'Send him in when he arrives.'

It is Geoff Levison. I remember him from last week. I observed him with Nidi a few times. He is a nice man, originally from Mongolia. He taught himself to speak English online. Very clever. As a result, he sounds like he is from seventeen different countries.

I dash back into my office to get ready for battle. I mean work. I glance at my wine cooler cabinet. Full of immediate answers. And possibly also home to problem number four. I suspect that I might be a bit of an alcoholic now. But one thing at a time.

I'll just quickly check up on Ryan Reynolds first to see if he's thinking about getting divorced again or at the least having a few marital complications. As I'm typing in 'Ryan' and 'marriage problems' to the search engine, I come across a quote that Nidi shared last week with clients, who were having a tough time coping with relationships and full-on careers. It says that filling their days to the point that they are physically and emotionally drained will mean that they end up with nothing by the end, but if they fill their days with nothing, they'll have something by the end. I literally have no idea what that is supposed to mean. An ugly thought occurs. Is that what I spent the whole of my twenties doing? Filling my days with so much work I was left empty by the end?

Oh Christ. Fifteen minutes just disappeared. *Where? How? Bloody TikTok.*

I just have time to remind my terrible assistant to answer any calls, especially client bookings or changes of appointments, and to under no circumstances let the awful man from the International Coach Federation book an appointment. In fact, I'll tell her to say I have left the country and do not intend to return. Even just the thought of Oliver brings back a wave of humiliation. I have a good mind to report him for unprofessional behaviour, never mind him reporting me. I mean, surely, I am not the first woman to be caught rolling around pretending to be on fire. It's in the Life Coaching Handbook. I'll make sure to remember to put that in my complaint. It's on pages 35 and 36, clear as day.

Now, I must find something for Geoff. I quickly Google something useful for us to use as a task. Within minutes, I've managed to find out what Ryan Reynolds really thinks about second marriages and fatherhood. I'm pleased to hear he finds it a struggle at times.

Gaaah! Another fifteen minutes disappear just like that! I fly into reception, ready to bark at Maria-José-Inmaculada-Carmen. There is no way that I can go through with this. No way. How can I possibly justify him paying me fifty euros for the hour? How would he be getting good value for money? I won't be able to take it if I feel like I've cheated him.

The sound of the door opening downstairs stops me in my tracks.

'He is here!' yells Maria-José-Inmaculada-Carmen at me. She's given up on the phone system entirely. 'He is on time as usual.'

God help him.

Just as I hear his footsteps on the stairs, an idea forms. I could help him with his English as an extra service, part of the package. A free English lesson from a native speaker.

Starting with helping him get to grips with pronouncing his own name correctly.

'I will give him a mint for his breath.' He is standing in front of her.

He looks at me apprehensively.

'Hello, Geoff,' I say, plastering on a smile. 'Remember me from last week?'

· ♥ · ♥ · ♥ · ♥ · ♥ ·

I take a deep breath, tap my wrists and third eye gently and exhale as slowly as I can. I convince myself to feel positive about today despite the universe's multiple attempts to sabotage it. I am determined to move Geoff from doing nothing about his business ideas to an action point. I found his last session with Nidi a bit frustrating. Plus, she never once tackled him on his phonics.

'Now, Geoff...'

'Jiff,' he corrects.

'No, your name's Geoff,' I remind him politely.

'Yis, thit's what ah sid. It's short for Jiffrey.'

Good Lord, this could go on for the entire session.

'What does success look like to you, Geoff? What would you say is the pinnacle?'

He's so distracted by this bolt from the blue that he dithers a bit.

'Take your time,' I say.

About sixty minutes would be ideal.

I get out some paper and suggest we throw some words

on there and unpick his thinking. I know the first few words he'll come up with. According to Google, they're the words that EVERYBODY says when asked this question, so I dive straight in and tell him that he is not allowed to use the words, money, achievement or happiness. This stops him in his tracks.

'Ah caaahn't write hippiniss?' he asks with eyebrows raised.

'No, Geoff. It's lazy sheep-like thinking. It'll get you nowhere. Now, success Geoff, what does it look like? What will spark joy in your life?'

He takes the pen I offer him and immediately comes up with words like sizeable profits, empire building and ten-berth luxury yacht. As I watch him scribble away, those material things seem suddenly childish and meaningless. I can't help but think of all those years I put in at work, slaving away, early starts, late finishes and not even a yacht to show for it. Why did I bother? Why did I sweat it out each day surrounded by that team of absolute pillocks? Where was the joy or fun in any of it? Have I let life slip me by? Maybe Oliver is right, and it is time I dusted myself off and stopped wallowing in regrets.

Suddenly I have an idea. I'll tell Geoff that success should define a way of life, not an end-point.

'It's all about the journey we take, Geoff. The day to day. Not the stuff we buy at the end. I mean what's the point in getting the yacht at the end if it cost you thirty years of being miserable? Working life should be fun and rewarding, shouldn't it?'

I watch as Geoff suddenly stops jotting down words and looks at me. Maybe I have got this wrong.

His face breaks into a broad grin, as if I've just announced that he's due a gigantic tax return. 'Thit's it!' he shouts at me. He stands up. He swivels about and sits back down. His hands fly to the sides of his head as he clutches his hair like a mad professor.

'Thit's flaymin it!' he shouts again and looks wildly at me. 'Thit's where ah hev bin going wrong all these yiz!'

'All these *years*, Geoff.' I look at him intently for signs of him taking the piss. I mean I've seen him and Nidi, more or less, get nowhere every session. This seems terribly out of character for him.

'A way of laff,' he repeats slowly, 'Ah need to change my way of laff.'

'Life,' I correct.

'Yis, mah way of laff.'

'MY way of LIFE,' I articulate carefully for him.

Jiff looks at me with such a sad expression it instantly makes me feel awful.

'I'm sorry, Geoff. You have a lovely accent. Very global. I was just trying to help but anyway, you don't need it. Let's just get on with it, shall we?' I say briskly. I need to act like an actual life coach, and not a speech and language therapist. I need to do the stuff in the handbook and what the internet tells me to do.

I get out some action planning tools, one of which is a pyramid of words. I can feel his excitement, it feels genuine and it makes me excited as well. I actually think I can help him. I do.

'You want to be a go-getter, don't you?' I ask him, drawing on my many wasted people-pleasing years at work. He nods enthusiastically back. 'But you are not sure of exactly *what* you want out of life so naturally you are stuck on *how* to get it?' He keeps nodding. 'You are searching for business ideas because you associate a successful business with *you* being a success, am I right?' He'll need a neck brace if he continues like this.

'Ah im so stuck raaht now,' he admits.

'Well, Geoff, with experience comes wisdom, which means that talent can often develop later in life for many people. So, for the next session, I want you to name one person you admire and whose career is similar to the one you would most like to develop for yourself. I want you to look *into* this person Geoff not *up* to them. Find out what their *journey* to success looked like. Understand?'

'Yis,' he says. 'Journey to success, stip bah stip. Got it.'

I walk to the door to see him off. He stops by Maria-José-Inmaculada-Carmen's desk to make another appointment.

'Nidi won't be back for three weeks,' I explain.

'Why can't ah see you for laff coaching?' he says, his face falling. 'Ah rilly think we are gitting somewhere. I really enjoyed this sishun.'

I gulp, the compliment almost too much. I nod to Maria-José-Inmaculada-Carmen to take the booking.

I am a life coach. I am a bone fide life coach with an actual client who wants to pay for my services. I feel like I've just done a line of cocaine as an instant hit of happiness pings round my brain.

'See you at the singles event Senor Jiff,' she waves after him as he leaves. I roll my eyes unable to keep from grinning.

'Not you as well? Honestly, it's Geoff,' I say slowly to Maria-José-Inmaculada-Carmen who looks confused.

'J- E- F' I pronounce phonetically.

She seems confused as she looks at me, then down at the appointment book, then back up at me. I watch her turn the book round so that I can see his name and signature. It says Jiffrey Livison. I peer at the signature and the printed name next to it. It does indeed say very clearly, for absolutely any idiot to see, Jiffrey Livison. JIFFREY effing LIVISON. Clear as day. Crystal clear. Un-fucking-mistakably clear.

I have been calling him Geoff, and he has been correcting *me*, not the other way around.

I tap my third eye rapidly and focus on my breath as the joy is sapped from my body.

You are on a journey. The beginning of a delightful learning curve. One of many. Breathe through it.

I can see that Maria-José-Inmaculada-Carmen is dying to smirk. I am not ready for that, so I swivel around to turn my back on her.

'It's okay,' I say, suddenly remembering a much bigger emergency. 'You can go home early.'

My sister is arriving tomorrow morning and I need to stop her boarding that plane.

Chapter 19

I am severely regretting my decision to knock back a whole bottle of vino in under an hour last night. Snippets of me ringing my father late at night to try and get him to talk Ava out of coming – pointless, utterly pointless – are coming back to haunt me, along with the unwise decision to open a second bottle after the exchange didn't go quite as planned. I replay the conversation in my head while I nurse a coffee.

'But Dad, you HAVE to stop her coming over.'

'Nell, my darling, she's already announced it on Instagram to all of her followers.'

'She can't come! There's nothing for her to do. She can't just turn up expecting to become a life coach overnight.'

Like I did.

'She's too unlikeable and... self-absorbed. Literally the opposite of what you need to be.'

'She's arriving in the morning, and she's staying for as long as she wants, darling.'

'FINE! She can stay two days.'

'As long as she wants, Nell.'

'OKAY! Three days max. Two would be better.'

'As long as she wants. It's her home too.'

'We'll just have to see, Dad. She may want to leave straightaway. Don't put pressure on her to stay. Two days is quite enough time for her to pull herself together and realise she belongs back at *home* with you and Mum. Tell her to only pack for two days.'

'Nell, are you a bit drunk because it sounds like you aren't listening to a word I'm saying?'

The rest of the conversation consisted of my Dad repeating himself until he was too weary to continue, and when he sounded like he was getting a bit annoyed with me, I accidentally roared, 'SHE CAN ONLY STAY FOR TWO EFFING DAYS, ALL RIGHT?'

Despite my colourful language, I'm sure he'll have passed on my message.

A sudden nausea spreads throughout my body. My head is banging, and my stomach feels incredibly queasy. I dry heave a few times and drag myself back to the bedroom. A sideways glance at the time tells me I am going to be extremely late to pick my sister up from the airport. I throw on the nearest clothes lying on the floor and haul my heavy body to the bathroom to give my black, red wine teeth a power scrub. Ava is the type to notice tiny red wine smile marks at the side of lips and unkempt dental hygiene.

Now where did I fling my car keys when I got back from work yesterday? And where is all that loose change I'll need for the toll road? And where did I hide my new bank card so I can fill the near-empty tank with petrol on the way?

While I'm frantically searching the oven and rifling

through bags of pasta for my bank card, I find the car keys in the sink.

I will add being better organised to the list. And by *better organised* I mean, *less pissed*.

The transfer of money from my UK account to the new Spanish one went as seamlessly as trying to access the internet with only a roll of Sellotape and a cabbage. I'm down to my last twenty euros and I've been putting off going to the bank to sort it out because of all this shit that's going on. That also reminds me, I must book a venue and caterer for the business singles event.

Gaaah! Later. I'll do it later. I have more pressing needs.

I set off in the car and try to drive like a normal person instead of one who is teetering on the brink of an emotional cliff, about to throw herself off into the deep end. Last night's binge drinking has done nothing to alleviate the knot of tension in my stomach, thus guaranteeing there was no chance of any jogging or yoga happening this morning. Or hot water with lemon. Or exfoliating for gleaming skin. Or any lasting joyful fecking thoughts.

As I drive along, the sea twinkles back at me. The sun shines brightly, but the scenic beauty is completely lost on me. There's no fecking bright side to any of this. I'm just fooling myself. No matter what my mother says, my sister is here for one reason and one reason only. To ruin my fecking life all over again. I feel the bile of too much coffee, too much wine and too much resentment swill around. The heat building in the car is stifling and making me feel ten times worse.

· ❤ · ❤ · ❤ · ❤ · ❤ ·

By the time I skid through the airport and park up, I get out of the car and instantly throw up burning liquid from the drink last night. My sudden and startlingly noisy outpour sends a family of four scurrying away from me, across to the arrivals and through the huge glass doors guarding the airport entrance. As it gushes out of me, I instantly feel better.

Unfortunately, that feeling is short-lived as I feel a pair of judgy eyes on me. My sister is standing by the entrance with her hand on her hip and her head cocked to one side. She's wearing an expression very similar to mine, but in a face that's a lot prettier and better plucked, moisturized and hydrated. With better-conditioned hair and notably stronger eyebrows. What a fucking hypocrite. It's me who needs to be annoyed, not her.

It is the moment I have been dreading. The scenario feels surreal now that I'm in it. Whatever I do, I must remain dignified and self-respecting. No more throwing up on the pavement in front of families with children. I wipe my mouth on my sleeve and hold her gaze. My mind is completely blank. The sun is beating down on me, the air is unbearably dry and it's not helping my hangover a single bit. All I can feel is a familiar rage simmering deep within. Dignity might just have to take a back seat for this one.

Feck! Feck! Feckerty, feck, feck!!

I simply can't move. Ava has come dressed as though she

may be called on to enter the Love Island villa at a moment's notice, in what is essentially a denim thong. When she walks towards me, lugging her huge cases, one of her bags slips off her shoulder to the ground, spilling its contents everywhere. I make no effort to help. I watch her stumble on her elegant high-wedged shoes, trying to juggle her phone in one hand and the trolley holding her cases in the other, while she bends to pick up her belongings from the road. The trolley is piled high with luggage. She *definitely* looks like a person who intends to stay for more than two effing days.

She quickly swoops a salon's worth of beauty products back into her bag, grabs the trolley and continues her march towards me. Her clean, thick hair shines in the sunlight and sways in slow motion like a glossy shampoo commercial. As she gets nearer, I notice she looks very trim and athletic. She's also wearing really nice, expensive-looking clothes that flatter her figure. I see her skimpy denim shorts hugging her award-winning legs, not a pick of cellulite to be seen. Her skin is gleaming. She looks shiny like she's bothered to have herself waxed from top to toe. I've always wanted to get myself thoroughly waxed. But unlike her, I don't have the time. I'm too busy starting a new frigging career from scratch.

Her beautifully annoyed face finally reaches mine and we stand for a moment, a foot apart, staring at each other. I really can't understand what happens next, what with me always managing to keep a professional lid on things, but somehow at the same time my sister puts her hands together in prayer, bowing down to say a polite but patronising 'Namaste', I bellow out 'GO TO HELL YOU PATRONISING, SELF-ABSORBED CRETIN!!!' at such a prize-winning pitch that startles even me.

I have never called anyone a cretin ever before, nor am I a hundred percent on what it means.

We stand staring at each other as my words hang in the air.

'Well,' she stutters, 'I'm glad you got that off your chest. It's important to own your truth. I learned that in Thailand. Can we make a move, please? I'm very tired... from waiting for so long? I'm thirsty and looking forward to a dip in the pool.'

Just like that. No apology, nothing.

I watch as she opens the boot and struggles to get the cases in. She beckons over to me for help. I stay firmly where I am.

Let her bloody struggle. My hand is literally stuck to my hip refusing to move anyway. Fused to the bone with anger. Then to my extreme annoyance we hear, 'Perdona, senorita.'

We turn to see *Senor Handsome Bugger*, sporting both a lazy smile and a head of bouncy, thick, wavy hair. He deftly lifts my sister's bags and cases into the boot as though they weigh no more than one of his toe rings. He shuts it with a slam, turns to give me a hard, disapproving stare, and then turns back to my sister to wish her a pleasant stay. Within seconds, I witness some outrageous, devil-may-care flirting as she tells him MY bloody address, says she'd absolutely LOVE to go for drinks with him and then gives him her phone to do some swapping of numbers. After an embarrassing series of selfies, where they take turns doing the peace sign, pretending to laugh and sticking out their tongues, she is finally ready to go.

Dear God! Has she no shame?

To make matters worse, while she's busy eyeing up his retreating buttocks, she turns unexpectedly and catches me tapping my third eye like a loon. The stress of seeing her has got me so rattled that I'm tearing at my scalp, causing a few flakes short of a snowstorm to land on my shoulders. She slowly shakes her head, taking it all in, with contempt, or maybe it's pity, ballooning from her big green eyes.

'Come here,' she says with her arms open wide and a terrible sympathetic look saddening her face. I can see actual tears in her eyes as she quickens her pace towards me. She feels sorry for me. She has the bare-faced cheek to throw her arms around me, sobbing out how much she has missed me and is here to help me get better.

'Get better? Me? GET BETTER?' My hand flies to clutch my pounding chest. I'm struggling to breathe. I open the driver door and throw myself in. Ignoring the shakes I've developed, I start the engine. My sister gingerly walks to the passenger side without comment.

I drive roughly out of the car park area through the barriers and clip the side of the car. Without even looking, I know there'll be a scrape on the paintwork. All totally her fault. I will inform Dad. There's absolutely no point telling our mother. At least our father has always tried to treat us equally.

We drive in complete silence and without air con so that she is as uncomfortable as possible. We are both dripping with sweat, our legs stuck to the leather car seats.

'If the aircon is broken, I'll just open the window,' she says, pressing the switch to lower the screen and let the cool breeze in.

'No!' I shout, pressing the master switch to halt the window and make it go back up again. Serves her right. She flinches and sits back, keeping her hands tucked between her knees where I can see them. Once we are through the toll booth and well on route, I see a filling station up ahead and pull in.

'You'll have to pay,' I say curtly. 'I paid on the way here.'

'You filled up on the way to the airport, but only put in enough to cover a one-way trip?' she asks, confused. She turns in her seat to face me, 'So that I could put the equal amount in on the way back?'

'Yes.' I lie. I mean, that's not so unusual is it, surely? She's deliberately making it sound weird. She better not make a huge deal out of paying.

Then her expression softens. 'Are things that bad? Financially, I mean. I'd heard that life coaches don't make much.'

I gawp at her. *See how she twists things?* This would be a good time to remind her that usually following a shock redundancy, one is out of fecking pocket until the twatting company eventually can be bothered to pay up. We were herded out so quickly that I can't even remember any details about the financial package we were offered or when we would receive it.

As I unpeel from the seat with a loud squelch and swing my legs out of the car, I slam the door behind me. I can feel her piteous gaze on me as I grab the petrol nozzle roughly from the pump. I watch as she calmly opens the passenger door and walks over to the petrol station doors which swish open to let her glide through.

I am totally losing the plot here. It's like I'm having an out of body experience. I cannot believe how awful and embarrassing I am being and yet, I feel powerless to stop it.

I fill the tank and get back in the car. Jeez, but it's boiling in here. I turn the engine back on and quickly blast some cool air around. I'm absolutely baking. My throat is as dry as a bone, my head throbs with the heat and all I can taste is stale wine.

I must rise above this. I must. I will continue the rest of the journey with as much decorum as I can muster.

The slidey doors swish open and I see my sister nigh-on skipping back to the car, all happiness and carrier bags. Not a remorseful bone in her entire body.

I quickly switch off the air-con blasters before she gets in, and when she starts rummaging about in the bags, I speed off, sending her flying into the dashboard. As she lets out an annoyed yelp, I smile serenely as if I'd simply not even noticed.

Now I will rise above it. That was the last blip. *Decorum, I'm all yours.*

'I bought you this,' Ava says, holding out an ice lolly. She knows I LOVE a good ice lolly. It's one of those extra fruity toxic orange and red ones. Full of hazardous chemicals and diabetes. So unhealthy for you. How typical of her to forget I hold my physical wellbeing in the highest regard.

I'd BLOODY KILL for one right now.

'No thanks,' I say stiffly. I'm so parched my tongue feels ready to blister at any moment.

'It'll just melt,' she coaxes me like I'm a sulky child. 'Go on, just have a bite to cool you down. It's low-calorie. Real fruit juice. No chemicals.'

I drive back in silence, watching out the corner of my eye, tormented as she slurps noisily away and takes selfies with her licking it suggestively for her followers. She's already removed most of her clothing so it looks like they've simply blown off in the wind.

'Ah,' she sighs unnecessarily loudly, 'that was so good.'

I can't help myself. After a few minutes, I slide my eyes over to her. 'All right then, I'll have one.'

My tongue is literally glued to the roof of my mouth.

'Too late. I've eaten them both,' she announces.

Rise above it.

I simply... breathe two, three....

Can't stand.

My.

Fecking.

Sister.

Chapter 20

We reach the villa in mercifully quick time, due to not much traffic and me breaking all the speeding laws that the European Union has imposed.

'Do you think you could help me unload the bags?' Ava asks.

I jump out of the car, shaking my head.

'I am now very late because our mother *ordered* me to pick you up, without any regard for either my professionalism or my clients, whose shit lives deeply depend on keeping their appointments with me,' I say, turning briskly to thump through the open-plan villa to my bedroom, slamming the door shut behind me.

Luckily, my room is the only bedroom, apart from our parent's room, to have an ensuite bathroom. My sister, who will take the guest bedroom, which of course I've left entirely unmade up without so much as a sheet on the bed (not because I'm being childish but because I have been very busy), will have to trek down the hall to the small shower room every time she wants the toilet or to get washed. It is also freezing in there, no matter what time of year. I shed my clothes and step into my white-tiled, pristine, cosy bathroom.

When I get out of the shower, I feel much better. I towel myself down and brush my wet hair. My scalp feels relieved. I poured tons of conditioner on my poor, raw skin. I decide to treat the rest of my body to the same and take a few moments to smother myself in thick, creamy moisturiser. The cool luxurious cream I 'borrowed' from Ava feels like nectar to my skin. I instantly feel revitalised and much firmer than usual, and my face looks its age for once. As I stare at myself in the mirror, I decide to up my game with a bit of make-up and some nice hair styling for a change. Just so my sister knows exactly how professional and important I can be. I do run my own business after all (according to my fictional Instagram grid).

I quickly click on Ryan Reynold's Instagram feed to see what he's up to. And even though he's still, disappointingly, very much happily married and isn't angry at anything at all, just the sight of his handsome smiling face soothes me instantly. I take a few minutes to do some deep nostril breathing.

I must admit, seeing my sister after two weeks of seething is not as bad as I feared, despite not throwing herself at my feet to beg forgiveness. I'm glad I haven't embarrassed myself by acting too bitter and will continue, as the older sibling by seven years, to show nothing but dignity and poise from now on. After all, it is I who has the moral high ground.

Once I'm happy with my face and hair, I walk over to the

wardrobe and pull out a shortish denim skirt and one of Ava's tops that I 'borrowed' when I packed to come over here. I slip my feet into a pair of flat pumps and give my legs a quick extra coat of moisturizer to highlight my tan. At least my legs will be much browner than hers.

I make my way through to the living room, passing by the door to the master bedroom. I have kept it closed out of respect for our parents, as it is their room, and I'm still very angry at them for not seeing my side of the whole 'my sister making me redundant, stealing my boyfriend and ruining my life' saga, but the door is wide open. I peer in to see my sister making herself at home, unpacking her cases, clothes and make-up all over the place, music is blaring out and she's opened the patio doors. This bedroom has its own private patio and terrace area, ideal for relaxing in peace and cocktails at sunset because of the wonderful view. I stand in stunned silence watching my sister prance about, wiggling her pert bottom and shaking out clothes as she hangs them in the wardrobe. The white linen toile curtains billow softly as fresh, pine-smelling air fills the room and sunshine pours through the doors like a luxury holiday villas advert.

'What the shitting hell do you think you are doing?' I bellow loudly over the music. My sister jumps a mile as she turns swiftly towards me.

'Unpacking,' she says a little too defensively for my liking.

'YOUR room is down the bottom of the corridor, remember?' I state bluntly. Surely, she can't have forgotten where the guest bedroom is. We spent every bloody summer here growing up.

'But that's only a single room and it's always freezing cold in there.' I know what's coming. I feel the familiar gurgling of dread forming knots in my stomach. I watch her calmly continue, 'Mum and Dad *insisted* I have their room if you hadn't taken it already. Otherwise, I would happily have had our old room,' she explains unnecessarily. 'You know, the one you're in?' Then she screws her eyes at me, 'The one you share with my GHDs, that top you're wearing and my gel nail kit?'

I've longed to be in this room since I arrived, but I couldn't bear the thought of having to ask my mother. And here Ava is, waltzing in, taking it over. Just like that. Just like bloody that. And all this time, it could have been mine. I could have had the sophisticated patio and the enormous ensuite and walk-in friggin' wardrobe and the TV that hides in the bottom of the massive bloody bed and slides up from the massive bloody film-star size bedframe.

'I've always loved this room,' she sighs sweeping her gaze over the twinkling chandelier, the luxurious rugs scattered on the marble floor and the twin his and hers designer chairs that occupy a little snug area with a glorious silver lamp and matching table. The whole room oozes charm and sophistication.

'I'm amazed you didn't move straight in here yourself. It's so spacious and...' I watch her search for the right word. 'Indulgent!' she declares, flopping down onto the sumptuous bedding, oozing over the sides of the Hulk-sized bed. She whips out her phone and looks sultrily into the camera, lips pouting, eyes half-closed. Click, click, click before turning her gaze back to me.

I take in her wide eyes and fake innocent expression. I smile blankly at her, as if the thought had not even occurred to me to want our parents' magnificent boudoir and leave her to it.

Click, click, click – nine likes already!

I walk out of the bedroom and calmly through to the living room. *It's got his and hers sinks.* I grab my car keys from inside the microwave as I walk through the open-plan kitchen. *It has a huge, lit, full-length mirror in the dressing room.* I catch my reflection in the shiny glass of the microwave door. My smiling face looks like a slightly melted mannequin.

Click, click, click – seventy likes!

It has stunning patio furniture perfect for entertaining. I open the fridge and pull out my purse and a Nutella sandwich that I made yesterday for breakfast and forgot to eat. Technically it's vegan as it's mostly nut based.

Click, click, click – fourteen retweets!

I close the fridge door gently and quietly leave the house. I walk over to the car and get in.

It has an eye-wateringly expensive designer bathroom with a jacuzzi bath.

I grab the wheel tightly and do some breathing exercises before I set off.

It should have been mine. Why did I not move straight into it? What the shitting hell was I thinking?

Breathe... two, three.....in, two, three...out, two, three...in, two, *feck!*

It's no use. I let out a jealous roar the likes of which no human has ever made. I simply can't help myself. She's taken a fundamental, basic human right away from me, and I am BEYOND furious.

'I WANTED THE BIG ROOOOOOM!' I bellow with the lungs of an overweight opera singer. 'I WANTED IT! I WANTED IT!'

After taking a moment to compose myself, I turn on the ignition but just as I reverse the car out of the driveway, I see my sister looking at me with wide, shocked eyes in the rear view mirror.

Chapter 21

I drive, in a bit of a daze, to the office. This morning has been more than a little weird, so what I need is the familiarity of sitting at my desk, the comfort of googling Ryan Reynolds to see what he's appalled about today, and to be assertive and in control. More importantly, I need to catch Maria-José-Inmaculada-Carmen in the act of not working. I creep into reception. Indeed, as predicted, I find her on the phone chatting.

'Put that phone down!' I bark.

As she looks up startled, I realise she may be booking in a client or changing an appointment for someone. She is surrounded by notepads and bits of paper and has a pen in her hand. Come to think of it, that does also look like our shared diary open on her desk.

'Never mind!' I quickly shout, 'Carry on! CARRY ON!' I stomp past her to my office, leaving her open-mouthed and gaping at me. I sit at my desk and let my head drop onto it.

I can't do this. I can't.

My desk phone ringing minutes later, jolts me out of my

trance. It is Maria-José-Inmaculada-Carmen warning me that I have two minutes before a new Zoom client comes online. She asks if it is okay to give me her notes.

What new client? How? Why? When?

'Can't you change the website to stop clients from making new bookings?' I ask as soon as she walks in.

She shakes her head. 'Nidi has not trained me how. I do not have access to website log-in.'

'You run the website but... you *don't* have access to it?'

This does not seem like the sort of oversight that Nidi would be guilty of. There has to be more. I wait it out.

Maria-José-Inmaculada-Carmen looks incredibly guilty. 'There is a training file she gave me, but I think I took it home and left it there.'

I shall try to remain serene. Fair but firm in my role as her new boss. 'I must say Maria-José-Inmaculada-Carmen, that this is very disorganised of you.'

She seems to take the hump at this. 'But I have printed notes for you. Information you need. For to pretend to be life coach.'

Thank God, Nidi is not here to witness this shameful display of disrespect.

Before I can tackle her cheek, my computer screen pings to life with an incoming video chat. I click accept and see myself flash up onto the computer screen before shrinking into the top right-hand corner.

'Hello Wendy,' I smile brightly. The client is mid-twenties and wants to learn some tools and techniques to manage the stress she is under at work. The time seems to fly by and we are getting on like a house on fire.

'I know all about stress,' I tell her with a sympathetic sigh. 'And it seems clear that the difficulties you're having are related to managing your bullish colleagues.' Turns out that she is the only female in an all-male environment. She feels left out at times because these men tread on eggshells, in case they offend her in any way. They fear she might yell 'HASHTAG-ME-TOO!' at them and they get sacked.

I glance down to the Life Coach Handbook open at page forty, a section called 'Your Boss Hates You' and remind her that how she thinks can profoundly influence how she acts and feels. I tell her all about the wankers that I had to deal with on a daily basis and their unacceptable behaviours in the workplace. 'It's all about the mindset Wendy, love. You don't spend eight years amongst a group of lazy, self-promoting dickheads without picking up a few tips along the way.'

Wendy seems delighted to have found a kindred spirit and promises to be in touch to book more sessions with me as we draw to a close. I can't help but realise that while I was helping Wendy to build confidence and identify some strategies to manage her staff positively, I on the other hand, am very guilty of letting Maria-José-Inmaculada Carmen get away with all sorts of terrible behaviour. I prompt myself to spy on her later this afternoon, to ensure she is not reading the *Hola!* magazine or chatting with her mother. Besides, we have a huge event to plan and I need her to bring her 'A' game. I must stay focussed and not let my sister's arrival or Oliver's treachery, distract me from the task at hand. But I keep experiencing searing flashbacks to the retreat, of Oliver and his beefy arms holding me tightly, and the way he kept looking at me.

I look around the office for some inspiration. Nidi has a ton of self-help books on how to be a successful entrepreneur and how to get the best from relationships, dotted round the office to make the place (me) seem productive. I should read them. I sweep my gaze over the new, shiny, untouched covers. And I will, right after I've had a good look at Ryan Rodney Reynolds' Twitter feed to see who he is helping today. He is such a kind-hearted man. Rarely a day passes without him looking gorgeous. I mean without him being compassionate and caring. No wonder he has almost eighteen million followers. Every single one of them, like me, following him with interest, keen to learn from his benevolent way of life, not simply to judge him on his magnificent looks.

As I'm researching Ryan Reynolds appreciation groups, the more I think about it, the more I think that it is perhaps me with the terrible behaviour, not Maria-José-Inmaculada-Carmen. As though she's reading my mind, my phone trills.

'Mees Weston, it's the one you call Boring Berry.'

Feck!

I watched Nidi get approximately nowhere with him last week. He comes in every single day because he is lonely, and I am simply not in the mood. I have much to worry about and much finger-pointing still to do. Just as I'm telling her to send him away, he walks straight into my office and sits down.

'Hello, Nell. I hope you don't mind me just turning up like this, but I had nowhere else to go.'

I take one look at his bony frame and milky, sad eyes and feel a pang of sympathy. We've all felt lost and hopeless at some time in our lives. I scan the chapter on loneliness while he shuffles over to the sofa.

'Okay. Even though you've clearly turned up *without* an appointment, let's see if we can close the gap between where you are in your life today and where you want to be,' I say briskly, trying not to sound exasperated with him. 'Now, tell me Berry, what makes your heart sing?'

Boring Berry is taken aback. We spend an hour rationalising why no one ever visits him and why he never leaves the house other than to come to our office. I hold back my professional opinion that it is, of course, because he's too bloody boring. But I'm going to get right to the heart of his fears.

Boring Berry looks at me. 'I see. What you mean is, why am I just sitting around all day waiting for someone else to make life more exciting, instead of getting up and doing things for myself.'

I remind him that sometimes we need to be the instigators. 'We need to issue the invitations to do things with family and friends. We need to reach out.' I push a leaflet into his hand. 'I picked this up for you after one of your sessions with Nidi.'

He looks down at the leaflet and back up at me, then down at the leaflet again.

'I want you to join this group, Berry. It might not be your cup of tea, but I've explained that you are widowed and severely lacking in conversation. Just go along and have some fun with other people.' I fix him a determined look.

His eyes go all watery, like old people's eyes do, and tells me today is the anniversary of his wife's death. He says his heart aches without her, even after all of these years, and that when he woke up this morning, he prayed to her to help him get through the day.

'But today,' he says, taking my hand unexpectedly, 'I asked her to give me a sign that she is still here, watching over me, waiting for me.'

I dare to look into his wet face, as he explains, waving the leaflet at me. 'I asked her to help me get back into playing bowls like I used to before she... before she.... and now here you are, giving me this, telling me to go and play bowls!'

I'm not sure where to go with this. I don't really want to burst his bubble and for all I know perhaps it *was* his late wife who put the idea into my head. Maria-José-Inmaculada-Carmen watches Boring Berry leave, sniffing up the last of his tears. She glances in my direction. I would stake my life on her thinking that it is me with my terrible Life Coaching that has reduced him to tears.

'Well, thankfully, apart from Jiff, Berry will be the last proper client I do before Nidi gets back,' I say relieved. Life coaching is a huge responsibility. People are relying on me to help them achieve their goals. Their life goals. For the one and only life they'll ever have. I let out a gusty breath, feeling the enormity of the pressure deflate. I close my eyes and pinch my nose, grateful that Nidi will return in a few weeks.

'Yes,' Maria-José-Inmaculada-Carmen agrees. 'The last one for today.'

An ominous prickle creeps up my back. I count to three in my head before speaking.

'Meaning?'

'It is this computer. It is allowing all the people to book sessions. Even the clients I tell not to come. See? It is the computer's fault.' She turns the monitor to face me, sits back and folds her arms accusingly. 'It's why this book is much better. I will use the book instead.'

I stare at a packed diary for tomorrow as anxiety sweeps me up. Names and times swim before my eyes. While she has been burying her head in the sand, clients have been booking sessions willy-nilly. There isn't enough time left in the day to ring every single one of them and reschedule.

'Some of these slots are double booked,' I say. 'The names on the computer don't match the names of clients you have booked in the diary.'

'Si.'

She has a defiant look on her face. It is clear that Maria-José-Inmaculada-Carmen won't be offering a solution any time soon.

'And also,' she says, moving the conversation on. 'We have many bookings for *The Coach Trip*. People are excited to know where we are going. Will the coach have air conditioning and toilets?'

'Coach trip?'

'Yes. The singles coach trip you are organising.'

'You mean *we* are organising? And it's not a coach trip. It's a coaching sort of journey.'

'Si. Journey as in trip?' she waves Google Translate at me on her phone.

Gaaah!

'No. It's not a trip. It's very much a journey.'

'What is the difference between a trip and a journey?'

I stop to think. I have been speaking this language since birth, and yet I have no clue how to answer her.

'Erm, the difference is that one is more of an actual trip to somewhere, and the other is more of a journey to somewhere.' *I'd never make a teacher.* 'Actually, no. It's the context. A journey can be a spiritual... no, what we are organising is much more of an event, really. It is a life coaching event to take people on a journey but without physically moving.'

Maria-José-Inmaculada-Carmen looks understandably confused.

'Please tell me you have not been booking people onto an actual coach trip. You've explained that it is more of a coaching *experience* with some singles and business activities involved?'

Whatever the heck that means.

'Si.'

She has done nothing of the sort.

'You can go now,' I tell Maria-José-Inmaculada-Carmen, trying to keep my voice from breaking.

I'm a grown woman. I will handle this.

Chapter 22

I spend the next two panicky hours rooting around the internet, looking for fun activities that would benefit both single people and sole-traders *and* involves some type of coaching. It is nigh on impossible but has distracted me from the dread of seeing Ava back at the villa.

Before I pack up to go home, I flick through the Life Coaching Handbook which is full of advice that makes me uncomfortable. I come across a quote that makes me stop and think. It says, 'Resentment is like swallowing poison and expecting the other person to die.' It recommends writing a list of all the things you resent about the person.

There isn't enough paper in the land. I simply wouldn't do that to all those innocent trees. But I could compile a mental list.

It's dark by the time I finally face up to returning home. Even driving up to the villa and seeing all the lights blazing away and knowing my sister is relaxing and enjoying herself fills me with resentment. I hesitate at the door. I almost feel like knocking. This place no longer feels like *my* place anymore. I really must get a grip. I can't keep going to pieces every time I have to face her.

People go through far worse, don't they? I mean, there are far worse things than being stabbed in the back by your entire family. Of course, there are.

Reluctantly, I hear Oliver's words about dusting myself off and getting on with my life echo round my brain.

It's time to confront Ava and sort it all out.

I take a deep breath in and open the door. The delicious aroma of something cooking fills my nostrils and lets my stomach know immediately that I forgot to eat again today. I can't really remember the last time I ate a proper meal.

The music is blasting out, and even I, though I hate to admit it, I can see she's managed to make the villa seem homely and inviting. The dining table is set with two plates, cutlery, glasses and a bottle of wine. She's obviously invited that handsome bugger from the airport over already. Probably to help her get over the break-up with my ex- on again off again boyfriend, Dan. Or maybe she is still seeing him. Maybe she is playing the field while she is here in Spain. She still hasn't even had the decency to admit that she was having an affair with him behind my back. Morally bankrupt. I will put that on the list. I watch as she opens the oven door to release a burst of heat and clouds of glorious-smelling meaty, garlicky fumes.

'Ta-dah!' she's sings joyfully. 'It's your favourite.'

I follow her gaze to the oven dish inside bubbling away. It's chilli chicken. It smells incredible. I see she's been chopping salad and toasting pittas and then I try to smother a gasp as I clock the huge homemade cheesecake. There's no denying that my sister does make incredible cheesecake. We once worked out that it contains over ten thousand calories.

'Look,' she sweeps her arm over to the table, 'I've gone to so much trouble. It's had 374 likes already.'

It's all about her. See how easy it is to be resentful? Much easier than NOT being resentful. My mind instantly pictures her wearing it and how many likes it might get then.

'I was looking forward to reconnecting and having a nice evening. Like always,' she says. Fake memories. She's just like our mother. Not once have we had a 'nice evening' together that I can remember. Not since we were kids anyway.

'I didn't ask you to.'

'But I thought maybe you'd...' she trails off. *This should be interesting.* 'I was hoping,' I can clearly see her choking on the next word. 'You'd hear me out so that I can own my own truth and move on.'

Flaming cheek. Me, Me, Me. I'm going to move that one further up the list and give it top priority.

'It's spicy chicken,' she says.

'I'm vegan now.'

'Are you? But you said it was for smug do-gooders, rubbery and over-priced when I did a whole TikTok thing on it. Well, never mind, there's salad?'

Honestly, is that all people think we vegans can eat? Leaves? And I hardly think a thirty-second video of her dancing in the kitchen in her pyjamas while she made a snack out of grilled tofu was Earth-shatteringly informative.

'Enjoy your meal,' I say stiffly, turning to go. If she thinks one delicious chilli chicken and a to-die-for cheesecake will make up for ruining my career, she is sadly mistaken.

'But we need to talk about what happened,' she calls out, with her wide eyes and dentist advert smile. All she'll do is go on and on about how it wasn't her fault and how that really, if I've *any* sense at all, I should see that it is, in actual fact, all *my* fault.

'Yes. We do.' I make sure to slam my bedroom door loudly. Oh my god, this darkness inside me is borderline embarrassing. It's like the voice I hear belongs to someone else, not me. It's like I'm deliberately trying to alienate people and take my anger out on them. The exact opposite of how I used to be. Maybe Oliver is right.

I need to be the better person here. I need to stop drinking the poison.

I catch sight of myself in the mirror. I'm surprised to see my stomach is concave and my hips look sharp. I've definitely lost weight over the last couple of weeks. I used to have a sparkle in my eye but now, they are dull and hollow-looking. My thoughts fly briefly to Dan and how he's never so much as sent a text after that awful day. Neither has Pippa and we were such great friends. Not one word from either of them. My reflection stares back at me, I look gaunt and not so pretty, dead behind the eyes. Bitterness is ageing, I don't care what anyone says.

I'll quickly freshen up and then confront her over dinner. We can talk through what exactly happened at work like two civilised adults. The emails. The promotion. The shock redundancies. And Dan. But when I step out of the shower a few moments later, I hear voices and music.

I throw on my mother's elaborately-coloured silk kimono which is hanging on the back of the bathroom door, to go investigate.

I nearly die when I walk in the kitchen and see Senor Handsome Bugger from the airport sitting opposite my sister, eating *my* chicken and drinking a glass of *my* wine. They are laughing their heads off. They both turn to me smiling.

'Oh, hi Nelly-Belly. This is...' but as my sister introduces him, I blank them both, swerve round to retrieve my keys from the plantpot, head out of the door and slam it loudly behind me.

I can barely drive, I'm so fuming. She hasn't been in the country for more than five bloody minutes and already she's got a bloody date. And the cock-faced fucker looks like some sort of super model. She's ruined the big confrontation I'd built myself up to, and now I have to go to sleep starving hungry, dressed in a peacock blue and burnt orange kimono.

Within minutes, I've reached my office, unscrewed the bottle top on the emergency wine and felt the cool liquid sliding down my throat. It's like watering a shrivelled-up plant just before it dies and watching it spring back to life. Like those speeded up scenes from nature programmes on the Serengeti or wherever, when the mudflats get a single drop of rain and suddenly burst into lush green meadows with gazelles leaping about while hippos roll in the water.

That's how my taste buds feel. Within minutes, the wine bottle is empty and I'm fast asleep on the good sofa.

· ♥ · ♥ · ♥ · ♥ · ♥ ·

I wake up the next day in my office, crumpled and drained but ready for a sturdy day of ignoring my sister and of course, a day of helping people with *real* problems. I am NOT going to have a meltdown today. I need to rise above it. I'm going to have to race home and change so that I can transform from this hideous, wine-soaked husk in a brightly-coloured silk kimono, into a professional-looking life coach who cares.

Deep breaths.
Deep breaths.

I have some of Nidi's regular clients today and I am determined to take them a step further towards their goals even if it is the only session they do with me. I will explain that there has been a computer mix up and if they complain afterwards, I won't charge for their session.

A momentary flashback of Oliver looking lustfully at my lips pings into my mind accompanied by a flurry of butterflies. And yes, he might have been a little heavy handed with the home truths, but he is perfectly tall, with dark mysterious eyes, unruly dark hair and a sort of commanding presence that adds a sexiness to him. Even if he was sent by the ICF to spy on me.

Snap out of it.

As I haul myself up from the sofa, my phone is ringing.

Without thinking, I answer it before I've even checked the caller ID. My determined mood immediately evaporating as I see who it is.

'How are you and Ava getting along?' my mother asks, blunt as ever.

'Fine, Mother,' I say, cramming some mints into my mouth to relieve the dryness.

'Well, that's not quite how your sister put it this morning when I spoke to her. She's says you didn't come home last night and over fifty of her followers were all worried sick about her being worried sick. Now listen to me,' she says all direct and cold-hearted. 'She is your SISTER.'

'Mother. That is hardly breaking news,' I reply petulantly. Honestly, she brings out the worst in me.

'Don't be childish,' she warns. 'You must forgive your sister and move on. Simple as that.'

I am gobsmacked.

'So, you are admitting that it was all her fault?' I ask incredulously.

'She knows what she did was wrong, but she was in a very difficult position,' my mother continues. *See? Always on her side.* 'You must give her a chance to explain herself. It's not as straight forward as you think.'

'Oh, I think it *is* straight forward Mother,' I say, my mood plummeting rather rapidly. 'She ruined my life, and you took her side. You ALL stabbed me in the back!'

I hear my mother take in a sharp breath. 'Oh, baby girl,' she says quietly. 'Is that what you really think?'

She sounds upset now. A lump is forming in my throat,

but I refuse to answer. I'm not being manipulated by this woman again.

'You were *ill* my darling. That job was squeezing the life out of you. We could all see it.'

I immediately stiffen. The familiar heavy feeling of anxiety descending fast. *How dare she!*

'Mother, I have to go,' I say, slamming down the phone. Trust her to ruin my morning. A quick look at the time tells me it's too late to go back to the villa to change. I thump around the office getting ready for my first client.

I stop for a brief moment to sigh heavily, allowing a wave of apprehension to engulf me. It's draining.

I'm still thrown, even as Maria-José-Inmaculada-Carmen arrives at the office. Exhausted, I find myself saying a pleasant good morning only to see her eyes balloon in surprise. She gingerly hands me the notes for my first client. She will be wondering why I am not yelling 'NOTES! NOTES! GET ME THE NOTES!' I simply have not got the energy for it today. As long as no one mentions The Coach Trip, which will definitely be a trigger, we should just about scrape through the day.

This little blip will not get me down. I am resilient. I am hardy and strong. I am still wearing a peacock-blue kimono.

'Who's next?' I call, disappearing into the sanctuary of my office.

'It is the laughing guy. The one you hate so much,' she yells through. 'He says it's urgent, but he makes no appointment for this morning,' she says with a roll of her eyes at the inconvenience, as I dart back through to reception.

'You mean the one from the ICF? The tall one? The Scottish one?'

My mind flies to our booking system. The one designed to prevent this sort of thing happening. *She has one job. ONE JOB.*

'Yes. I tell him that you are in the Bahamas for avoiding tax reasons, but he still says he is coming.' She shrugs her shoulders as if to say 'Meh, what can you do?'.

Shite. Between my sister turning our home into a knocking shop within hours of her arrival and my mother, I forgot to check the diary.

No, this cannot be happening. And the fact that I slept here and didn't bring an overnight bag isn't helping. I race back into my office and over to the mirror. I have no spare make-up, no spare set of beautifully lined expensive suits and no sexy footwear. I cleaned my teeth with an extra-large mint.

A knock at the door has me jumping out of my skin. I swivel round to see Ava standing there. Could things get any worse?

'Fuck off!' I yell at her. Her face immediately crumples as she turns to leave. 'Wait!' I shout and wave her in. It's like I've developed Tourettes around her.

'Look, you've caught me at a bad moment, okay?' I explain. She looks at me and nods in understanding.

'It's okay,' she says, 'I'll go.' Before she leaves, she turns and tells me that I have a really nice office. I nod back at her. Then she asks, 'Is it anything I could help with?'

Like I'd need *her* help.

'No, not unless you have a magic wand that can make me look amazing in less than...,' I take a huge breath in and yell through to Maria-José-Inmaculada-Carmen, 'Maria-José-Inmaculada-Carmen? What time is he coming?'

'In ten minoots!' she shouts back. My sister and I trade glances.

'Of course,' my sister says, grinning at me while she rummages around in that massive bag of hers, the one she dropped at the airport that had a salon full of toiletries in it. I also spy a toothbrush. I stare at her. That is indeed the answer. But I can't let her near me, never mind ask for her help.

'Let me at you for five minutes. Nell, I practically do this for a living. What do you say?' she asks kindly. I'm caught in a moment of hesitation. I'm not proud but I let vanity get the better of me.

She leaps towards me. 'Go do your teeth. You've a red wine smile.' I do as she says. 'Sit here by the light.'

She tears open the bag, yanking at my hair with a brush, gets out some straighteners and dusts my cheeks with powder, swishes make-up brushes all over my eyebrows, lips, eyes. She runs the straighteners through my hair super quick, stands me up, gives me her shoes and jacket. She fiddles with the kimono, making it look more like a dress, and says, 'Ta-dah!'

She turns me to face the mirror.

Oh.

Chapter 23

I look great. Unbelievable even. She leaves me staring in wonder at myself and heads out the door with her head hanging down. Well, the jokes on her because for short bursts of time, I can be quite nice. I begrudgingly say, 'Thank you. Much appreciated.'

She spins around all hopeful, so I shoot her a warning look not to get too carried away. I'm still majorly furious with her. It's all I can do to manage a small, grateful smile but only on one side of my mouth.

I see her jaw drop open as the entire doorframe behind her is filled with my man from the International Coaching Federation. This time he is not covered in sandy shorts and a t-shirt. He's wearing a dashing suit. His shirt unbuttoned at the top and no tie. His hair is still floppy and his arms still beefy, even *through* the suit jacket he's wearing. My, but he looks sophisticated. He takes one look at me, and we stand transfixed. I don't even notice my sister slide out of the room and more importantly, neither does he! I think I have just fallen madly in love with Mr Beefy Arms, solely based on the fact that he did not pay my sister or her award-winning legs one ounce of attention. He has kept his penetrating gaze fixed on me the whole time.

If it were still okay for women to swoon, I would. My mind is blank from lust, so for want of anything better to do, I just keep gawping.

Oliver speaks first. 'Can I come in?' he asks politely from the doorway. He sure fills a doorframe nicely enough.

'Of course, of course,' I say, snapping back to my professional self. He closes the door behind him, and I catch a glimpse of two nosy faces behind him, leaping up and down to see what is going on. I watch mesmerised at his commanding walk across the room to stop inches before me. I look up at him. I'd forgotten quite how tall he is. It's very impressive.

'Sorry to barge in like this,' he apologises, 'but I wanted to tell you in person.'

My mind flies to the International Coaching Federation. A sudden flashback of when he came into my office to find me rolling around on the floor pings into my brain. Oliver is towering incredibly close to me. No wonder he's come all professional looking.

'Yes?' I whisper uncomfortably, looking away from him. How mortifying this must be for him, having to revoke my licence, put me out of a job and possibly be the cause of me having to turn to online topless ironing to make ends meet. But even the sweaty tension of imminent exposure can't dampen how attracted I am to him.

'I've got to fly off this morning to deal with some urgent business up in Madrid,' he says with an apologetic look.

I guess this means the date, I mean session, is off.

'Which means I'll have to take a rain check on our next session,' he says softly.

'Is everything okay?' I ask. 'Are you having trouble with your board of wankers?'

I must look devastated because he steps closer and lifts my chin up so that I meet his gaze. 'Yes. I am having trouble with my board of wankers. But I will be back in a day or so,' he says. 'Let's fix a date.'

I nod slowly, still lost in his eyes. A date date? Or is he merely suggesting rearranging the session? The session where he reveals he has been sent by the ICF and declares a conflict of interest?

'What about the ICF and the board? Won't they mind?'

'What about them? What I do outside of work has nothing to do with them.'

I like his thinking. A lot.

'So, you still want to honour our special arrangement?'

Could I be any more unclear?

'Very much so.'

And what special arrangement am I talking about exactly? He's so overpoweringly good-looking that I have lost the thread entirely of whether a session means a session. Or is this sizzling undercurrent of metaphors between us is all in my head.

'And you won't tell the ICF?'

Oliver shakes his head. 'Why would I tell the ICF?'

Hello, because you work for them?

'And you won't be breaking any codes of conduct? There

aren't going to be any imminent job losses? Namely, mine.'

Oliver looks amused. 'As long as we work within the standard regulatory perimeters of employment law, I don't see a problem.'

I stare at him. He's matching my crazy.

'So you still want to put a *date* in to do some *actual* life coaching with me?'

He nods causing my heart rate to increase by a million thumps per second.

Could it be possible, beneficial even, to have a client-coach relationship with a man this attractive? *Despite* the distraction of sexual tension?

I take a beat to reflect on it while I gaze into the depths of his incredibly dark eyes.

It could. We both simply need to remain professional.

As if reading my mind, he leans in and kisses me lightly on the lips.

I very much admire his unprofessionalism.

'Give me your number,' he demands, masterfully holding out his phone to me. I take it and quickly put my number in his contacts.

'Do not,' he warns, 'do anything crazy until I am back.'

My eyes balloon with indignation.

'See?' he says, 'I don't want to miss any rolling around on the floor or tapping of chakras or whatever nonsense it is. It's all... captivating.'

'That *nonsense*,' I say, in as haughty a fashion as I can muster under the circumstances, 'is an ancient form of emotional healing. That I can personally vouch for.'

I am met with what could only be described as an intensely smouldering and sexual look.

'Go on,' he encourages huskily.

Do not engage. Repeat DO NOT fucking engage.

My voice comes out all raspy and two octaves lower than normal. 'Tapping the meridian points on one's body is a centuries old mechanism for helping one to cope with anything from...' I stop to lick my lips. '... an overly dismissive mother to, I don't know, toxic issues in the workplace.'

Oh Jesus.

Thankfully, he interrupts me before I can talk any further shite at him. Taking hold of my arms, he says, 'I find you utterly...' his eyes searching mine, '... bonkers.'

The atmosphere in my office suddenly becomes heavy with lust. I blink slowly, my breath coming in short bursts. He grabs me roughly to him and gives me a hungry look before kissing the life out of me. A surge of electricity powers through me and I am consumed. He must feel it too, his breathing is all ragged and his hands start to wander over my body, pulling me in close. The silk kimono falls open at the front to reveal plump breasts tumbling from my balcony bra. His eyes light up.

'Magnificent,' he says, cupping one of them then the other as our lips melt passionately together. My fingers tangle in his soft hair as I pull him towards me. I have never wanted anyone this much. The chemistry between us is electrifying.

After a while, we break off, both of us panting and wild-eyed.

'I'll be back soon,' Oliver says, flying out of my office,

leaving me gobsmacked.

I stare after him. Not only have we both broken every rule in the Code of Ethics about not having any romantic intimacy, but more worryingly, I haven't given Ryan Reynolds a thought in over an hour. Not one thought.

·♥·♥·♥·♥·♥·

I'm still rooted to the spot in a daze as Maria-José-Inmaculada-Carmen walks in. Ava is hovering behind. I wrap the kimono back around my top half and pat my hair back into shape as though I've simply been on a vigorous dusting spree.

'Okay, let's sort out this *Coach Trip* disaster,' I sigh rather dreamily, because I'm still reeling from that kiss.

What lips Oliver has. Powerful I'd call them. No, soft, but then again, hard. No, bouncy. No, firm and springy. No, that's how you'd describe a good mattress. *Good lord...* I must concentrate. Being present in the moment is, in fact, *key* to good life coaching. Being able to give one's full and absolute attention to the person in front of them is essential. And to really listen to them. Like Oliver really listens to me, and how he finds me utterly *captivating*. Captivating and bonkers. No one has ever, EVER called me captivating before.

'How many people have you booked onto it so far?' I ask, dragging myself back into the present. I really must try to stay here, in the here and now.

I hear her mumble something. Lust has affected my hearing. I wonder if Oliver has a strong surname to go with his strong beefy arms and his overall general strong beefiness. I simply must find out.

'How many?' I say, sighing happily. I'm so giddy. Giddy is the only way I can describe it. Light and fluffy and high on endorphins. Oliver's kisses are... commanding. Yes, commanding. No, they're sweet. No, promising. That's what they are. Full of promise. A shoot of lust pings through my body and dances around in my lady parts.

Maria-José-Inmaculada-Carmen considers me for a moment and pushes back her thick dark hair. It could do with a brush. Oliver has perfect hair, as one could probably imagine.

'What do we do?' she asks me with knitted eyebrows.

'Yes,' I answer, still smiling as my mind wanders. Oliver has such a great body. I have a flashback to him touching me inappropriately, only a few minutes ago. I wonder if we'll do it on this very couch. On this carpet. My eyes roam the office for bits of furniture we might have sex on.

'What do we do?' Maria-José-Inmaculada-Carmen asks again. 'We have booked people on to a Coach Trip. Where are you taking them?'

Gaaah! But she's right. And also, wrong.

'It's *we* and it's less of a trip and more of an experience. A Life Coach Experience.'

I have literally told her a hundred times.

'Sounds interesting,' Ava says.

No. It really doesn't.

'Leave it with me,' I say. I'll sort it out later. I have some daydreaming about Oliver's lips to do.

· ♥ · ♥ · ♥ · ♥ · ♥ ·

A while later, I wander through to reception to see my sister sitting next to Maria-José-Inmaculada-Carmen behind the desk. They are giggling away like old friends. I can see they have Ryan Reynold's Instagram up on the screen. He is lounging in bed with a tuxedo and a pair of shiny shoes.

'What is going on?' I bark as they leap to attention. 'This is a professional place of work, not a girly catch-up. What next? Bottomless brunch?'

'I'm sorry, Ms Weston,' says Maria-José-Inmaculada-Carmen, but she is interrupted by Ava.

'It's not her fault. I asked her to show me the ropes.'

'Show. You. The. Ropes?' I ask incredulously.

Ava lifts her chin and smiles broadly. 'Yes, I'm training to be a life coach. I thought you knew.'

My scowl is all the answer she needs.

Chapter 24

'Seeing as you are the boss, I thought I'd learn from the best?' Ava says, a slight shake in her voice. Nice try, but she's not going to win me over that easily.

'Did you now?' I say, folding my arms and glaring at her. There is no way on earth that I am going to train my own back-stabbing sister up to be my competition, even if I were the boss, which I'm not. Besides, I've literally only been doing it for a day, and I'm not even qualified to do that. Also, things are already complicated enough.

'I can help you. I bring a lot to the table in terms of skills and experience.'

She thinks *she* will help *me* to sort out the business. SHE can help ME to sort out the business. SHE! SHE! I see what she's doing. Trying to take over.

'So, did Mum ring you this morning?' she asks, changing the subject. I know her game. I bet she bleated on all day yesterday about how awful I was. Boohoo, isn't my sister terrible? Well, two can play at that. I nod stiffly.

'I told her not to interfere,' she tells me. 'I know you are still very angry with me and quite understandably so.'

What? Am I hearing her right?

'I am more than prepared to do anything to win back your trust and earn your forgiveness.'

Holy feckers. This sounds almost like an apology. THE apology.

'Furthermore,' she continues solemnly. 'To prove that I am serious, I am going to turn my life around. Starting with how to fix our relationship.'

This takes me completely by surprise. I'm not even sure what to say as she hands me a coffee and looks me right in the eye. She seems genuine. She's got tears in her eyes, and her voice is wobbly.

'I'm building to an effective apology,' she explains to Maria-José-Inmaculada-Carmen.

These are the words I have wanted to hear since the day it happened. I have played out multiple scenarios in my head about how she admits she is to blame and now she's saying them. I can't quite take it in. My sister smiles hopefully at me. I am completely thrown. Until she whips out her phone, checks her eyes are glassy, sexy and tearful and takes a selfie.

'Hashtag broken relationship?' I guess.

Ava shrugs her shoulder in response as though it is all out of her hands. 'My followers are waiting to see a pic of us reunited. This is for the build-up. Then I thought we'd do a reel for the making up bit. Me owning my own truth. As part of a live energy cleanse. Then, I'll put a link in the bio, and we can be like *actual* life coaches together, and help people with their own hashtag broken relationships.'

I should have known. It's all about her.

'I would have thought that you'd have enough money from your enormous redundancy pay out, not to *ever* have to work again,' I say sarcastically, 'what with you having managed over TWO hundred staff across TEN regional offices.'

She goes bright pink and hangs her head, 'They shafted me. I got barely anything. Enough to come here and live for a few months. That's all.'

'What goes around, comes around,' I say. *I'll never last a few months.*

'I know,' Ava says, looking very sorry for herself. 'I should never have trusted them.'

I feel a sudden pang of sympathy for her.

'Well, if you must hang around, Ava, then at least learn how to manage the phone system, which is about as difficult as blinking, and then please show Maria-José-Inmaculada-Carmen how to use it.'

'Of course. I love helping people,' she says, turning her kilowatt smile on my gullible assistant. 'When I was in Thailand, searching for true meaning and happiness...'

Oh, here we feckin go. I can see Maria-José-Inmaculada-Carmen being drawn in. Impressed by the way Ava is flicking her hair and gazing into the middle distance.

Ava puts her hand on her heart. '... I became a fully qualified shamen which is basically the same thing as a life coach, isn't it? What's that quick qualify website called again?'

That's it. That's quite enough. I knew this would happen.

I close my office door. I don't want to go back out there with those two in cahoots. I need to sort out this singles event mess. I'll quickly check on Ryan to see what he thinks of veganism and then do something calming. I haven't stroked my crystals for a good while. Yes, I'll do that. I'll pick the big green one to soothe and heal. No, I'll go pink and energise. It's so hard to choose as they are all powerful tools when it comes to transforming my energy fields, according to Nidi and Endless Cloud, at any rate. I grab one of Nidi's crystals and rub it furiously.

The only problem with stroking crystals is that it can be bloody boring. Still, it has taken up twenty minutes. I press my ear to the door to see if my sister is still there. I can hear some faint giggling through the door. Very unprofessional. I think I'll tell them both to pipe down. I swing open the door swiftly to catch them in the act, but I'm stopped in my tracks. I witness my sister on the phone talking to what sounds like a prospective client while my vacant assistant looks, for all intents and purposes, like she is finally filing away that mountain of papers and confidential client information into proper files.

I best look as if I needed to check something, so I walk over to the desk and peer at the appointment book. I casually turn the page. Ava looks up as she is talking and gives me a thumbs-up sign.

I should probably thank her for loaning me her shoes and jacket and making me look nice for Oliver. And for working reception. Maria-José-Inmaculada-Carmen is bloody hard work. I'm secretly impressed that my sister got her to put down the *Hola!* magazine for a start, never mind keep her off the phone to her mother. Maybe I should treat Ava to lunch as a sign of my maturity and stoic nature. And as a tiny step towards tolerating her company. I give her a half smile and she returns it with a mega-watt beam of shiny, white, bleached teeth and sparkly hopeful eyes. Bit much but yes, it feels like the right thing to do. We need to clear the air between us and it's going to take me to be the bigger person. Plus, I'm starving. I will use my last twenty-euro note to get a menu del dia between us.

She puts the phone down and chirpily calls to me, 'Me and MJ are going to grab some lunch, if you fancy joining us?'

I stop abruptly. Prickles of alarm stabbing every inch of my skin.

MJ?

Lunch?

Me join THEM? There's a THEM? I swivel back around to glare at her. One fecking morning and she has already stolen away my assistant. She probably stole that client she was speaking to and booked them in to see herself. After all, she'll probably think she's qualified now, having spent an hour working reception. I feel a familiar knot tighten in my stomach.

'MJ?' I query.

'Maria-José-Inmaculada-Carmen, MJ,' she smiles innocently back. Then here comes the dagger. 'That's what all her friends call her. You didn't know that?'

She has friends?

I glare over at Maria-José-Inmaculada-Carmen, who is tactfully buried deep into a pile of papers, acting like she cannot hear one word of this conversation, but her bright red cheeks are giving her away. A wave of self-pity engulfs me. For two weeks, I have suffered near pulmonary failure with each conversation, just getting to the end of her bloody name.

'Of course, I knew,' I say tightly, flicking Maria-José-Inmaculada-Carmen a hard glare, as I force a smile out of my rigid face. 'And no thank you to lunch. I'm very, very busy.'

'Are you sure because… ohmygodohmygodohmygod!' Ava yells, excitedly waving her phone at Maria-José-Inmaculada-Carmen, 'He just liked my Live Your Best Life post!'

I see Maria-José-Inmaculada-Carmen's eyes light up.

'Who?' I say tightly, hoping she isn't going to say Dan.

'Ryan!' Ava beams.

I can't look. The thought of it would make me sick to my stomach. 'Which one?' I can barely keep it together.

Say Gosling. Say Gosling.

'Reynolds, of course,' Ava says, sighing happily. 'He's so amazing.'

Gaaaaaaaaaaaaaaaaaaaaaaaaaaaah!

I have loved him for over ten years, and she has only loved him since this morning. Besides, Gosling is still a perfectly respectable but-not-quite-so-good Ryan. Why can't she pester that one? Why does she have to muscle in on mine? I try hard to keep the fury from my face as I pull the jacket off my back and the shoes roughly from my feet, gathering them all up and pushing them back into my sister's arms.

'Enjoy yourselves,' I manage as I close the door behind me.

Once back inside the safety of my office, I flop down on my sofa. Nothing ever works out for me. I still haven't booked the venue for the singles business event slash business singles event or whatever the fuck it is. The only thing I do know is what it *isn't*. It isn't a coach trip. I haven't thought about the food or drinks or games to play or how to run it. I haven't a clue where to start with the invites but since I mentioned it on the radio, I'm going to have to make it happen somehow, because we've had a flood of enquiries. And on top of that, I have no fecking friends.

A text pings into my phone.

It reads 'I can't stop thinking about you'.

I take a deep breath and press delete, one hundred per cent sure that he will be far better off not getting involved with a bitter, twisted mess like me. It would never have worked anyway. He didn't even put a x at the end of his text. If you kiss someone like that then decency dictates that an x must be put at the end of a text to that someone. Forget him. Him and his freakishly beefy arms. And his abnormal height. And his ridiculous girlish giggling.

Then he sends another one. 'Too busy staring at pebbles?'

Cheeky feck.

Just because he's some sort of life coach expert sent to discredit me, doesn't mean he can patronise me. He barely knows me. He can't judge me on what he has seen so far.

My mind flies back to the crying at the airport, the lies he overheard on the bus, the stealing at the retreat, the begging him to pretend to be a client, the rolling around on the carpet, the wailing and the sobbing in his arms about how much I hate my life.

Now I think about it, maybe he has seen *too* much. Maybe pursuing this relationship would be a waste of both our times. I have been down this road before. This texting is indisputable proof of rule breaking, and will only lead to me being humiliated on record.

I will put a stop to it. I don't want to seem impolite. But I do want to seem decisive. 'Under the circumstances, it's probably best if you don't contact me again.'

I take a deep breath in. At least that is one less thing to worry about. I've done the right thing. He will know that I am serious about my profession and think twice before taking my licence away. Plus, it will only be a matter of time before Ava gets her claws into him anyway - taking everything that is mine as usual. I tap my wrists a few times and rub my chakras with a bunch of dried sage leaves, the one thing that Gandalf did get right.

I'm not sure I should have sent that text to Oliver. It sounds rude now that I've thought about it.

He hasn't replied, not that I blame him. I can't help but ruin things for myself. I lie back on my couch and take a deep breath in.

Chapter 25

The late afternoon is so quiet, the heat from the sun pouring in through the window has the effect of a horse tranquilizer, and what with all the rubbing of crystals, I doze off by accident.

I'm surprised to be shaken awake. *Why? Why? Am I elderly now? Is that it?*

It's my sister. 'Hey Nelly-Belly, are you okay?'

I struggle to sit up. I feel stiff and achy. She tells me that she's heading home, the paperwork has been successfully filed away and she asks if it is okay to get a lift with me. In my groggy state, I agree, and then she asks if we could also drop Maria-José-Inmaculada-Carmen off on the way, as she lives not far from us. This is news to me. Again, I hear myself agreeing.

Christ, I'd better wake up quickly before I commit to anything else that I'd normally say a firm *no* to. But she hits me again, by the look on her face, with the world's best idea.

'Or even better, we could go for a few drinks right now! MJ, HOW ABOUT A FEW DRINKS RIGHT NOW INSTEAD?'

'CLARO QUE SI, ABBA, MUY BUEN IDEA!' Maria-José-Inmaculada-Carmen answers with an excited bout of hissing.

Christ! BFFs already. Not once has Maria-José-Inmaculada-Carmen EVER asked me to go for a drink after work. I am determined not to let my feelings show and almost split my face trying to conjure up a smile.

'Great,' I say, not quite meeting my sister's eyes. 'I'll drop you both off on the promenade.'

'Actually, I meant all three of us,' she says. I fix her a look and I can see pity emanating from her eyes.

'I have my spinning class,' I say stiffly.

Well, I would have my spinning class if I'd bothered to join a gym.

'Oh,' she says, sounding disappointed. 'I was hoping that I could just buy a few rounds to say a sort of thanks from me for, well, everything, you know.'

I glare at her.

'My treat,' she adds.

My head is full of misery over what I did to Oliver. I'd do anything to take that text back. He must think I'm so rude after he's been nothing but lovely and supportive. Even if he is an ICF spy. Maybe I should go out and get shitfaced. It might help me cope with Ava and this awful situation between us.

I nod slowly. 'Yes, whatever, just one.'

In a daze, I drag myself up. I take two minutes to splash water on my face to wake up a bit. I hear Maria-José-Inmaculada-Carmen call through, 'Miss Weston? Abba ees doing our make-up before we go for thee dreenks!'

I walk through to reception to see it has turned into a pop-up salon with hair and make-up products scattered all over the desk. My sister has put on some Latino music, and they are dancing about and swishing blusher over their cheeks and posting endless selfies of their nose-contouring journey to her Instagram. She has managed to transform Maria-José-Inmaculada-Carmen from sullen vampire to very gorgeous vamp and she is emitting that familiar but strange hissing sound again.

'Sit down,' my sister says to me and before I know it, she's going at me with make-up, hair straighteners and the like. In an unusually generous about-turn, I suggest we open my *emergency* emergency bottle of wine in the cooler, literally the only surviving bottle.

Within seconds Maria-José-Inmaculada-Carmen is holding out three plastic cups brimming with wine.

Soon after the bottle has been drained, Maria-José-Inmaculada-Carmen makes a shy suggestion. 'Miss Weston, would it be possible for us to eat first and then go for thee dreenks?' She explains that she has only eaten four times today. She fears that she has not lined her stomach properly. She reminds me that the Spanish simply do not have the capacity for drinking alcohol that the Northern Europeans have. This is very true. The Spanish will often nurse a small beer for hours and hours, whilst we Brits will have drunk ten or so, in the same time.

I immediately wonder if my last twenty-euro note is going to cover it. Not likely. Shame. I've not eaten out at all since I got here because I've not had anybody to go anywhere with or any money to do it. I really must sort out the money transfer somehow. It still hasn't gone into my account here, but I haven't had time to face the countless hours on the helpline, the endless queueing and numerous trips it will take to the bank.

'You two go ahead,' I shriek way too chirpily. 'I'm not really hungry.'

My stomach has already eaten itself and made a start on my kidneys.

I've lost track of who owes what for the coaching. Nidi mentioned something before she went, but what was it? And I'm sure I asked Maria-José-Inmaculada-Carmen to do a spreadsheet or something. At that moment, my phone pings. It's not Oliver. It's from Nidi asking if me and Maria-José-Inmaculada-Carmen have booked the date and times for the singles event yet, and how the preparations are going as she can't see any advertising on our Twitter or website for it. She has also had loads of enquiries to the work email about a coach trip. And another one asking if Jiff is alright because she received an unusual message from him asking if she had any contacts for a speech and language coach. I leave the texts unanswered and feel anxious.

Drinks was a stupid idea. I'll wait until they leave and then rub the feck out of some crystals. 'I forgot, I have the finances to do. And this event to organise,' I say flatly, turning to go back into my office.

'Please, Nell, even if you only have a few bites. Come with us,' Ava pleads.

See? It's them against me. They're a firm 'us' after only one day doing admin together. I'm always the outsider. Always the one left out. But I could eat an entire family of cows.

'Okay,' I sigh making sure they both know that I have MUCH more important things to do with my time, 'Just a quick bite and one drink, if I absolutely must.'

OMG I sound like a right ungrateful twat.

Maria-José-Inmaculada-Carmen pipes up. 'My parents have restaurant by the marina.'

What? And she's waited until now to mention this to me?

'Wonderful!' my sister chirps, turning to me. 'What's it like, Nell?'

One look at the embarrassed exchange between me and Maria-José-Inmaculada-Carmen gives Ava the answer she is after. Maria-José-Inmaculada-Carmen tells us quickly that it is Italian because her father is from southern Italy.

'Small place, nothing fancy. La Bella Maria,' she says.

'That's your parent's restaurant?' we say in unison.

'That's our favourite restaurant in the whole world, isn't it, Nell? We used to go there all the time with our parents, didn't we?' Ava gushes. 'I LOVE that place!'

Jeez, next Maria-José-Inmaculada-Carmen will be telling me that they've got a yacht and are embarrassingly wealthy. She beams at my sister and then looks shyly at me.

'It's really sweet how they named it after you,' I say, remembering how crammed full of people it used to be. Tourists coming from up and down the coast to eat there. I know this for a fact, as it is always number one on TripAdvisor. 'Your parents must be really proud of you.'

Maria-José-Inmaculada-Carmen blinks at me. 'My family is... our relationship is muy complicado.'

Ava and I exchange a look.

'Aren't they all?' I say stiffly.

Chapter 26

After being talked into leaving the car at work, the three of us walk in awkward silence towards the main promenade, taking in its beautifully clean stretch of ornate paving, lined with pretty streetlamps and palm trees every few feet. The white pebbled beach gleams as it reflects the late evening sunshine. Our parents picked a lovely spot for their holiday villa.

As if reading my thoughts, Ava sighs happily, 'I've always loved this place. It's so soothing.'

She's right. The mountains surrounding this bay slope gently down towards the sea. The lush green land between is dotted with white villas, and the skyline is dominated by the magnificent, cobalt blue tiles of the church dome, high up on a hill, overlooking the marina. We would often walk up the cobbled streets of the white-washed village to the church, to drink in the atmosphere, to listen to the live music and watch the artists draw cartoon caricatures of tourists. The four of us would eat tapas in one of the many lively restaurants that line the square. I catch my sister's eye. I think we are sharing the same happy memories.

I hastily look away.

Once we reach La Bella Maria, we see a queue out of the door.

'It looks full,' observes my sister, 'what a shame.'

We are startled by an almighty shriek from a crazed lady in an apron at the far end of the restaurant. I watch as the lady barges through the tables whooping and cheering, to scoop up Maria-José-Inmaculada-Carmen into an embarrassing hug, kissing her cheeks many times. You'd think she'd not seen her since she was a baby.

'Your mother,' I say knowingly to Maria-José-Inmaculada-Carmen, who glances across at us with a withered look. Even the diners around us stop eating to see what all the fuss is about. Maria-José-Inmaculada-Carmen is clearly uncomfortable and rapidly tells her mum in Spanish to calm down as she is making an embarrassing scene. Her mother laughs this off and continues to hold her face in both her hands, yelling 'Look who is here!' over the diners to, presumably, her husband and other family members.

Out from the kitchen troop a line of chefs and kitchen staff ready to make a huge and unnecessary to-do over Maria-José-Inmaculada-Carmen. *How stifling.* I catch her eye and for the first time, we exchange a look of understanding. She eventually rolls her eyes, emits a little hiss and allows herself to be fussed over. I suffer a pang of nostalgia and regret. It has been too long since I last enjoyed interacting with my parents.

Breaking me from my thoughts, I hear my name being mentioned. 'This is Miss Weston.' Suddenly, I am being launched at by this overly passionate family. People are kissing my cheeks and shaking my hand and speaking in pigeon-English to tell me how happy they are that at last their Maria-José-Inmaculada-Carmen has found a job that she is good at.

For a moment I almost choke. Good at? *Good at?* How on earth have they reached that conclusion? Then the penny drops. I flick her a look and she goes bright red. I listen as her parents praise me for training up their daughter to be a successful businesswoman.

'We always knew she would run her own business one day. She's just like her Mama,' Maria-José-Inmaculada-Carmen's father says, looking proudly from his daughter to his wife.

I raise an eyebrow. For a split second, I am sorely tempted to burst this little bubble, this web of lies. I see Maria-José-Inmaculada-Carmen take in a sharp breath.

Like me, Maria-José-Inmaculada-Carmen has not been entirely honest with the people who should matter the most.

I turn to her family, and in Spanish, tell them that their daughter is indeed a valuable member of the partnership and announce that she will very soon be overhauling our accounts system, as well as a new online booking system which means we can expand OUR business. This elicits lots of 'oohs' and 'aaaahs'. I receive a grateful look of thanks from Maria-José-Inmaculada-Carmen, which I return with a firm look of expectation.

Maria-José-Inmaculada-Carmen nods in understanding.

Well, I'm just going to assume that is what it is, as she can be very compliant at times, and I simply have no idea if she means it.

We are whisked through the restaurant to the private outside dining area. It is a small, square courtyard filled with tables covered in checked cloths, lined with trees covered in twinkling fairy lights and dominated by a fountain in the centre. I breathe in a nostril of the delicious Italian cuisine filling the air. The scene before us is breath-takingly pretty.

'Wow,' my sister and I say together. She gives me a little embarrassed look. When we were kids, we always said things in unison despite the age gap. She'd follow me around everywhere. A sign of our closeness. All the men in white overalls and chefs' hats disappear, leaving Maria-José-Inmaculada-Carmen's mother to usher us to a glorious table by the fountain.

'On the house!' beams Maria-José-Inmaculada-Carmen's mother at me, grinning away and I find this bit extremely, extremely embarrassing, she takes my hands in hers and thanks me profusely for putting up with her daughter. I give Maria-José-Inmaculada-Carmen a confused look. Surely, I misheard.

Her mother leans in close and whispers to me in Spanish, that if possible, could I get her daughter to stop ringing her every five minutes, as she has a busy restaurant to run. She winks at me and bustles off, wiping her hands on her apron as she trots into the kitchen and disappears out of sight.

'What did she say?' Maria-José-Inmaculada-Carmen demands.

'Um... well, she said that she's very proud of you, and she understands that her speaking with you during working hours is distracting you from running a successful business. So, she will speak to you when you get home after work. Face to face. Instead of every ten minutes during the day.'

I wait to see how Maria-José-Inmaculada-Carmen will react to this potentially devastating news.

I'm relieved to see her face light up.

Within seconds, glasses of red wine are shoved into our hands along with menus. Plates of dough balls, olives, assorted dips and breadsticks are plonked down for us. My eyes are on stalks. It looks amazing.

Now, I know I've told these two that I'm not at all hungry and that I detest garlic and that I am staunchly vegan now, so I'm not remotely surprised to see my sister and Maria-José-Inmaculada-Carmen trade glances when I order a cheesy garlic bread starter and spicy wedges, and I am also not surprised to see my sister stifle a giggle when catching sight of me wolfing down an enormous pepperoni pizza, half the size of the table itself, even though I've declared meat-eaters to be contributing to the end of the world's eco-system.

And when three hot chocolate fudge cakes with homemade vanilla ice-cream are plonked down afterwards, I ignore their wide-eyed stare and dive straight in. I can barely move as I listen to Ava, who appears to be on a break from taking pictures of the food instead of eating it, asking 'MJ' all about her life here in Spain.

Turns out I barely know this girl. Shame on me. As another bottle of red wine is opened and poured for us, I notice Maria-José-Inmaculada-Carmen looking shyly at the waiter. My sister notices this tiny giveaway too. The waiter, however, does not notice and barely looks in her direction. Maria-José-Inmaculada-Carmen's face deflates for a split second before she recovers herself.

'Who's the hot waiter guy?' Ava asks instantly. We watch as Maria-José-Inmaculada-Carmen feigns ignorance, shrugging her shoulders as she looks away from him.

'Here, have a confidence drink,' says Ava, topping up her glass, 'and watch this.'

Maria-José-Inmaculada-Carmen and I are treated to a masterclass in flirting as Ava calls the waiter over, orders some water and deftly pumps him for information. In less than two minutes, we know his name - Alejandro, how often he works out – too often, what his views on feminism are – he likes it - his Instagram handle and, most importantly, we learn that he is single and available next weekend.

'This is my sister Nelly-Belly, and you must know MJ already? She's like the owner of this restaurant. It's named after her.'

Maria-José-Inmaculada-Carmen's cheeks flame instantly as the handsome waiter says of course he knows her. He gives her a lingering smile. She immediately protests that she is definitely not the owner of the restaurant and starts to release that strange hissing sound again, her lips curled into an awkward smile. It's certainly a unique laugh, I'll give her that.

Alejandro rushes off to get our water.

'Well done,' I say to her. 'He's very cute and totally into you.'

Maria-José-Inmaculada-Carmen's face is beaming as she protests that Alejandro is nice to everyone and probably wouldn't look twice at a girl like her. A former vampire, she must mean.

'You're a beautiful, strong, independent woman who doesn't need a man to complete her,' I trot out. *You just need a regular supply of fresh blood and a nearby empty coffin to lie down in.*

'But if you fancy a snog then Alejandro would definitely be up for it. I can sense these things,' Ava boasts.

My mind instantly pictures Dan and Ava clinking drinks and flirting at work. All behind my back. Men can be so weak and pathetic. Except Oliver. He seems to be a decent sort.

She glances over to a group of lads on a nearby table who are eyeing her up. Ava waves back, raising her glass up to them.

'Won't Dan get jealous of you flirting with other guys?' A dig that I simply can't resist.

'Dan?' Ava turns to me all confused, 'Dan, who?'

'My boyfriend that you stole,' I remind her, 'from work?'

Maria-José-Inmaculada-Carmen follows what we are saying, and looks horrified at Ava.

'Yes, MJ. It's true,' I say slurring slightly. 'Meet my cheating, job-stealing, computer-hacking sister traitor.' It's an enormous surprise at how not bothered I feel all of a sudden.

'Oh, Dan?' Ava hiccups loudly, ignoring what I just said. 'Yes, of course. Total dickhead.' She turns to Maria-José-Inmaculada-Carmen, drink spilling out of the glass as she waves her arm about. 'He was no good for my sister. I had to sack him. He's a cheater. Him an' Pippa.'

Oh my fucking God.

'What?' I croak. 'Seriously? He was cheating with Pippa? Not you?'

'Me? Urgh. Fuck no. As soon as I found out, I managed him out without a single penny. Same with Pippa.' Ava stares at me. 'Didn't I tell you?'

'No.' My mind is all over the place. I suppose I did just assume the worst. And it is weird that Pippa or Dan didn't reply to any of my texts after we had all left work.

I watch as Ava processes this. 'Some prick from an international company took charge. Sacking Dan and Pippa was literally the only decision they allowed me to make. I wasn't in control of any of it. Even the computer hacking to get evidence against Pippa. I had no idea they would use it against you too. Especially not to make you redundant. I'd never do that. Sorry Nelly-belly. I thought I had told you. But then it was a bit of a nightmare time for me.'

I suppose it was, now I come to think about it. And all this time she was saving me from Dickhead Dan. I'm not sure what to say. My whole world has just been turned upside down again. Or maybe the right way up.

'So, MJ,' my sister says as though this isn't a huge, life-changing deal for me. 'Are there any good clubs we can go to near here?'

'Benidorm?' Maria-José-Inmaculada-Carmen says, her eyes sparkling brightly.

Over my dead body. There's no way that I am going to Benidorm. I need to process this miraculous piece of information.

I need to meditate.

I need to make peace with myself.

I need to heal.

I need to reflect on the somewhat unnecessary psychological damage I have inflicted on myself and those around me.

Chapter 27

A mere three hours later, I find myself shoulder deep in a half-soaked, scary-eyebrowed Hen party. Maria-José-Inmaculada-Carmen has suddenly become best friends with them even though she has no idea what any of them are talking about.

'Where is this place called Saff-landan these chickens are from?' she is asking. I quickly translate for her, explaining it is more generally referred to as South London, and that these squawky women are hens not chickens, but she keeps flapping her elbows and clucking. She is clearly not listening to me as usual, but the *Hens* are finding her terribly amusing. They are quick to plonk a pink satin sash and some pink, fluffy deely-boppers on her head to take her under their wing and claim her as their own. They are also tremendously full-lipped and heavily made-up, like pantomime dames, which seems to be having a powerful effect on the menfolk around them. It is making it impossible to hear what Ava is shouting above the music and spontaneous bursts of squealing.

'How could you not tell me, though?' I ask her again. We

have had this same conversation on a bit of a drunken loop, but it is taking a while to sink in.

It could have saved me weeks' worth of emotional pain and could have avoided an embarrassing amount of unsolicited whinging.

'I texted you, like, a BILLION times!' she yells at me. 'Did you not get any of my messages? What about all of those posts on my grid?'

Shite. I blocked her number, didn't I? No wonder I didn't get any texts from her.

The realisation that this could all be as much my fault as hers has me in an immediate spin.

I'm a fool.

A complete fucking idiot.

A terrible sister.

An awful human being.

'Wait. Did you unfollow me?' she gasps.

And the rest.

'So, all this time you thought I *deliberately* made you redundant? That I gave all those emails to Karen as evidence against *you*?' Her hands fly to the sides of her head, just like Geoff – I mean Jiff. 'Oh my fucking God. And you thought I was having an *affair* with Dickhead Dan?' She makes vomiting noises.

I gulp. When she puts it like that it sounds... well, it sounds...a lot like I'm the dickhead.

'I'm so sorry,' I say.

'Me too,' Ava says, flinging her arms around me. 'I should have been there for you when it all kicked off. Instead of making assumptions and being bossed about by Karen and some faceless prick they brought in to fire everyone.'

'Let's try to forget about it for tonight.' I desperately need to process this properly, with the help of some pebbles or a babbling brook or even some throat singing. 'We'll circle back to it in the morning.'

'Great idea,' Ava says. 'Let's get shitfaced!'

· ♥ · ♥ · ♥ · ♥ · ♥ ·

While I battle the sticky floor and bits of broken glass that litter my path to the bar, I watch my sister and Maria-José-Inmaculada-Carmen dancing like someone is poking them with electric cattle prods. I'm pleased to see they look carefree and happy.

There is a lot of braying going on. Grown men, wearing neon-coloured mankinis, are treating innocent bystanders, like myself, to an intimate glimpse of their hairy chests and bums which are covered in an assortment of barcode and Welsh dragon tattoos. It is highly unappealing not to say unhygienic, but what is abundantly clear, is that they are playing the world's loudest, rugby-themed drinking game. By the looks of them, the game started twelve years ago and is still in full swing.

'I love men with thick necks, Gav,' I hear my sister saying. She is hanging from a man wearing a lilac-coloured bra and knicker-set. It appears to be made of industrial-strength stretchy lace and he is punching the air in celebration.

I shudder and take a step back from the heaving throng,

who have now turned an area of the bar into a dancefloor.

I much prefer a tall, long-legged man myself. My mind wanders to Oliver. I've completely blown it with him. I knock back my drink, and order three more cocktails.

While I wait for Ava and Maria-José-Inmaculada-Carmen to finish dancing, I slip into a nice little fantasy where Ryan has just come over with a bottle of Crystal and is dangling the keys to his helicopter at me, when, before I can dart away, one of these hairy beasts, Jimbo, throws an arm around my neck. He winks lasciviously and waggles his appendage at me.

I unpeel his arm and watch as he starts doing, what I assume *he* assumes, is a routine from *Magic Mike*, using a dirty bar cloth and a cocktail umbrella stuck between his teeth.

'No thanks,' I say, turning back to the bar.

He throws his head back and howls with laughter, 'Squinty! I've got a live one here mate! Gorgeous knockers mind.'

Absolutely charming.

'You have such a beautiful way with words,' I yell back as he yanks me in close, so that I can enjoy the view of his hairy chest from up close.

A thunderous cheer goes up around the bar and I discover that these male strippers, behaving for all intents and purposes like posh lads *are,* in actual fact, posh lads. They are a professional rugby team full of heroes, newly arrived here to celebrate their recent cup win dressed in slithers of Lycra for two whole weeks. We quickly learn that they have also been out for a vindaloo, which apparently tapped into their natural competitive streak, and now several of them have recently experienced an explosive rear end discharge.

Their manager must be so proud.

My sister and MJ, as she insists on being awkwardly called by me this evening, dance over to see what the fuss is about. I take this opportunity to slide out from the headlock.

'That's my sister,' Ava says, pointing at me. 'She's a very successful life coach. And this is MJ. She's her... company director. And I'm an influencer!'

Me and MJ exchange a guilty look.

'We can come clean tomorrow,' I tell her. There's no need to overegg the pudding. We've had all the confessions we need for one day.

'And you're all invited to come on our excellent coach trip next week!' Ava yells.

A huge cheer goes up and before we know it, the rugger boys are pushing glasses of prosecco in our hands and booming out things like 'Jimbo has massive balls!' and 'Go Team Tits!'

If they weren't constantly replacing our empty glasses with full ones, we would probably have scarpered by now. And even though I have been thrown wildly about on the dancefloor and have managed to fight off numerous gigantic wandering paws, I am relieved to be more successful at avoiding their straying lips than my sister and MJ, whom I have spotted locking lips with the two hairiest of the group. *Urgh.* And now there are tongues being flapped about.

I take out my phone to capture this glorious moment lest

we all forget. In my drunken state, I capture my sister's desperately poor lifestyle choices. I fumble with the buttons and end up taking a few accidental video clips and a selfie. I remind myself to take a selfie of me and Ava for our parents. I think they would love that.

The next thing I know, the rugger boys take it in turns to show off, lifting people off the ground and spinning them round above their heads to hoots of laughter, starting with Ava. Then we are herded into a roped-off VIP area where we are treated to some champagne and a long and detailed account of why Rugby Union is better than Rugby League. MJ has brought all the Hens with her, and they are so ecstatic they have draped themselves over a rugby hero each.

'I LOVE this song!' Ava suddenly shouts at us, jumping up and spinning around. 'Come on!' she yells throwing her arms above her head.

MJ and I jump up. 'Who is it?' I shout above the music, joining in as we gyrate as if our lives depend on it. It has been years since I last went out dancing.

'No idea!' Ava yells back to us, 'But I never want it to end!'

'Me neither!' I yell, slinging my arms around both of their shoulders. We all beam ridiculously at each other. And just for a moment, everything seems perfect.

· ♥ · ♥ · ♥ · ♥ · ♥ ·

My phone buzzes a while later as we prop ourselves up on

stools to take a breather from the flash mob dancing. It's like we have become best ever friends with all the ladies from the hen party and all the rugger boys. We are like one huge hairy family. I have been sorely mistaken about them. They couldn't be more charming, and their skimpy outfits are a hoot and not at all offensive. And they are all heroic and handsome.

Ava has been taking millions of selfies with them, especially Squinty the captain, who is seriously good-looking and quite debonair despite the scarring, the black eye and broken nose bandage.

My phone pings and I glance at it to see who would be texting me at this very early hour in the morning.

I swish open my messages.

Oh Christ. It's him.

My last text stated clearly for him not to get in touch. But that was before I knew the truth about Ava. Before my epiphany.

'How are you?' it says.

I quickly tap in 'Fine, thank you so much for asking.' I can be exceedingly polite when drunk. And bizarrely, I make fewer spelling errors. It's one of my best features.

He quickly replies, 'Working late?'

He'll think I'm working late into the night on my business, helping people. Saving lives. I should tell him I have embarked on my own life-saving journey. I should tell him my soul has been healed and my aura has had a thorough cleanse. Like my vagina.

'Yes, thank you. May I enquire as to your own working

practice?'

I'm simply charming, aren't I?

'Unlike yours, it doesn't involve grown men dressed in nappies.'

Shite.

Chapter 28

My eyes swivel around searching the bar, but it is impossibly crowded and I'm not tall enough to see over the rugger boys, until a sixth sense crawls over my skin and I feel his eyes on me. I turn around to see Oliver staring right at me. He doesn't look too pleased. He takes two gigantic strides through the crowd, and he's reached me.

'I FLEW STRAIGHT BACK!' he bellows over the thumpingly loud music.

I have no answer to this, mainly because I'm a tiny bit drunk (shit-faced). I give him a confused look. I look from my sister to Maria-José-Inmaculada-Carmen who are simply rivetted by this exchange between me and the handsome giant from the ICF.

'How did you know I'd be here?' I ask him.

He plays a video clip. 'You sent me this.'

I watch mortified as my camera is trained on a load of hairy bums and then myself looking really rather pissed, and then back to the bums.

'I recognised the bar straight away,' he points out, showing me the neon Jolly Roger sign above the bar that comes briefly into view in the video clip. 'I was worried! Your text, it said that you... I mean it sounded like, y'know, uh... you found something out about me. I can explain. Just hear me out.'

Maria-José-Inmaculada-Carmen leans over to my sister and whispers something in her ear. They slip discreetly off their stools to disappear onto the dancefloor.

I take a moment. What on earth is he talking about? I found something out about him? Then I have a moment of clarity. Of course, he knows that I'm onto him.

'You're an ICF spy,' I say, tapping the side of my nose.

He is staring at me with wild eyes. For want of anything better to do, I keep on staring back at him. And swaying slightly. And hiccupping. But in an alluring way.

He helps me clamber off the stool as we make our way outside, away from the music.

'You're fine with it then, I take it,' he says at last. He looks sexy and dishevelled.

'Yep,' I point to myself. 'I'm certainly no picnic myself.'

He looks slightly perplexed. But that's okay because I happen to be extremely self-aware.

'I'm no walk in the park. Even though it's my job at stake. To be the helper of ones...hic...who need help. I'm the helperer. I am the help who helps,' I explain articulately. 'But I am a terrible person, so don't you feel bad. You. You are lovely. And big.'

He gives me an exasperated look. Almost like he has immediately regretted flying back. This makes him instantaneously a thousand times sexier. I'm a bit drunk and finding him very handsome. I take a step towards him, swaying slightly as I go.

He reaches out to steady me. Just at that moment, Jimbo, Gav and their esteemed team captain, Squinty, barge past braying and honking. They have deely boppers on their heads, with a pink sash lady under each arm cackling away because these rugger lads are so, so very funny and charming. They stop to politely ask if I'd like to join them back at Squinty's hotel room.

'Just for an orgy of booze, sex and drugs, mind. No funny business,' he winks.

For some reason my response is to laugh hysterically, rather than politely decline.

'See you soon,' he yells over his shoulder before they disappear round the corner.

No you won't!

He pops his head back around, 'DM us the deets of the coach trip thing, yeah? We'll all come.'

'Will do!' I yell back, waving.

Oh my God.

'Judging by the state of that lot,' Oliver finally laughs, 'maybe I do need to save you from yourself. Coach trip?'

Oliver is becoming increasingly handsome as the minutes fly by, but I do feel the need to put him right on a few things. Namely about him having to accept who I am. I am a strong, independent, *extremely* hot, sexy, attractive man-magnet. Coach trips and orgies with hairy toffs might be a fundamental part of my identity for all he knows. I am a free spirit. I am what I am and what I am needs no excuses.

I might sing this at him. I have a beautiful singing voice. Beautiful. I take a deep breath in and prepare to wow him with my hidden talents.

'I am what I am,' I suddenly sing into his face, waving my arms in the air. 'And what am I? I'm my own special creation, no that's not it.' I jab at him, missing his chest. Suddenly the words come to me. I bellow them out. 'I love each sparkle and each bangle. So what? You can take me from a different angle!'

I get a cheer from a nearby table. Who knew the lyrics were so sexual?

'Listen, why don't you forget the song?' Oliver says quickly. 'I'll get you some water instead. I need to explain a few things to you.'

'What song?' I say, watching Oliver stride over to the bar and back again in under a second. He catches me in his beefy arms as I sway towards him, and because I must look terribly thirsty - he is so kind - he gives me a bottle of designer water, and I drink it down.

'Will you get into trouble for just aband...abandning-nig...abadnoning...leaving work like that?' I slur in amazement. I can't help but wonder at his impulsiveness. I could never be like that. It takes me half an hour to choose an avocado at the supermarket.

'Yes,' he says bluntly, raising an eyebrow and looking at me like I'm a naughty minx who has caused him nothing but trouble. The atmosphere between us is suddenly heavy with lust.

'So, you flew to Madrid on important ICF business and

flew straight back?' I can't help wanting to clarify. *Oh my.* I am in lust. Deeply in lust. 'Just for me?' I ask, staring into his eyes in wonderment.

He takes a step closer, never once breaking eye contact. This is the most romantic thing anyone has ever done for me. Even if it is because he thinks I am a complete loon. It still counts.

The water kicks in, sobering me up.

'Feeling better?' he asks. My breathing has become raspy because his gaze has slipped to my mouth. I bite my lip slowly.

'Are you sure?' he says softly.

I nod. I've never been so sure in all my life.

And just like that, we fall into each other unable to keep from kissing a moment longer. When I finally take hold of my senses, and break apart from him, I gasp out something about the moral code and ethics, only for him to burst out laughing and shake his head.

'I don't give a shit about your code,' he says easily and pulls me to him. 'I'm not sure the ICF cares as much as you think it does.'

I like this maverick, and his devil-may-care attitude to work and his easy kissing technique.

I fully enjoy his varied kissing procedures for another ten minutes, before I become aware my sister, with camera phone held aloft, and Maria-José-Inmaculada-Carmen, are hovering by our sides, grinning away.

I break instantly from Oliver's embrace and turn to face them.

The important thing to remember here, I think, is my manners. I turn to Maria-José-Inmaculada-Carmen first. 'You remember the nice gentleman from the ICF, don't you?'

She gives me a strange look. Her eyes are slightly crossed. 'Yes, yes, of course! Of course, yes. YES! You are mister... the laughing man. Of course. Mr Laughing Man.' She is exceedingly pissed.

Oliver continues to laugh, shaking his head. 'Don't you have some sort of booking system? How can you not know my name by now?'

She's on her own. She can take one for the team.

'Oliver,' he says, introducing himself. 'Oliver Reynolds.'

Then me and Maria-José-Inmaculada-Carmen look incredulously at one another. For once we are locked in mutual understanding. We make big 0s with our mouths.

Reynolds!

Reynolds! I've always wanted to be MRS REYNOLDS!!! I wonder if he'd mind changing his name to Ryan.

'Meester RAYNOLDS!' she yells. A small hissing sound emerging from her lips.

Oh god, Oh god, Oh god.

'Meester RAY-NO-W-LDS,' she repeats super slowly in case I didn't get the inference. She gives me a pantomime Widow Twanky type wink.

Thankfully, Oliver allows this to go straight over his head. 'And you must be the infamous sister.'

Oh shit.

But before I can explain, my sister suddenly looks alert

and about to make a Nobel-prize-winning revelation.

'I have nearly a million followers on Instagram. I post videos... you know, on TikTok? You've probably seen them? I do life hacks? To help people like... live better, y'know? Milly-May follows me?'

This means very little to Oliver, and he doesn't flicker. *I LOVE HIM!* Then my sister looks at him all wonky-eyed and points to herself, 'I used to manage over two hundred staff...'

I step in and cut her swiftly off, 'Yes, yes, he knows.'

Oliver gives me a look and says that he's off to the bar to get us all a pint of water each. *So kind. So, so kind.*

'If I was going to steal any of your boyfriends,' she says, looking mischievously at me, 'it would be Oliver. He's absolutely off-the-chart good-looking and so unbelievably sexy. In fact, he reminds me of someone... '

I am momentarily stumped by this. I wouldn't put it past her to only pretend to be joking.

'You're not my type,' says Oliver, swooping in suddenly, to take us by surprise.

Ava looks like she's just been given *nul points* in the Eurovision song contest, as Oliver winks at me, puts three pints of water down on the table and throws his head back giggling like a little girl.

It takes only a second for her to get over herself. 'Ohmygodohmygodohmygodohmygod!' Ava shrieks waving her phone around. 'He liked my post!'

'Who liked your post?' I've never seen her this excited before, not since...

'Ryan!'

'Which one this time?' I steel myself ready for the answer.

'Oh,' she says, her face falling. 'Gosling.'

I try hard to keep the relief from my face.

'You two are a nightmare.' Oliver butts in. 'You're as bad as each other.'

Ava and I stare at each other before we turn abruptly to Oliver to put him right on a thing or two.

But before we can get a word in, Maria-José-Inmaculada-Carmen says, 'Yes Ryan, they are exactly the same. Yes. Two beans, no peas, two peas in a...'

We wait while she takes a slurp of her cocktail. I greatly admire her command of the language. Far, far better than anything I could do.

'Where was I? Ah yes... you have lovely eyes Ryan, and huge arms.' We watch as she squeezes Oliver's bicep. '... and Ms Weston is very good life coach. Very good. The best.'

She strokes my face.

'... and Abba ees very good friend for hair and clothes. We are BEE-EFF-EFFs.'

She flicks Ava's hair extensions and makes a heart sign with her hands.

She has known her for less than a day.

I take a moment.

It's her lack of judgement and any sense of loyalty that is the real worry.

Chapter 29

I can barely open my eyes the next morning. It's as though I'm coming round from a general anaesthetic where I've been given a last-minute epidural to prevent my limbs from moving while the surgeons take turns going at my head with an ice pick.

I lie back against the pillows, taking it all in. Last night. The pizza. The drinks. The all-night dancing. The braying toffs. And that wonderful kissing. Even through my banging head, I feel a wave of excitement. I wonder if Oliver will get in touch with me today. Last night was like a dream come true, the way he just showed up like that. All beefy and handsome and full of heroics.

I hope he isn't disappointed when he finds out that, day to day, I'm exceptionally ordinary. I just went through a bit of a difficult patch, as we all do. That's all. I mean surely everyone has had to deal with shock redundancy, family disloyalty (imagined), dysfunctional staff, cheating boyfriend, global economic and environmental meltdown brought on by very poor political decisions, and the overuse of plastics, at some point in their lives, haven't they?

I think back to how Oliver and I parted ways.

Now, did he say he would text me, or did I say I'd text him? I can't remember which one of us said what.

After the introductions, my sister decided we must all do shots to mark the occasion. After the third one, I remember desperately trying to stand up straight and Oliver helping me because he's extremely attentive like that. He then left me briefly, after propping me up on a stool against the DJ booth, to look after my sister who had thrown up all over the table we had been sitting at.

Yes, that's right, that's why Oliver moved me to the stool, so that I wouldn't get any more vomit on me. He is such a gentleman. So, while he escorted my sister to the toilet, I vaguely recall that he then had to go back to get Maria-José-Inmaculada-Carmen.

Ah, now. It's all coming back to me. Oliver had to put his huge beefy arms to good use and give her a fireman's lift out of the club and over to his car, because she had passed out and was also covered in my sister's sick. That's right. Then he came back in for me, and returned with my sister, who apparently had also passed out mid-wee, in the ladies' toilets.

Phew, what a night. It must have been two o'clock before Oliver managed to get us back out of his car and into the villa.

Then there was a right hoo-hah when my sister and Maria-José-Inmaculada-Carmen woke up, and briefly exclaimed that they were having a second wind, and demanded to be taken straight back to the club. Luckily, the second wind lasted only long enough for the tantrum and tears to stop, the hugging to begin and then for them to reach the sofa and pass out again.

I remember asking Oliver if he wanted to stay over and him saying, 'Absolutely not' in a really exasperated voice.

The more I think about it, maybe he was a teeny bit annoyed with us by the end. I hope he has also forgotten that I called him Ryan when I waved him off. Maybe I should wait until *he* texts me.

I stumble out of bed and into the shower. It's a good job I've a strong constitution for the drink. It's one of the perks of living alone and having no friends with whom to go out with. I don't wish to brag but I can easily drink a bottle of wine and not even be tipsy.

While I'm washing the powerful stench of booze from my hair and skin, I hope that Oliver hasn't been put off me. I think back to my sister and MJ treating him like their personal Uber. I'm now certain Oliver was quite annoyed with them.

Mind you, I hardly made the greatest of impressions myself. I've got a hazy recollection of doing a sexy striptease for him outside of the club, only to do it quickly in reverse when he barked 'Put those back on!' at me.

Oh god.

Unable to resist, I grab my phone and text Oliver to say thanks for getting us all home last night and that I hope to see him soon. I stare at the phone for ages, but he doesn't reply. He must be really angry. I quickly send another text apologising for our awful behaviour, saying that he doesn't have to see me soon after all. Not if he doesn't want to.

Nothing.

Now I think about it, it might be best to leave him to cool off. I notice a string of Instagram alerts and click to see what's going on.

Feck.

Ava has drunk posted a string of reels on her story from last night. There's one of her with deely boppers on her head and her arm slung around the Welsh rugby captain with some blurb about how she is cheering the team on, hashtag winning at life, hashtag live your best life. As if she is the life coach behind their success! They both look pissed as newts. It's nothing short of a mockery.

I keep scrolling, there's one of Oliver giving Maria-José-Inmaculada-Carmen a fireman's lift out of the club, hashtag my fire fighter hero. Lord knows who must have taken it (me?). There's one of Ava looking adoringly up at Oliver, hashtag fanny magnet. It's already had over a thousand likes, and several replies saying what a cute couple, and many more saying they would *do* him. OMG there's a reply from Milly-May, ordering Ava to send him around, as he can put her fire out any day of the week!

Then there's one of Oliver looking annoyed, yet extremely handsome, with neon lights highlighting several hairy bums in the background, and a caption saying he simply can't get enough of these guys. And even more replies than before from men paying him lots of compliments.

I flick through a string of embarrassing photos of me looking worse for wear with my arm slung drunkenly around an assortment of rugby players. There's one with a cigarette dangling from my lips that looks suspiciously like a joint (How? When?), one with me standing on a bar stool about to fall off, and finally, there's one of me sitting on Squinty's broad shoulders with a rose between my teeth, and waving what could be a pair of knickers around (mine?). Ava has written that she's very proud of her big sister and how I have managed to bounce back from professional disaster and disgrace and for EVERYONE to come on my singles coach trip, where I will hashtag find love for you all, hashtag LOVE COACH hashtag THE COACH TRIP. Every word is spelt wrong except our website address. And she's tagged in Milly-May AND Ryan Reynolds!

I hardly know whether to laugh or cry, it's so ridiculous. But one thing I know for sure, is that it is a mammoth relief to know the truth about Ava. And it was the best night out I think we've ever had. Even MJ had a blast.

As I'm looking at an image of Maria-José-Inmaculada-Carmen being held upside down over a bucket of beer, a cold realisation dawns. What if Nidi sees how we are carrying on? What if Oliver sees?

Once my hair is dried and my make-up is on, I'm ready for some water and ibuprofen, and I might even manage a hot water with lemon. Didn't Endless Cloud say the slice of lemon detoxes your whole system or something? Or was that the apple cider vinegar?

The whole place is in darkness. I can just make out my sister and Maria-José-Inmaculada-Carmen sprawled on the two sofas, covered in a blanket each. Oliver must have done that while I was looking for ingredients to make him a chickpea and flax seed pancake. I'm not sure why that popped into my head, considering the fact that I have never once thought to cook it in my entire life. But I do recall eyeing his taught muscular body up and down, before deciding he must be a real health food enthusiast, and that I would make him a spectacular VEGAN supper for his trouble.

I'm not sure, but I think I remember him saying a firm 'You will do nothing of the sort' before taking the frying pan off me.

Oh God, how embarrassing.

Why? Why? Why? My chakras are going to need some serious unblocking.

Chapter 30

As I let myself in to the office, the phone rings immediately. I have barely gotten through the door. I'm only two steps into the hallway. I pick up the post from the floor and race along to reception. My eyes are already burning into my sockets with tiredness. I must have only slept for four hours at the most.

Is it too much to bloody ask that I have two fucking minutes of peace and quiet so that I can tap my third eye? Is it? IS IT?

I reach out to answer the phone and it stops ringing.

Good.

I open the post and see one of the envelopes is from the quick qualify company and rip it open. My Life Coach Certificate has finally arrived, but I'm too shattered to even give myself a little whoop whoop never mind frame it and hang it on the wall.

I quickly check to see if Ryan Reynolds has any allergies that I should know of. He hasn't. I check my phone to see if Oliver has texted. He hasn't. I rub a couple of crystals and tap my base chakra to loosen off the hangover. It doesn't work. The book says I should release any blockages, before

I do anything meaningful. I quickly grab the gong and ding it a few times.

I must stay focussed. I have an event to sort out that has run wildly out of control and I have two helpers who are currently of no use to me whatsoever.

I quickly click on our Instagram and Twitter accounts and slump back in my seat.

OMG. Nidi's Life Coaching sites are now as bad as Ava's.

There's one picture after another of drunken cross-eyed rugby players cavorting with the Hen ladies. Several photos of a scantily clad Ava, with a pondering look, hashtag life, what's it all about? And many, many memes of kittens with sad eyes. KITTENS!!!

How am I supposed to work like this? How?

The bookings are a shambles. I have no idea who is coming in or when. Half of the bookings are for the wrong time anyway. There are no notes. NO NOTES! No payment records. NOTHING!!

Nidi has been gone barely a week and I have single-handedly RUINED her business. I wonder if Ryan has these same worries when he is running his production company or his Welsh football team? Probably. I wonder if I should message him. I decide not to. Even I can see that this fantasy escapism of mine is a mere disguise for procrastination and truth avoidance.

The singles event, my missing redundancy payout, the client payments must be dealt with today. I will start by laying out and rubbing my green crystals. It should help me visualise my financial goals.

I reach for the biggest crystal and wave it about in front of my face and upper body. I have no idea what it is doing, but the rhythmic motion is instantly soothing.

My phone pings.

It's Oliver! My heart skips a beat at the sight of his name. I quickly scan the message.

Shite.

He's asking if I can take down ALL of the photos of him from ALL of our social media. AS SOON AS POSSIBLE PLEASE if I wouldn't mind. He has been bombarded with DMs and thinks it is very unprofessional. He is flying back to Madrid because his board have also called for him to be suspended from work.

Oh God. It's started already. The repercussions. The backlash. Another career down the drain.

For my own sanity, I switch off my phone and turn my attention to some deep nostril breathing and some active relaxation involving me imagining that I'm somewhere nice and doing something calming, like kneading bread or stroking horses or better still, unwinding in Ryan Reynold's sauna.

I'm so wound up, I have to force myself to relax into the dream, lowering my shoulders and placing my hand on my stomach to feel the gentle rise and fall of each breath. Just as Ryan is asking me all about my worries, before suggesting we take off our towels like Scandinavians, so we can sit there looking at each other naked, two things happen.

One is that there is an almighty racket from outside my office and the other is that the reception phone shrills.

I dash outside to the reception to witness Ava tutting and making throaty annoyed noises at a shrieking Maria-José-Inmaculada-Carmen who is gesticulating wildly with arms and hands waving about.

I calmly walk past them and round to the other side of the reception desk to pick up the phone.

'Hello, you are through to The Life Coach. How can I help?' I say politely, taking in this bizarre scene. They haven't had the common decency to stop arguing. It's like I am invisible to them.

Last night they were swearing to be BFFs and soulmates.

I also stare in wonderment at the three big buttons in front of me. One has a large green telephone on (to accept a call), the middle one has a large red telephone on (to hang up a call) and the other a black telephone with emanating sound (to place call on loudspeaker) and marvel at how on earth Maria-José-Inmaculada-Carmen manages to always, always, fucking ALWAYS press the loudspeaker by mistake.

An official-sounding woman tells me that she is calling from the ICF to arrange a talk with Nidi, an observation with me, which is routine practice, and other important checks.

I mouth to the girls to be quiet.

Maria-José-Inmaculada-Carmen slips onto her seat at reception with last night's clothes on, her hair wild and she is positively stinking of drink. I am delighted to see that she is incredibly late for work, and her face has a sickly green hue to it, as though she has very recently recovered from the plague.

Ava is chewing on a nail, looking very dishevelled and dark around the eyes.

'I will ask her to ring you as soon as she returns from the funeral,' I say, relieved she's not ringing to fire me or close the business down. 'Although, I am surprised Oliver hasn't told you that she is away.'

'Oliver who?'

'Your inspector. You know the really handsome one?' I simply can't help myself. Even if he is very annoyed with me at the moment. 'The tall one with lovely kind eyes and a sort of attractive bossiness to him. Oliver Reynolds. And by the way, those social media photos were not his fault. You should not be suspending him from work. If anything, it is all my fault.'

Least I can do under the circumstances.

'I've never heard of him and we never value our staff by their outward appearance,' she snaps. 'As far as I'm aware, we have no operatives, handsome or otherwise, in your area. And now you've mentioned it, please do take down those awful photos you have posted on your socials immediately. They are not in keeping with the ICF values.'

Maybe I've misheard, or maybe it is because Oliver is working undercover like a mystery diner.

'Oliver Reynolds,' I repeat. 'He works for you. Your Madrid branch unfairly suspended him.'

Ava and Maria-José-Inmaculada-Carmen lean in to hear what is going on. I press the loudspeaker button. They may as well hear first-hand the consequences of their drunk social media posting.

Maria-José-Inmaculada-Carmen looks at me as though I've just pressed the button for DEFCON 1.

It's a teaching moment. An ironic teaching moment.

'Miss Weston, I assure you, no one of that name works here at the ICF. We do not have a Madrid branch and we certainly haven't suspended anyone.' She sounds annoyed. 'I'm going to push for your monitoring visit to take place as soon as possible. Goodbye.'

We take a beat to stare at each other.

Apparently, Oliver is lying about working for the ICF or the ICF are lying about him.

I switch my phone back on.

Five missed calls from Oliver.

Chapter 31

Before we can digest this startling information, the phone trills again. Maria-José-Inmaculada-Carmen gingerly picks up as though the handset weighs more than a baby elephant.

'Hello, is that The Life Coach?' asks a polite voice.

Of course, Maria-José-Inmaculada-Carmen has pressed loudspeaker. Of course, she has.

It is Wendy, the lovely Zoom woman, who wanted help dealing with her men fellas. She is wondering if she could book another session with me in a few days' time and she has an idea she would like to discuss.

'Also,' she says, 'would it be possible for us to go on The Coach Trip? I've just seen it pop up on my socials. It sounds like an ideal team away-day. Will we be life-coached when we get there? How do we book places?'

GAAAH!

Maria-José-Inmaculada-Carmen tells her that I'll be in touch really soon with all of the information. *Me*. I will be in touch really soon with *ALL* of the information.

I stand with one hand on my hip and my other arm raised,

my finger pointing towards my office, ready for when she clicks off the call.

'You two! In my office NOW!' I sound like a very cross Headteacher. They both wilt under the force of my instruction and meekly head through the door.

I catch sight of my reflection in the gigantic mirror across the office. My hair is all over the place. I reach up to pat it down. Is that a yellow post-it stuck in there somewhere? Maria-José-Inmaculada-Carmen and Ava are standing sheepishly over by the window. I look no better than either of them.

I push thoughts of Oliver to one side. One thing at a time.

'I'm so sorry,' says Maria-José-Inmaculada-Carmen. 'I am late. I have no notes. I have mixed up the bookings again, and I think... I may have been sick in your fridge.'

Ava is staring at her toes. They are poking out of her wedge sandals and seem to be absorbingly fascinating.

I take a deep breath and instantly calm down. I need to be at my best. I want to be a more effective life coach. I have the tools I need to run this business *and* help Maria-José-Inmaculada-Carmen, rather than abandon her like I have.

'I'm sorry too,' I say to Maria-José-Inmaculada-Carmen. 'I shouldn't have yelled. It's not your fault. Well, not entirely. Or yours, Ava.'

I realise that I also need to help my clients. They have been paying me good money, even if I have no idea where it has gone, to do a job and so far, I am failing them.

'We'll figure it out together.' I invite them to sit down.

'But first, I need to be honest with you, Ava.'

Maria-José-Inmaculada-Carmen beats me to it. 'I am not the managing director. And... I am not entirely sure what happens here.'

Ava sniggers.

'And I'm not the CEO,' I say, causing Ava's jaw to drop open. 'I don't run this company. Nidi does. She's the qualified life coach. I'm more like an apprentice. I only just qualified.' I point to the envelope on my desk.

'Yes. This is true. Quick qualify,' Maria-José-Inmaculada-Carmen says helpfully. 'She made the last client cry.'

One time. And they were happy tears!

We wait for Ava to say something judgemental involving a hashtag.

'So, where's Nidi?' she asks, surprising us with this simple question.

'Funeral,' I say. 'In the UK.'

Ava closes her eyes and presses her fingertips to her temples as though meditating. 'Hmmm, go on.'

'She's left us in charge and we need to put on an event to drum up new customers. An event that showcases our services and gives them excellent value for money. An event that will leave them inspired and ready to take the first step towards living their best life. And thanks to a plethora of misunderstandings... now involves a *coach trip* and needs to link being single and being a small business owner with being...' I'm struggling to find the right word.

'Human?'

I look at Maria-José-Inmaculada-Carmen and inwardly sigh. 'Isn't being human what fundamentally links us all, Maria-José-Inmaculada-Carmen?' I should give her a chance to explain.

'Yes, exactly.'

What can she mean?

'I agree,' says Ava. Suddenly, her head jerks up. Her eyes flash open, lighting up her face. 'I've prepared my whole life for this moment!' she announces, slowly removing her fingers from her temples. 'I have the answer.'

It's as though she's imagining a drumroll.

'Nell, the answer to all of life's problems is... '

This better be worth it.

She claps her hands together in prayer, tilting her head to one side. She's really milking it.

'... to be kind. The world would be a much nicer place if only we were kind to each other. And recycling. We need to recycle more. And the trees. We need to do something about them. That's what the event should be about.'

Futile. Completely futile.

I plaster a smile to my face. 'Okay, why don't you both go for some food and come back in an hour, refreshed and ready to sort this out properly? We'll get some ideas and information together.'

· ♥ · ♥ · ♥ · ♥ · ♥ ·

Once they've left, I sit and stare at the crystal on the table. I'm instantly reminded of Nidi.

'How are you, my lovely?' Nidi says, answering my call.

I close my eyes and allow myself to be immersed in her lovely warm voice. It's time to come clean about everything.

'Nidi, I have to tell you something and you're not going to like it.'

She listens to me pour it all out. The ICF complaining about the embarrassing social media photos and Tweets. The mess up at the bank with my money transfer from the UK. The singles event that is now being called The Coach Trip, even though it doesn't involve a coach or a trip. The mix-up with the website and the bookings. The sister I said I didn't have. I leave nothing out except that Oliver, my fake client who we all thought was from the ICF, is no longer the spy we thought he was.

I just think that at this juncture, it seems a bit far-fetched, and I'd hate for Nidi to suffer any further undue stress in her delicate condition.

'I'm so sorry I lied.'

'Nell, honey, I won't say I'm not disappointed, but you've got to look failure straight in the eye, be resilient and learn from it. I knew you were a complete mess the moment you walked through my door. But, you know what? That's why you need this lifeline, and why I took you on. You are a great listener. You have empathy. You're a quick thinker and have a creative brain. You're kind, compassionate and will make a great life coach. Now, let's deal with one thing at a time, starting with the things you have most control over.'

It feels like a hand reaching into the water and pulling me back up to breathe the air. We talk for a while about how I have managed to avoid dealing with my family issues for almost all my adult life. My reaction to Ava making me redundant was the straw that broke the camel's back. We have carried this rivalry since childhood.

She helps me see that when I booked the flight to Spain, I thought that I'd be leaving the angry, resentful, embarrassed me behind, to start a fresh new life, but sadly all that internal stuff boarded the plane with me.

'Don't underestimate yourself, honey. You've had to face such a huge life-changing situation alone, and instead of challenging the very people who are supposed to be the cornerstones of your emotional and social support, you've simply 'run away' from them. You've learned a really big lesson here about not jumping to conclusions. Allow yourself the time and space to heal properly. It's not the end of the world.'

She's right.

I flop down against the sofa feeling light and unburdened. I breathe deeply in through my nostrils, hold for 4 seconds and gently exhale.

Oliver is not who he says he is. I have five missed calls. Rather than jump to conclusions, I will call him back to find out what is going on. We will discuss this like rational adults.

His phone is switched off.

Everything will work out. I know it will. I can do this.

Chapter 32

I take myself off for a walk along the promenade. The fresh sea air invigorates me while I think things through.

When I eventually return, and walk into Nidi's office, I'm greeted with a hive of activity. Ava is filing away things onto shelves and Maria-José-Inmaculada-Carmen is organising the diary and tapping away on the computer.

'Our new online booking system!' Maria-José-Inmaculada-Carmen announces proudly. 'We want to do nice things for you because we think you are very sad about Oliver.'

Ava turns like lightning, 'BUT I SHOWED HER WHAT TO DO AND HOW TO DO IT!'

I smile serenely at both of them. 'Thank you.'

What a sweet gesture.

Maria-José-Inmaculada-Carmen turns to me excitedly. 'We have an idea!'

I listen as they outline their marketing plan.

'Big coaches will take clients from the office to this amazing retreat we found,' Ava says. 'To do holistic activities. Ones involving trust falls and team work. They have a fountain that cries healing tears. We will take clients on a Life

Coach Trip.'

Warning bells are ringing in my head.

'Because it involves a coach,' Maria-José-Inmaculada-Carmen explains when I do not respond immediately. 'And you are a life coach too. It is a play on words. The coach does the coaching during the trip on the coach.'

The bells are getting progressively louder.

'We will do fun *stretch and think* activities,' she says. 'We spoke to the owners. They look like old wizards on the website. Clients will love them.'

Ding. Ding. Ding.

Love them? It will be more of a bad, hallucinogenic sort of trip. Involving two cobwebby warlocks. Besides, once Gandalf finds out it is me – the liar and the thief – he may not want to host our event.

Maria-José-Inmaculada-Carmen gushes, 'Ava has booked Meals in Heels. They are ladies from Benidorm who do all the parties. Very classy. They are coming very soon to tell us about their services. Special food. Music. Dancing.'

What music? What dancing? What special food? I have not pre-approved anything of the sort. I clearly said to get some information and ideas together. Not, do what the bloody hell you like.

'Edible soil. Edible flowers. Everything vegan,' Ava joins in.

I've had to zone out. People will think they are at a garden centre not a business networking event.

Gaaah!

See what happens when you give people an inch?

'But this isn't a party,' I say to them.

Their faces drop.

'Look it may have potential. I just need time to process how it might pan out and how to pay for it. Coach hire is not cheap. Guests could make their own way to the venue. I'm not sure the retreat is such a good idea.'

Ava and Maria-José-Inmaculada-Carmen trade guilty glances.

'We have already booked it,' whispers Maria-José-Inmaculada-Carmen.

'And we've sent out the invites and posted to our socials,' Ava says quietly, looking at her feet. 'You did say to use our initiative,' she mumbles. 'Sorry, Nell.'

I take a deep nostril breath in. 'It sounds like you've invited the whole of the Costa Blanca. I need to see that invitation. Right now.'

Ava gingerly turns her screen to show me.

I want to yell, 'I TOLD MARIA-JOSÉ-INMACULADA-CARMEN TO USE *HER* INITIATIVE BECAUSE I KNOW SHE DOESN'T HAVE ANY. NOT FOR YOU TO USE YOURS, AVA!'

But I don't. Remarkably, I look at their petrified faces and say calmly, 'Okay then, let's get planning!' I keep my smile tight.

The door swinging open distracts us.

'That will be Meals in Heels,' announces Ava.

'Buenas dias,' a familiar voice cackles. I am greatly surprised to see Juniper, the journalist from the Costa Blanca News, with one of her divorcée friends in tow. The pair of them looking like dark leather skeletons clad in skimpy French Maids outfits and pillar-box red six-inch stilettos.

'Hello, Juniper,' I say, trying to avert my gaze. 'Nice to see you.'

We listen for a few minutes as Juniper explains the service they provide.

'Naked waitressing is extra of course,' she says in her gravelly smoker's voice, taking a long drag on her cigarette and eyeing me with a heavily kohl-rimmed stare. 'And of course, you'll have to provide the food and the serving plates and the booze.'

'So, basically, Meals in Heels is just a waitressing service? There's no meals involved?'

'No.'

After a few moments, it is clear we are all at cross purposes, but the lovely Meals in Heels ladies say they will show up to the event anyway, as it could be good for their own business which they'd like to expand (Deals in Heels, Wheels in Heels, Squeals in Heels, Feels in Heels), they are both also in the market for new husbands and/or lovers, and they offered to cover our event in the newspaper for free. I promise to introduce Juniper to Boring Berry.

'Juniper and Berry, we sound like the perfect match,' she cackles. 'We'd make great gin together.' *Poor Berry.*

We wave them off and discover that a similar misunderstanding has occured over the date. Instead of two weeks time, the event will now be held in a five days.

I gulp.

'That might have been my fault,' admits Ava. 'For some

reason my phone's a bit glitchy, and the number two no longers works on the keypad apparently.'

A flashback of her dropping her phone in my cocktail comes to me.

Maria-José-Inmaculada-Carmen whips out her phone. 'Don't worry, I have idea for catering.'

Me and Ava look hesitantly at each other. This is the same woman who has also argued for us to invite the Hen ladies. Five minutes later, she has executed a rescue plan. Unbelievably, her parents say that they can cater and give us an amazingly low cost per head.

Maria-José-Inmaculada-Carmen's face changes from surprised through to flustered, as she listens to them on the phone and begins hissing and making nervous raspy sounds. We see her cheeks flame. She ends the call and turns to face us.

'They have put Alejandro in charge. They have asked me to come and meet with him to discuss the menu and staffing.'

'Okay, good,' I say. 'You take charge of catering and numbers. Ava, you take charge of socials, invites and bookings. And I will manage the ICF mix-up, the venue and the life coaching activities. Nobody is allowed to Google Ryan Reynolds. We all need to focus.'

They nod in agreement.

'I need to get something from my office. Back in a moment.'

Deep breaths,
Deep breaths.

I close my office door behind me and ball my fist into my mouth and let out a silent scream. Once it is fully out of my system, I feel instantly better. I straighten up and glance round at my many pictures of pebbles and sayings on the wall. They are all versions of the same message; in the middle of difficulty lies opportunity, strength comes from overcoming the things you think you can't do, don't give up.

I can do this.

After the last few weeks, I feel changed.

A few dings and a quick rub on the crystals, and I'm awake to new possibilities.

I make my way back to Nidi's office. 'What are they going to get out of their time with us? We still need something to weave through all the activities like a golden thread, bringing them together.'

We sit around the table staring at one another blankly.

The minutes tick slowly by.

'Between us we have what it takes to come up with something brilliant,' I say, trying to sound hopeful. 'After all, which one of us here speaks a second language fluently?'

I receive a grateful look from Maria-José-Inmaculada-Carmen, who then tells us she speaks fluent French and Italian too. And she is a talented photographer and a trained yoga instructor.

Who knew?

You'd think Nidi would have read her CV properly. Ava and I exchange impressed looks.

'Meditate with me,' I say, suggesting we close our eyes and

let the answer come to us.

· ♥ · ♥ · ♥ · ♥ · ♥ ·

After half an hour of deep meditation, I open one eye to see Ava scrolling on her phone, and Maria-José-Inmaculada-Carmen has disappeared.

'I know,' Maria-José-Inmaculada-Carmen says, breezing back in, smelling of cigarette smoke. 'The Law of Attraction. It is everywhere and inside everyone.'

Oh my word.

She's right. SHE'S RIGHT!

'Go on,' I encourage.

Maria-José-Inmaculada-Carmen walks over and picks up the Life Coach Handbook, flicks to the middle section on manifesting and reads. 'Positive thoughts produce positive energy, which produces positive outcomes for everyone.' She slaps it shut. 'Whether they are single, running a business or just want more from life. We can all use it.'

Ava looks a bit put out. 'I'm sure I did a post on the Law of Attraction once.'

'It's okay for someone else to have ideas,' I say. 'We're a team, remember?'

Ava looks sheepish. 'Sorry. Old habits.'

While Maria-José-Inmaculada-Carmen shows Ava the Life Coach Handbook, the time suddenly feels right for me to heal the rift between me and my family once and for all.

I whip out my phone and text my mother.

Chapter 33

The upside of having much to do at work, with a sudden influx of new clients, thanks to Ava's raunchy posts, and not one single word from Oliver, is that Ava and I have been keeping to a jogging routine and our realistic and achievable goals. Except for the green tea and the vegan slop masquerading as breakfast. A line had to be drawn somewhere.

The downside to organising this event has been catastrophically horrendous. Between the pair of them, Ava and Maria-José-Inmaculada-Carmen have bounced around the most ridiculous ideas for how the business networking singles launch Coach Trip is to be organised and they have not been able to agree on one single thing. I have listened to them arguing for days now about every little aspect. On and on they have rowed. They can both be spectacularly stubborn. And violent with it. My sister threw her precious notebook across the room during an argument about penmanship over writing out the badges. Maria-José-Inmaculada-Carmen, in a fiery vampiric explosion, retaliated by knocking over the flipchart and upending a tray of biscuits.

Ava has invited all the rugger boys and Maria-José-Inmaculada-Carmen has invited all the Hens. Ava then suggested we don't invite the Hens because really, they are simply here for two weeks of heavy drinking and will think they are coming to a party for free booze, won't be remotely interested in the free life coaching. There was a delightful bust up over that little revelation, I can tell you.

Obviously, I had to step in and administer some nursery nurse-style facilitation.

Today, in a bid to heal rifts, Maria-José-Inmaculada-Carmen has invited us to do yoga with her down on the beach at sunrise. It turns out Endless Cloud was also right about this too - it *is* a really invigorating start to the day.

'I will go to the retreat this morning to firm up the details of the activities,' I say, trying to sound casual as I bend myself into Cow's Pose. I will have some explaining to do when I arrive, and I'd rather not do it in front of these two.

'I'll come,' says Ava, looking at me upside down from between her ankles.

'Me too,' says Maria-José-Inmaculada-Carmen. She has positioned her leg up high, perpendicular to her body. 'I hear they have a cauldron.'

I collapse into a sitting position on my mat. 'Unfortunately, I need you both to stay in the office to field any calls. I also need you to confirm all of the bookings we have for the coach trip so far. How many people can the coach hold? Which company did you book with?'

The event is only a few days away and I have suddenly realised that I know nothing about the transport arrangements.

'Coach?' asks Maria-José-Inmaculada-Carmen.

'Yes,' I say. 'We need to know how many people it can hold and match that with how many people you have invited.'

It's basic Maths.

'I naturally assumed Maria-José-Inmaculada-Carmen had booked them,' says Ava quickly. 'What with her being from the area.'

'And I *naturally* assumed you would book them,' says Maria-José-Inmaculada-Carmen, looking at me. 'Because you are the boss.'

We all stop to take a minute.

I had naturally assumed one of them had booked them seeing as it was their idea.

'So, no one has booked the coach?' I ask.

Silence.

'And how many people do we have booked on?'

Ava and Maria-José-Inmaculada-Carmen look blankly at each other.

'So how do we know how many people to feed?'

Silence.

'So while I've been busy life coaching and pre-assessing all the new clients, what exactly have you two been doing these past two days?'

Bickering about Instagram posts and catching up on celebrity gossip from the Hola magazine?

'It is Ryan Reynold's fault. He has been very busy on social media,' Maria-José-Inmaculada-Carmen explains, 'meeting sick people in hospitals and giving poor children free holidays.'

Ava nods along. 'And of course, his football team are doing very well at the moment.'

This might be on me. I have allowed this to happen. My every waking thought has been about Oliver and where he is, what he is doing, why he is ghosting me.

· ♥ · ♥ · ♥ · ♥ · ♥ ·

Back at the office, the phone on Maria-José-Inmaculada-Carmen's desk is flashing. We have a telephone message.

Maria-José-Inmaculada-Carmen presses play and we listen to the officious-sounding voicemail.

'Hello. This is Andrew calling from the International Coaching Federation in Alicante. I'd like to book a time to do an assessment with Nell Weston, please. I also would like to book four places for me and my colleagues to attend your networking event. Are there are any places left on the coach?'

Good question. At this point in time, the whole event exists largely in our imaginations.

There is a second voicemail. I hold my breath hoping it is from Oliver.

It is the owner of this building with an angry message for Nidi. He bellows down the phone that he hasn't received the rent. He is giving her a day to get it sorted and the money transferred into his bank, otherwise, he says we are out by the end of the week.

OMG.

'Leave it to me,' I say to two shocked faces. 'I will book the coach and deal with this wanker. Ava, you book the ICF places and respond accordingly, please. Maria-José-Inmaculada-Carmen, can you ring the retreat and reschedule my appointment?'

My phone pings with a message.

'I just landed. Can I see you?'

My heart leaps a mile. Where's my calming crystal and my good karma body spray? I will begin my manic getting-Oliver-ready spree with a little aura cleanse.

·♥·♥·♥·♥·♥·

A short while later, my meditation is broken with the sound of the girls arguing. I walk into the reception to see Oliver standing with them.

'Sorry,' says Oliver. 'I just came by to apologise for the text I sent earlier. I should have phoned you.'

He looks very tired.

'It should be me apologising to you. I got you suspended from work. From the ICF?'

The girls are quick to stand by my side, arms folded in a hostile manner. We wait for him to deny or confirm. Either way he has some explaining to do.

He shrugs. 'I don't care. I need a break from them.'

'Oh, that's funny,' I say. 'Because when I spoke to them two days ago they hadn't heard of you.'

'Ah,' he says, looking guilty. 'There's something I need to explain. I just haven't had the chance to discuss it with you yet.'

'Look at his shirt,' yells Ava.

We look at Oliver. He looks mighty fine. His shirt is stretched tight across his chest giving his pecs incredible definition.

'It looks lovely. Very... snug,' I say, ripping my eyes from his biceps.

Traitor.

'Look at the logo,' she tuts.

I switch my gaze to the letters printed on the shirt pocket.

'See? It's him,' Ava yells, pointing at Oliver. 'I knew I recognised the ICF logo from somewhere. He's the one. The prick from the transformation company I told you about. '

Oliver immediately looks backfooted.

'*He* made us all redundant. *His* company.'

I turn to Ava. 'What are you talking about?'

'He's not from your ICF. He's from the International Corporate Finance company that Karen brought in to streamline the business. And by streamline, I mean put us all out of jobs.'

We all take a beat. Even Maria-José-Inmaculada-Carmen takes a step away from him. 'I preferred when he was a spy.'

It is suddenly very hot in here and my head is starting to swim.

'She's right,' Oliver says. 'There have been some crossed wires. It's what I've been trying to tell you, but you haven't been answering my calls. Then I had to fly to Madrid to face the board. I'm from the other ICF. I'm sorry.'

His eyes are full of regret.

'That's why you've been so interested in helping me? Guilt?'

Pieces of the puzzle suddenly fall into place. We were on the same flight. He seemed to know a lot about losing jobs. He seemed so keen to know how I was doing. No wonder the life coaching ICF had never heard of him.

'Wait. Have you been stalking her?' Ava shouts at him.

Oliver gulps. His face says it all.

I have never felt so gutted in my life.

Chapter 34

There's a gentle knock at the door. 'Go away!' I yell, watching as the door handle turns slowly.

Oliver pops his head around the door. 'Just give me two minutes to explain,' he says softly. 'There's been no stalking. None whatsoever. I would never.'

We stare at each other for a few seconds before he closes the door gently behind him and walks towards me. 'I swear, I only put two and two together when you kept going on about the code of conduct that night in Benidorm. Not before.'

I look over to the door wondering if Ava and Maria-José-Inmaculada-Carmen will be running to my rescue.

'The others have gone,' he tells me. 'They're not speaking to me, apparently. I'm so sorry you got caught up in the redundancies. I really am. It's an unfortunate part of any transformation and not personal. It's purely business. Redundancy is awful. It's the one part of the job that I hate but without it, most companies would go under, and everyone would lose.'

'Where have you been?'

'Madrid. Sorting out my severance package. Signing disclosures and agreements, and not signing legal documents that stop me from setting up my own company. That's why I couldn't reply to you. They took my phone to wipe the contacts. I've been locked in negotiations non-stop.'

Sounds very heavy but I totally believe him. He's always had kind, honest eyes. And they're looking at me right now.

'Are you okay?' I ask him. 'Do you want to talk about it?'

After all, I'm qualified now and almost know what I'm doing.

He smiles for the first time.

'I can help you sort out your wankers,' I say, feeling suddenly thrilled that I can help him. As a peer. As a bona fide, high-calibre professional. 'It's my speciality. Dealing with pricks in the workplace and the bedroom... I mean boardroom. I love dealing with wankers in the boardroom.'

I've ruined it.

'I'd value your input,' he says, his face breaking into a huge grin. 'Now that we've cleared the misunderstanding up.'

Something doesn't quite add up for me though.

'All this time, you thought I was talking about your ICF? Didn't moral codes of conduct seem a little out of context? A little bizarre?' I say. 'Didn't I sound completely ridiculous?'

He refrains from answering.

Ah. How humiliating. I guess everything he's seen me do

and say so far, has been bizarre.

'Let me help,' he says. 'It's the least I can do after I made you redundant and then ghosted you by accident.'

He thinks I'm worried about the redundancy.

'I'm not bothered about the redundancy now,' I tell him. It's the truth. 'I'm actually where I want to be for a change. I *want* to do this job. You don't need to feel guilty. If anyone should feel guilty then it's me. I've behaved like a colossal bellend since the day I met you.'

'Have you?' Oliver says. 'I hadn't noticed.'

He has a dry sense of humour with almost perfect comic timing. It's a very lovable quality.

'I'd still like to help. I help businesses for a living.'

Now he thinks I'm worried about being incompetent.

'You can't help. The ICF... the *other* ICF will revoke my licence after this, so there's literally no point.'

I won't tell him I've only had it for less than a day. Or that it is still in the envelope it came in. Or the irony that I've been put out of work by two separate ICFs.

'What licence?' he asks, sounding all confused.

'My Life Coaching licence.'

'Jesus, you need an *actual* licence to do this? It's an *actual* qualification, is it?' he blurts out all incredulous.

I try not to be offended. This is new territory for us all.

'From an *actual* university?'

'Yes,' I say patiently.

'A proper one? An *actual* university?' he continues undeterred.

How are we still on the subject of my certification? How?

'Well, it's more of an online university. Well, less of a university and more of a... an online centre.'

'And they give *actual* degrees out in this kind of stuff now, do they?' he asks, still sounding baffled. 'After only a couple of weeks?'

Honestly! If he says 'actual' one more time... I swear I will slap him. I will slap.

'Yes!' I nod. 'Well, it's more of a Diploma, if you must know.' Then I spoil things by blurting rather childishly, 'Level four. Ofqual approved!'

One look into his wide eyes and I can tell they are filling with mirth.

'Look, I'm an accountant, well, and a lawyer,' he says modestly. Then he spoils it by giggling. 'Ofqual approved, of course.'

He gives me big apologetic eyes when I tut loudly.

'Now,' he commands, stepping towards me. 'Problem-solving and negotiating are my strengths. Tell me what's wrong.'

'It's not the running of the business that has upset me,' I say. 'Well, it is, but I'm more upset that you—'

'Ah,' he says. 'Of course. Of course. I understand.'

I'd be amazed if he did.

'Nell,' he says, taking hold of my hand gently. 'I'm not here out of guilt. I haven't been deliberately hanging around to make up for putting you out of work.'

One look into his soft kind eyes compels me to relax and take a deep breath. Oliver smiles at me. He really does have a set of superior lips. 'I'm here because I like you.'

Oh. What do I say? What do I do?

I gulp and carry on, as though he has just admitted to needing a haircut or a new pair of slippers. 'I see.'

He is still holding my hand. He is standing an inch away from me. My entire body is lit up from within like a sky full of stars. I'm drawn to him. I experience a sudden flashback to him lying stretched out on the bed, legs akimbo.

'Magnificent,' I say.

'Sorry?'

'I mean...'

Yes. What do I mean?

'I like you too.'

There, I've said it. I've made myself vulnerable and exposed. And I don't like it one little bit.

Oliver visibly relaxes. He lets out a gusty breath.

I make him nervous, I realise. I make this gorgeous man-mountain flustered. *I* make *him* nervous!

OMG.

I'm suddenly desperate to show off. 'Okay, you can help me work out a plan to get this business back on track.'

He seems glad of the distraction and asks what sort of plan. I get out the Wheel of Life diagram and show him.

'This is very similar to how I unpick complex issues. The eBay hostile take-over attempt, cryptocurrency destabilisation,' he says, sitting down next to me at my desk. I ignore the fluttering taking place inside me and try to concentrate on what he's saying. 'In fact, I could have used this for a cross-governmental contract I worked on recently, to finalise a deal over fishing rights off the coast of Iceland.'

Oh my. He sounds incredibly intellectual and competent. Too intellectual and *too* competent, if anything.

'Once we've sorted your issues out, I'd like you to walk me through this to sort out mine. It's time I set up my own company.'

I take a second to digest what he is saying. He is asking me to help him using my life coaching skills. He is after me to administer some *proper* life coaching. He smirks and directs my attention back to the diagram. 'Look, your finances and bookings are a mess. You have unexpected clients walking in. You're missing online payments. No wonder you seem swamped. Every day is spent fire-fighting. You are so busy working *in* the business, you have left yourself no time to work *on* the business.'

He has hit the nail on the head there.

'But,' he says. 'it was rather dumped on you last minute, so how are you supposed to know how everything runs? Credit to you for managing to get this far.'

I feel enormously uplifted by this but he's swiftly moved on to ask if I can show him the accounts, ledgers, tax returns and balance sheets.

Oh Christ.

'Do you know,' says Oliver, breaking my thoughts. 'It would be much easier to sort this all out if we could train Maria-José-Inmaculada-Carmen up properly.'

I admire his optimism. I do.

He proceeds to tell me that at least we'd be able to show her how to manage the finances and cash, cheques and online payments, receipts and petty cash, overheads, rental agreements, liability insurance, Spanish autonimo tax payments so that I won't have to.

'That will free you up to concentrate on the coaching,' he explains. 'And if you delegate the marketing and PR to Ava then she could organise the events. I'll draw up roles and responsinbilities so that there's accountability. It'll prevent any mix-ups.'

God, he's bossy. And sexy.

Even though I know this second chance is merely an opportunity for Maria-José-Inmaculada-Carmen to find new and inventive ways not to do any actual work and for me to keep complaining, I'm determined to give it a go.

I ring Ava to let her know everything is okay and that Oliver is on board.

Surprisingly, she takes the news with gusto. 'Nell,' she says patronisingly. 'Tell Oliver I'm also a guru in spiritualisationology. I can teach clients the basics of magnetism and how to draw the universal energy towards…'

'Fine. Whatever,' I say, desperate for Ava to shut up. 'We can discuss it later at home. I've told MJ to meet us early tomorrow morning for a staff meeting about roles and responsibilities.'

'You seem to be handling your sister rather well,' Oliver tells me when I click off the call.

'I found out a few things. Turns out I jumped to a few wrong conclusions.'

That is surely the understatement of the year. I brace for a barrage of questions.

'Yep. I've been there and done that a few times. Glad you

seem to have it sorted. Was it the crystals that helped or the sage?'

I'm so relieved he's going to let it go, I feel slightly light-headed. I have a smile as wide as my face.

We lock eyes and suddenly, instead of getting to grips with the ledgers, we find ourselves snogging on my couch and rolling around lustfully on the floor.

'I've been dying to try this ever since I saw you doing it the other day.'

Cheeky fecker.

My skirt is right up to my waist, his hands roam all over me and we are panting like excited puppies. His eyes have glazed over with lust, and he is saying my name with a desirous groan.

In an inexplicable moment of clarity, I break free and pull my skirt back down. I tell him that we should not get carried away as, technically, he is my coachee, and as much as I'd like to, I cannot continue to snog him until he is satisfied that we have achieved his goals. He is looking at me like I have gone crazy.

'Would it help if I told you that my only goal for this evening is to keep kissing you?' Oliver rolls off me and props himself up.

He catches me staring at his muscles. *My oh my*, but I feel like licking them.

'A hundred press-ups every morning.'

And it is totally paying off.

We both stand up, arranging ourselves.

'How about I come by tomorrow afternoon? As your

lawyer, we will need to see each other regularly.'

'Will you be charging by the hour?' I ask, trying not to make it sound so sexy. Although, I would like some clarity around whether his services will be free, in exchange for my own.

'Pro bono,' he says, making it sound like a sexual position. He then kisses me very slowly. It is full of promise.

He likes me for who I am. Even *I* like me for who I am.

Wow. I have finally got my shit together.

Breaking free, Oliver stifles a yawn. 'What a few days. I've hardly slept since Benidorm.'

No need to go into detail and drag up unpleasant memories. I'm hoping he can't remember a lot of it.

'I'm so very sorry. It was such a messy night. I'll pay for the car to be cleaned.'

'Absolutely not,' he says, pulling me back towards him. 'I'm looking forward to seeing what happens next. You're like the gift that keeps on giving.'

'Well, I'm sorry to disappoint you but I don't plan to be involved in any more dramas, breakdowns or catastrophes from now on.'

'Shame,' he says. 'I was beginning to quite like it.'

Chapter 35

I awake the following morning with what I can only describe as two hundred vodka red bulls surging through my veins. By nine o'clock, I'm showered and dressed for a day of business-rescue. I can't deny that the prospect of seeing Oliver today and showing him that I do have a 'highly functioning' side, is very exciting. Thus far, he has been treated to the side of me that's as mad as a game of meat ball tennis.

I have even made time to apply some 'no make-up' make-up, a liberal spray of perfume and have dressed in a pretty, floaty floral dress that is flattering and chic when teamed with shoe-boots and not mismatching flip flops, which I'm ashamed to admit has happened more than once. My hair is piled on my head in a loose type of bun thing and my lips are stained red.

More importantly, I am oozing positivity. I am a grown-up, mature professional businesswoman.

And just because my sister and I seem to ALWAYS rub each other up the wrong way, I will rise above it. It will be a challenge. And I am going to have my hands full today, training up both Ava and Maria-José-Inmaculada-Carmen, but I've never felt more ready in my life.

Ava is in the kitchen making the good stuff coffee and does a double-take when I fly in, grab the cup she has just poured out for me, down it in two gulps and bellow, 'LATE! COME ON! MOVE! LATE! LATE! NOW MUST GO!

That's petty. I can see that, but I honestly could not help myself. I am delighted to see she almost shat herself with fright, and nearly spills coffee down her white top and skimpy denim shorts. She swings her highly inappropriate sky-scraping wedges, designed to elongate her coltish, stick thin legs, off the stool and races after me.

Because of her genetic disposition, Ava says, 'Don't worry. I'll help you and MJ get the business sorted. I have such a creative brain.'

I take a deep breath to centre my inner calm. 'That's great. I'm really looking forward to your input. Thank you.'

I'm pleased to see her caught unawares. And I'm equally pleased to see Maria-José-Inmaculada-Carmen is waiting for us when we arrive. She is without cigarette breath and without, as far as I can tell, an *Hola!* magazine. It's time for me to put my plan in place.

We all make our way up to the office. The sunlight is pouring in through the windows. I instruct them both to grab a coffee and bring it through to Nidi's office which is just down the hallway. It is a beautiful room, tastefully decorated in soothing pale colours. Large sash picture windows overlook the bright blue sky, the not-too-distant mountains with sunlight dancing on their peaks and sharp, gradients that slope gently down to a twinkling sea. It is breath-taking. The room oozes calm and serenity.

I have already set up what I need for our planning session this morning, on the large conferencing table. When Maria-José-Inmaculada-Carmen and Ava sit down, I outline the main principals of life coaching and what the benefits are to the customer.

Ava immediately wants to tell us that she has most of a business degree. 'And I used to...'

'You used to manage over two-hundred people in over ten offices, we know.'

Honestly, if she's told us once, she's told us fourteen million feckin times.

'Regional,' Ava looks to me then to Maria-José-Inmaculada-Carmen. 'Ten *regional* offices,' she repeats.

Instead of taking offence at her sulky tone, I smile brightly. 'Of course, ten *regional* offices, how could I forget?' It has the desired effect of making my sister look petty. Which she is. But it no longer bothers me. 'It must have been so demanding.'

Twelve days she was in charge. Twelve. That's all.

Ava brightens at this and sits up straight, puffing out her chest. She reminds me of our mother.

'This coach trip,' I say. 'So far, we've been like the blind leading the blind. What are we going to do with the people once we have them on board? The future of the company depends on it being a success.'

Ava rolls her eyes and gives Maria-José-Inmaculada-Carmen a conspiring look. 'Honey, success is my middle name.'

It isn't.

Nidi warned me I'd need the patience of a monk. She also advised me to see through my sister's ignorance, and to embrace it as a chance for me to enlighten her.

After ten minutes of gritting my teeth at all of their wildly inappropriate suggestions, my phone buzzes.

It says, 'I'm here.'

Immediately, I am all a fluster. A heat rises in my cheeks and I pray that I am not outwardly blushing. I look up into two pairs of inquisitive eyes.

'YES! NO! NOTHING!' I bark. 'I will leave you two to it,' I instruct. 'I have a meeting to go to. I'll be back in an hour. See if you can put some solid ideas together,' I add, noticing that Maria-José-Inmaculada-Carmen is delighted to have been given a proper grown-up task to do that is unrelated to three telephone buttons.

I can hear Ava bossily taking charge, because of course she's the world's expert on all things marketing and being single, as I quickly race down the corridor to my own office, to check my face, my hair and my teeth.

All fine.

I have an air of excitement about me. I have not seen my face look so young and carefree for a long time. It won't be long, I hope, before I have the tranquil manner of one who does regular yoga (now we know Maria-José-Inmaculada-Carmen can teach us for free!) and one who drinks wheatgrass for a living (Endless Cloud was right!). My hair seems to want to show off today too. It's looking thick and glossy. I've not even had any itching scalp today. I give my lashes a quick flick of mascara to thicken them just in case they are called upon to waft slowly up and down throughout the afternoon.

In the same vein, I apply a thick coat of gloss to my lips which, I am also led to believe, will part involuntarily when looked at by the object of one's desire. I still have much to learn about Oliver Reynolds.

Just as I am about to step out onto the street an alarming thought occurs.

Now normally, at the start of the working day, I would immediately leap onto Twitter to see what Ryan Reynolds has made of the previous day's tweets and his opinions on the world and the idiot behaviour of some people. And yet, I have not checked up to see what Ryan thinks about any of it.

The thought did not even occur to me. Not once.

Chapter 36

'You look different,' says Oliver turning to greet me with a kiss on the cheek. 'Happy and glowing.'

I have to stop myself preening at the compliment. Oliver is standing outside the entrance to my office block under the shade of an umbrella-shaped tree. 'Is it me?' he asks cheekily, while I avert my gaze from his penetrating stare.

I mean of course it is, but he's a man, therefore he can never, ever know. He is quite ridiculously attractive. I take the opportunity to sneak a surreptitious glance at his toned arms, only to see that he flexes them into perfect round melons for my viewing pleasure.

I remain poised and keep my eyes looking to the middle distance, as if something important, beyond his understanding, is occupying my mind. I am, of course, imagining him flinging me over his shoulder like a Persian rug and rolling me out onto his bed.

'What's the number of the landlord?' he says, getting straight down to business. He rings the number, introduces himself in fluent Spanish as my lawyer, which is a massive turn on, and swiftly takes the landlord to town, like he's negotiating a Middle East ceasefire. Oliver is essentially telling him off for harassing me for something that is likely to be a banking error.

I am hugely turned on by his professionalism. We trade lustful glances. I imagine Oliver is struggling to keep from sweeping me up into his beefy arms and carrying me back to my office, for a mammoth sexual marathon on the chaise longue.

I can barely think straight.

'Would you like to do our coaching session first, in exchange for your help sorting out my finances?'

Oliver tears his wandering eyes away from my legs. An unspoken understanding hangs in the air between us. It clearly screams that if we are left alone for any length of time then life coaching, whilst meaningful and full of merit, is the last thing that we will be doing.

'Don't the banks close for a four-hour lunch break?' I suddenly remember.

Oliver nods. 'Yes. That's right.' His eyes are drawn to my chest like magnets, and no wonder. I gaze down to see my nipples are standing to attention and reporting for duty. This flimsy dress is clearly no match for them.

'Which bank are you with?' he commands briskly.

· ♥ · ♥ · ♥ · ♥ · ♥ ·

After we take a ticket and wait in line at the bank, I take the opportunity to find out a few things about Oliver. I will do it skilfully so that he will barely know that I am collecting information. After all, I do this for a living now. It is my job to find out about my clients without it seeming like an interrogation.

I slyly rake my eyes over Oliver, taking care that he doesn't notice me doing it. I have trained for this.

He is very well proportioned, I must say, and I am somewhat unaccustomed to feeling such waves of desire.

'I can see what you're doing,' he states matter-of-factly. He is staring straight ahead at the screen above us, as it clicks through numbers, sending people in the queue scurrying over to various desks. A smile is playing on his lips.

'I have no idea what you are talking about,' I say in my defence. 'I am merely queuing like everyone else. I'm not *doing* anything.'

Without moving a muscle, he says, 'I can feel you undressing me with your eyes.'

For goodness' sake.

'Don't be so ridiculous. That's simply preposterous. Ludicrous.' I say, mortified that he's bang on the money. It's not helping that my voice has risen a few octaves. I have to look away from him as I feel my cheeks flame immediately.

'See?' he giggles. 'You go all turn of the century when you've been caught out. It's hilarious. Now stop staring at me. It's nearly our turn.'

Such a bossy lawyer-type. It's hugely appealing. While he turns away to stare back up at the screen, I look at his profile. He must have immense self-control, unless he doesn't fancy me as much as I fancy him. I *must* play it cool. I must.

Do not speak. Do not. I will try some self-hypnosis.

Thirty seconds go by. It feels like an eternity.

'Tell me everything about yourself!' I insist.

'No, absolutely not,' he says, turning to grin at me. 'Look, it's our turn. Come on.'

I am absolutely buzzing. Oliver and I approach the desk. She gives Oliver an appreciative look and starts clacking away.

Within minutes, she has sourced the problem with the payments and explains that the direct debit for the rent on the office must be renewed annually in person. She gives me a form to fill in and sign, another ticket and tells us to join the growing queue, back over where we just were.

'Can't you do it for us now?' I ask politely in Spanish. I mean I know full well she won't because the long, drawn-out bureaucracy of even the most straightforward task is all that is holding the Spanish economy together. She gives me an apologetic look as Oliver sighs irritably.

We join the queue again.

'It's infuriating,' he says.

'And I'm sure you have much more important things to do.' I feel my mood begin to evaporate.

'Certainly not,' he says, catching me off-guard with a wide smile. 'I'm used to the Spanish doing things the awkward way. Of course, we need to queue all day. This is why people bring packed lunches for a day out at the bank. It's a cultural thing. If they adopted German efficiency, and combined it with the impatience of the French, then they'd all be out of jobs. The country would run like clockwork, with only a tiny fraction of those currently employed.'

I find his socio-economic commentary highly amusing.

Oliver is a very good influence on my crackpot mood swings. Just looking at him makes me feel lighter and upbeat.

'We'll be in here for hours. What do you want to know about me?'

'Erm, well, erm, just you know,' I say shyly, suddenly caught on the hop, '... just things.'

Are you the romantic type to tell a girl you love her every day? Would you be willing to surprise her and make sure she feels adored? In short, could you see yourself being in love with someone like me? Forever.

'Things?' he enquires innocently. *Poor fool.*

'Oh just, you know, where you grew up. That kind of thing.'

'I have three older sisters,' he says. 'Which means that I fully understand the subtext in what you are asking.'

He has no idea. Menfellas simply have no idea what we clever women really mean. No idea at all.

His eyes are dancing with merriment.

Surely not. He'd be the first man in the history of men to ever figure...

'I've been single for just over a year,' he adds, giving me a look. 'I've never been in love because until now, I've not managed to find a funny, clever, entertaining woman who makes standing in a bank queue for hours, even remotely worthwhile.' He squeezes my hand and fixes me an intense sort of look, 'Anything else?'

'No,' I whisper. I have to avert my gaze from his burning

stare because my heart is going like the clappers.

Suddenly, he starts rubbing his thumb seductively across my palm. It is a loaded action. The electricity between us is building.

Then a miracle happens. Our number is called. I fly over to the desk to find the lady speaks English, and rapidly beg, beg, BEG, her to activate the direct debit for the rent. I nod towards Oliver, who is standing across the waiting area in a splendid display of handsomeness. The girl gives me an appreciative nod and an unnecessary pantomime wink, immediately getting my drift.

'And while you're at it,' I plead. 'Why isn't any money going into my account from the business or the money I transferred two bloody weeks ago from the UK?'

She taps away and looks up questioningly to say nobody (me) has bothered to authorise the online transfers or the Paypal.

'Do it! DO it!' I hiss, nodding frantically. We both take a beat to admire Oliver, who is looking at us from afar with a bemused grin. He straightens up so that his pecks strain against his shirt buttons. The girl lets out a slow breath.

Two minutes later and we are out of there.

'Lunch?' he says.

I nod. Not because I'm hungry, but because I don't want to be parted from him or this energy that is crackling between us.

I'd love to know what colour my aura is right now. Probably neon sky blue pink.

'I know a place you might like,' Oliver says, leading the

way.

Walking side by side is excruciating. We try not to walk too close to one another yet, there's a magnetic force pulling us together, and every now and then, our arms brush causing shoots of electricity to run up my spine.

We arrive at SnappySnacks to hear lots of dogs barking.

Oliver looks super-pleased with himself. 'I know you like dogs.'

'Not to eat,' I say.

Oliver looks at me and bursts out laughing. 'No, it's a petting café. You get to pet the pooches while you eat.'

I peer through the window to see lots of puppies and dogs bounding around, leaping onto people's laps. There's a huge sign up on the wall announcing which dog is star of the week (Daisy because she waits politely for treats and doesn't bark for them) and which dog is in the doghouse (Pickles because even though he's tiny, he keeps jumping up onto people and farting out loud sulphuric fumes).

'I remembered you told me you worked at an animal shelter. These little guys are all rescues.'

I am taken aback at Oliver's thoughtfulness.

'Fancy a Yappy burger?' he asks. 'Or are you more of a hotdog lover?'

· ♥ · ♥ · ♥ · ♥ · ♥ ·

After thirty minutes of joyful petting and stroking, Oliver and I have bonded over a shared love of sad-eyed puppies. They were all over him, and seeing his caring nature and the way he handled them all so gently, made my feelings for him balloon out of all proportion. When I picked up one of the puppies and diagnosed a swollen kidney, Oliver went on as though I'd saved its life. Which I might have done, but didn't do it for any sort of fuss to be made. We ended up getting some free doggy biscuits to give out, and I couldn't help offering to volunteer a few hours a week.

Oliver is giving me big cow eyes.

'So, you have one of those fancy whitewashed townhouses, do you?' I breathe huskily when we break out onto the sunny street. No sooner are the words out of my mouth, than he has grabbed my hand, and we are almost halfway to his house.

We scurry past the marina and its bobbing yachts, past Maria-José-Inmaculada-Carmen's restaurant and over to the start of the cobbled lanes that wind their way up to the church. All the houses are centuries old, whitewashed stone with hanging baskets outside spilling over with bright pink and purple flowers. The picture-perfect scene would have any normal person *oohing* and *aahing* but the beauty is lost on me, because I am a person blinded by carnal lustings.

We stop abruptly outside a grand-looking, terraced house covered in colourful, flowered vines and, as we rush through a giant blue wooden door that Oliver deftly kicks shut behind us with one foot, we start kissing the lips off each other.

Somehow, we manage to kiss our way upstairs to a giant soft bed in a room with enormous patio doors overlooking terracotta roof tiles down to the twinkling blue sea. The view is breath-taking. It feels wrong not to mention it at least.

Oliver allows me two seconds of polite small talk.

'Ooh, what a simply stunning view of the....' Before he launches me onto the bed, and straight into heaven.

My floaty floral dress practically disintegrates under his touch. My bra needs even less encouragement and, unusually, instead of preferring to be wrestled off, pings off with just one smouldering look. Oliver yanks his clothes off and lies next to me naked. I can barely look at him. He is unbelievably well-maintained. I run my hand across his chest and slowly down towards his stomach. I am suddenly overcome with longing when he takes a sharp breath in. My touch is sending him wild.

'Oh my god,' Oliver mumbles, his mouth unable to decide which nipple tastes best. He breaks off to kiss my face, my lips and then my neck. His hands roam down to my knickers, slipping inside to cup my bare bottom and haul me on top of him.

'You are so gorgeous!' he cries, holding me tightly to him. I can feel his erection throbbing against my nethers. After some frenzied, passionate kissing and rubbing up against each other, the mood shifts, and he kisses me slowly. I feel his hands gently roam across my body, snaking down my spine, peeling down my knickers. It is unbelievably sensual. He rolls me onto my back and lies on top of me.

'I am going to kiss every single inch of you,' he says, looking into my eyes, sending shoots of desire through my whole body. Now is definitely not the time to mention that we are breaking several rules in the Life Coaching Code of Conduct.

My mind is immediately cleared of all things regulatory, because Oliver, it turns out, is a man of his word.

Chapter 37

I discover Oliver has taken the whole day off work to help me. Well, he's certainly helped with a few things so far. I haven't felt this buzzed for years. I'm all giddy and high from endorphins.

Hoorah!

'What now?' he asks, as we lie entwined together in a tangle of sheets.

My mind is ablaze with possibilities. Does he mean what now in terms of sexual activity? What now for the rest of the afternoon? What now for our relationship? What now for the rest of our lives together?

Men, they ask the most loaded questions, don't they?

I gaze lustfully into his sparkling eyes. They are full of something. Adventure, passion, mischief. I never want this magical moment to end. I should try to impress him with how fun and spontaneous I am. After all, that is a very hard act to follow in terms of vibe and endorphin-levels.

'Erm, maybe we could go swimming with dolphins? Or paragliding?'

Or looking for rings and wedding venues?

'I meant back to the bank to register you as autonimo for your taxes, or to the office to sort out the ledgers?'

He even makes ledgers sound sexy. I sigh dreamily.

'No,' he says. 'Definitely do not look at me like that. We'll never get anything done otherwise. I'm barely keeping it together as it is.'

Against my better judgement, we get dressed in a fit of girlish giggles as we hunt for our clothes which have been flung about the room. I catch a glimpse of myself reflected in the glass doors leading onto the balcony. My face is radiating bliss and my hair is twice its original size. I can't help but notice that I have a positively sexy aura about me.

I turn to give him a look. It must be smouldering because he growls sexily and grabs me to him, kissing my neck and peeling down my bra straps. 'What did I say about giving me that look?'

Instantly, we are lost in another frenzy of passion. We start kissing again and I am flooded with endorphins that take over my entire brain. Before I know it, my underwear has evaporated against his manly, hot body and we are going at it like rabbits again.

Oliver is definitely one Happy Bunny.

· ♥ · ♥ · ♥ · ♥ · ♥ ·

All the excitement has made Oliver incredibly hungry again. I, of course, am not hungry in the slightest because endorphins have suppressed my appetite. As we walk hand in hand along the promenade back towards my office, it's all

I can do to refrain from skipping. I am trying not to, but I'm smiling as though I've just won the Euromillions jackpot rollover. Oliver has a dewy-eyed look about him too.

'Let's buy lunch for the others before we go back and sort out your business affairs,' he says.

He is EVERY lovely word I can possibly think of.

We stop off to buy crusty sandwiches, crisps and diet sodas to take back to the office.

'Milly-May has agreed to support our marketing for free,' screeches Ava excitedly, as soon as I walk in. She waves her phone at me so that I can see lots of photos of Milly-May in skimpy swimming suits draped uncomfortably over beds, balconies and sun loungers with the hashtag law of attraction hashtag live your best life. It has attracted lots of interest from her many, many followers. 'In exchange for some life coaching from you.'

Not free then. I rise above it. This is a massive coup for us.

I am also over the moon to see Maria-José-Inmaculada-Carmen looking flustered every time she mentions the cute-looking waiter, Alejandro, and the catering requirements.

'Are we all set for tomorrow?' I ask them both. 'Coach? Catering? Clients?'

'Yes, all sorted,' says Ava. 'Plus, re our corporate look… I'll style us so we look on brand, yeah? And we took a few new bookings for you, and Boring Berry rang to say he will need to rearrange tomorrow's session as he has been invited to the bowling club luncheon. He said to pass on a massive thank you, and that he can't wait to tell you all about it.'

In my high state, I actually *am* looking forward to hearing all about Boring Berry's bowling club luncheon.

'And the Zoom lady with the troubles has asked if you can go to their workplace and do something with her terrified men before the Coach Trip,' adds Maria-José-Inmaculada-Carmen proudly.

'Mrs Fanny, the author with writer's block, called to ask if she can interview you,' Ava says, looking impressed. 'After her session with you last week, she's decided to write a novel about a barmy life coach. She sounded super excited.'

Huzzah! Isn't life wonderful? Oliver must surely think that I am a successful life coach in the making. I go to puff out my chest and sing my own praises before stopping myself just in time. I'm happy but not that happy. Not happy enough to turn into my sister. Or worse, my mother.

'And Ryan Reynolds has bought a new house,' she adds enthusiastically. 'I have sent you the link in the email.'

Oliver has the decency not to look my way as Maria-José-Inmaculada-Carmen continues ardently, 'You will LORVE it because he is by the pool, not wearing his....'

'Right... right... yes. Wendy, the Zoom lady. Excellent work, you two. Carry on! CARRY ON!' I yell, grabbing Oliver's hand and whisking him down the hall to my office.

As we munch our way through roast chicken baguettes, happily forgetting, once again, that I am supposed to be vegan at all times now, for the sake of the planet and future generations of poor defenceless children, who will never know the feel of fresh air or sunshine on their innocent freckled cheeks, or clean drinking water for that matter, or fish because there'll be none left, Oliver suggests we log on to the computer to see if we can find the missing financial information.

I have explained that Nidi, what with being heavily pregnant and in a fragile state, must not be contacted by me (with my many problems) again until she returns.

'Oh yes,' I say, tapping away on the keyboard while Oliver sits distractingly close to me. 'It's all here in the Admin and Finance folder. See? I do have a clue what's going on.'

'Excellent,' he says. 'Who would have thought to look in there?'

Cheeky. But so very charming with it.

One click and the folder opens to reveal a ton of mind-boggling documents and files within files with baffling names like *Ledger01.34* and *fiscal.accounts_2023*. My heart sinks.

'The double taxation laws out here require submission across two different fiscal years, so it can be complex,' Oliver says.

I have no fecking idea what he is talking about. But I have noticed a small scar high on his cheek bone. Very mysterious and debonair.

'Yes, that sounds just the sort of timeframe, and the sort of circumstances in which an action such as that payment...' My voice becomes more of a whimper. '... would require that what you are suggesting.'

'Please try to behave yourself,' he pleads. 'Or I'll never be able to concentrate.'

·♥·♥·♥·♥·♥·

It takes him only an hour of tapping away and murmuring *Jesus* under his breath while I stare blankly at the screen, watching him scroll down spreadsheet after spreadsheet, numbers flying past as he deftly unscrambles accounts and sifts out the information he needs. Turns out that Nidi could also do with a masterclass on how to set-up and run a successful life coaching business too.

'Don't beat yourself up,' Oliver says kindly, turning to me and taking in my downcast expression. 'You wouldn't believe how many companies I work with that are in the same sort of mess.'

Charming.

'Just follow what I'm doing, and you'll be able to understand it all, no problem,' he says encouragingly, giving my shoulder a light squeeze with his strong masculine fingers. He's got lovely nail beds.

I really must concentrate on what he is doing and learn from him. After all, I will have to do all of this for myself one day soon. I sit up straight and nod. He is exactly right. It's not so uncommon. Nobody in their right mind likes anything to do with Maths or taxation laws. I must rise to the challenge.

'Now,' he says all business-like, 'that's the taxes sorted and up to date. Let's see where the rest of the money has gone.'

I watch, mesmerised, as he taps away, absorbed in the

task. He has such fine hands. Slender, yet the size of shovels. His arms are like pistons pumping, and his shoulders are solid and dependable. Perfect for crying on. His neck is... how would I describe it... yes, it's resplendant. His jawline is... powerful yet accommodating. His hair is thick and perfectly....

'So, did you get all that?' I hear him ask in that super manly, important voice of his. Another great selling point. I can't help but marvel at why he has not been snapped up already, like a dreamy two-bed penthouse apartment with amazing views across to the sea with access to a luxury pool, gym and easy walking distance to all the amenities *and* all way under budget because the kind owner simply wants it to go to a good home.

He clicks the enter key with a flourish and states, 'What do you think?'

Ah, now well... I think you are gorgeous, that's what I think.

Oliver politely pretends not to notice that I have been so easily distracted from the important task of sorting out my business affairs, to which we both remember me pledging, only moments ago, to give my complete and full attention. He probably has a photographic memory and can recall the tiniest of details about what people say and about every aspect of the law, which he will know everything about of course. While I've been busy dreaming of licking Oliver's thighs, and thinking of inventive ways to entertain him.

He stands up and stretches, giving me a cheeky glimpse of a bare, flat stomach. He is a wondrous specimen of masculinity and I am behaving shamefully, even by my own low standards.

'Well, that's all I can do for today,' he says leaning across to kiss me. 'See you tomorrow?'

I nod enthusiastically, not trusting myself to speak as I watch him walk away.

I. AM. SMITTEN.

Chapter 38

'It feels like yesterday that we were being hurled around in that campervan,' Oliver says as he drives me in his incredibly fancy car, up through the forests towards the retreat. 'I'm a bit nervous about seeing Endless Cloud and Starbeam Night Sky, are you?'

I nod, not looking forward to it one little bit. 'I owe them a proper apology for being such a hot mess. I hope they forgive us and agree to do the event.' I glance over my shoulder to the peace offering Oliver and I picked up for them. Wine, cheese and a bunch of dried sage tied neatly with a ribbon and little card saying 'sorry'.

'I was as bad as you,' Oliver says. 'Maybe we should come back here for a few days. I hear they do a resentment cleanse.' Oliver does a mock-chortle.

He is referring to his board of wankers. It has not been a clean break and may be ongoing for some time.

'Don't worry. I'll help you resolve those issues and build your new company into something you can feel really proud of,' I reassure him.

'Looking forward to it.' He turns to give me a grateful

smile. 'Sorry, I might not make the coach trip tomorrow. I'm needed to sign papers in Madrid.' He looks genuinely gutted. 'So, tell me all about this app idea of yours.'

Oh dear. He has opened the floodgates.

'It's a new life-coaching service aimed at bite-sized sessions for people who want a healthier existence either at work or in their personal lives. The app will keep clients on track, keep them inspired and also to make it super easy to book another session, either online or face to face,' I gush while he's navigating the hairpin bends. 'We've called it *The Law of Attraction – how to get everything you want.*'

'I'm feeling the Law of Attraction right now,' Oliver says, swinging in through the retreat gates, causing the temperature in the car to rise substantially.

'Do please behave professionally,' I reprimand jokily, as we walk to reception with the gift bags. 'After all, they don't know we are a coup... erm, I mean acquaintences in a professional capacity.'

Gaaah! I almost said a couple. I stop myself in time. I'd hate for Oliver to think I'm jumping ahead. After all, he did once refer to us as 'fooling around'.

Oliver's smile leaves his face as he gently takes my hand. 'I'm sorry I ever referred to us as fooling around. I panicked. I wanted to see you, and I came over as obnoxious.'

'Oh, thank God for that,' I say, grinning. 'You were beginning to become unbearably perfect.'

Oliver's eyes widen with mischief. It's as though I can't say a single thing without arousing him. I have never felt more desirable in my life. It's thrilling. He leans down to kiss me, slowly sliding his lips over mine. It has the effect of a sugar-rush and has me tingling from top to toe.

'Aah, vee knew you two vud be couple. Lovely couple,' Endless Cloud greets us, floating with open arms over to where we are standing.

'Yah, favourite naughty couple,' agrees Gandalf, wafting in through the patio doors. 'Feel zee energies. Beautiful energies you have. Powerful aura.'

I am somewhat taken aback as to why they are not annoyed with me.

'Anger doesn't solve anyzing but it can destroy everyzing,' Gandalf says, reading my mind. 'Now come. Vee are werry excited to do this event tomorrow. But first, vot are your thoughts on doing a communal scream ven your clients arrive? Then vee do group psychic handshake.'

They both look stoned off their tits.

· ♥ · ♥ · ♥ · ♥ · ♥ ·

The following day, I spot Boring Berry cowering alone in the far corner of the office, having turned up two hours early, and cannot resist. I go over, grabbing Juniper on route.

'Juniper, I'd like you to meet Berry. Juniper, Berry. Berry, Juniper.'

Honestly, if that's not a match made in Heaven what is?

I leave them after a few moments when they latch on to beetroot as a secure topic of conversation, and make my way, meeting and greeting across the room.

I spot Mrs Fanny, the author, chatting to Wendy, the nice

Zoom lady, who has brought all of her menfellas along. They are mingling with the Welsh Rugby team who have come along on the last day of their 'bonding' holiday to make it look like they haven't just spent it boozing.

And from what I can see, Squinty, the captain, has taken a real shine to Wendy. She is positively glowing, and he appears to be taking her number. I think we may have just made our first perfect match.

There is much excitement in the room.

Mrs Fanny yells, 'Nell!' as if she hasn't seen me for years. Then she swings me around to face her husband. 'This is Nell!'

His eyes balloon, 'I tried the lot,' he says. 'The vagina-scented candles, the herbs, the crystals, and you'll never guess what?' he booms across the small crowd of potential new clients I had been hoping to impress with a good first impression. 'I've never slept so well in all my life! At first, I thought this is mental, a right con, hippy codswallop. But it turns out it's not!'

God how embarrassing! And yet I simply cannot resist adding fuel to the fire.

'Yes, Mr Fanny, the soothing, metaphysical properties of howlite release enough energy to help insomnia and reduce anxiety. Although, it's more of a *stone* not a crystal,' I correct him unnecessarily.

'See?' Mrs Fanny shrieks to her husband, 'What did I tell you?'

I'm not sure what she is insinuating but it's time to get on the coach.

'Wait for us!'

I turn to see the Hens charging down the street. The group has doubled in size.

'We invited all of our Hen activity people. They are all entrepreneurs and single!'

There's a huge cheer from the rugger boys as they pile onto the coach. I learn that one is a mixologist. There's a naked waiter business. A few beauticians. A few tarot card specialists. Some water sports people. And generally, lots of creative, enthusiastic small business-owners.

Once everyone is on board and seated, I walk up and down the aisle counting heads and ticking names off the guest list. The buzz is incredible.

Jiff Livison is deep in conversation with the IT guy, Max. Jiff has turned up in an outfit that can only be described as thought-provoking (jaunty, yellow, double denim) but they seem to be getting on extremely well. Max has come dressed as a washed-up porn star. His top has a very low V at the front, and he has had the courage to team this with a beaded necklace and a matching beaded bracelet. Even though he is very clearly not a Maori nor an Indian spirit healer.

'No woman ever said *ooh I love a man in crocs*,' Ava whispers in my ear. 'They are clearly meant for each other.'

My eyes swing from the foam clogs to the pair of battered espadrilles that Jiff is sporting. I overhear Jiff discussing business opportunities with Max who says he is a business development consultant. They are getting on very well. So well, in fact, they are going on a date. I could have sworn that Max worked in IT. Come to think of it, I almost *accused* him of working in IT. And *insisted* that he get a *girl*friend.

I stop to apologise, and they are quick to forgive. 'I hope you two manage to find love this evening,' I say, causing them both to blush profusely. 'I mean, I hope you find the Law of Attraction works for you.' Again, I have created an awkward pause and slide away.

·♥·♥·♥·♥·♥·

On arrival at the retreat, Maria-José-Inmaculada-Carmen's mother rushes up to her daughter, holding her face in her hands. She is clearly bursting with pride. Thankfully Maria-José-Inmaculada-Carmen is taking all the fuss with good grace. The love between the pair of them is almost palpable. I notice Ava is also watching this exchange of motherly love with a sad look on her face.

'I invited our parents,' I say, watching Ava's face fall in disbelief as she turns to find them in the crowd.

'What the actual fuck?' She is not happy when she spots them walking through the door.

I make my way over to the entrance, a wide smile on my face. Admittedly it's a bit awkward, but I'm going to slice right through it with some top coaching. I'm getting my own house in order and I'm moving onwards and upwards. I've never felt more determined in my whole life. Plus, it's nearly speech time and I need to get this over with as quickly as possible.

'Listen, before you both say anything, I just want to

apologise for the way I have behaved,' I say to my parents, stopping them in their tracks. 'I handled it all terribly, and I very much appreciate the space you've given me to work things out. I feel much, much better now. Sorry it has taken me so long to realise it. And of course, thanks for allowing me to stay at the villa.'

I envelop them both in a huge hug. They cannot believe it. Both parents have mouths hanging open.

Ava scuttles over.

'What are you two doing here?' she blurts rudely.

'Good to see you too,' my mother says stiffly. I notice she and Ava bristle. Dad gives me a look and a tiny eye roll. My hunch was right. I knew she was hiding something. I beckon them over to the Serenity fountain. Dad is positively beaming. He takes me to one side, leans in and whispers, 'I'm so relieved to see that you're much happier than when I last saw you. Has your sister been behaving herself?'

I give him a big hug. I'll just keep it simple because for one, he's a man and two, it would be awkward to tell him that the root of all our family problems, may lie with him just sitting back and doing nothing, while our mother pitted me and Ava against each other to live out her own delusional fantasy, resulting in none of us getting what we really wanted out of life or our relationships. Ava, Mum and I need to spend time together and be rid of this 'thing', this wedge, that we have allowed to build up.

'I think your mother is still annoyed at Ava for leaving her job like that,' Dad says nodding in their direction.

Glancing over, we see them locked in heated discussion.

'Wait, what do you mean? I thought Ava had been made redundant.'

Dad shakes his head, 'That's what she told your mother initially, but we soon found out. It's such a small town and I mean, it was a great job, she used to manage over two...'

'Yes, yes, I know, I know....' I politely cut him off. I quickly tap my third eye and my inner wrists. I close my eyes and rub my temples, letting out a low rumble of sound for a count of five. Dad is looking at me aghast. 'I'm perfectly fine Dad, but are you saying that Ava threw away her career, and followed me to Spain to try and repair our relationship?'

'From what I can see it's all she has ever wanted. To be close to her big sister,' my father says looking at me. 'She has followed you around her whole life, Nell. Always trying to get your attention. Mind, she can be bloody annoying at times, just like your mother, but the intentions are genuine. She had a whole surprise organised for your birthday. She wanted us all to pretend we'd forgotten, and then when she found out you'd left home she was very upset. I had to eat a whole cheesecake, and your mother had to drink all the champagne.'

If this is true, then it has been me who has been too pig-headed to see it. I look over at Ava, just as she looks over to me. As our eyes connect, we share a brief moment of understanding.

'Come on Dad,' I say and walk him over to where our mother is standing with a pinched face.

'Ava, can I borrow you for a minute, please?'

I call Maria-José-Inmaculada-Carmen over. It's time.

'Thank you so much for all the effort you've both put in to organising this event,' I say to them. Maria-José-Inmaculada-Carmen gushes about how her family keep saying how proud of her they are. Ava looks a bit sulky that I never told her our parents were coming and, quite rightly, doesn't believe me when I say I thought it would be a nice surprise for her, and that surely, she must miss them terribly. I ignore her protests when she argues that it's only been two weeks since she last saw them.

After a few minutes, the background music that has been playing is turned down and suddenly all eyes are on me, standing on a small podium. It's time to put my life coach face on. I'm a million miles from the fake who spends her days googling Ryan Reynolds instead of facing up to what she should be doing.

For a second, nerves get the better of me and I want to run away.

Then I see Ava and Maria-José-Inmaculada-Carmen looking up at me. Their faces are beaming.

Ava gives me the thumbs up and mouths, 'You've got this.'

I take a huge breath in.

It's time to shine.

Chapter 39

'To coach is a privilege. The opportunity to help someone help themselves is one of the most rewarding things that we can do for each other. Some people want to change their lives to pursue a life's dream, or sometimes they want to have a better relationship with a family member or friend.'

I pause to sweep my eyes across the small crowd.

'For some the goals are personal and for some the goals are business-driven. One thing, that each of us here today has in common is that we all want to see what the best version of ourselves is capable of. How high we can fly. How daring and brave we can be. How successful we can become. My team and I,' I stop to smile at the faces shining up at me, 'can help you create the life you want. We are dedicated to making sure you achieve what you set out to do. Nidi and I will be leading the coaching for business for those of you who would like to be more productive in the workplace or challenge yourself to a new career. Ava is our new Social Media coach to help you bring balance to your 'on and offline' worlds. And Maria-José-Inmaculada-Carmen is our Wellbeing coach, offering yoga and holistic solutions for those wanting to adopt planet-friendly lifestyle choices.'

There follows an almighty thunderous cheer as Maria-José-Inmaculada-Carmen's whole family erupt at the mention of her name. She looks like she will burst with pride. I see she is making eye contact with Alejandro, who is grinning back at her. 'And for this we are partnering with our favourite local retreat and hosts for this evening, Endless Cloud and Starbeam Night Sky.'

Both warlocks begin wafting their robes, humming loudly, 'Shanti, shanti. Shanti, von wibe von tribe,' ending in a piercing ding from the gong hanging around Endless Cloud's neck.

There's an odd beat of silence as we all watch with no idea how to react. Suddenly, the whole place erupts with applause.

Ava helps me off the podium as I am wearing ridiculously high heels and a very tight dress.

That was exhilarating. I feel high. That nervous energy from before, has turned to adrenalin and relief, and is coursing through my veins. I immediately wish that Oliver was here to share this moment. Flustered, my eyes dart around the room for him. I would definitely have noticed if he'd arrived. I've developed a real a sixth sense over the last few weeks. A nose for these things. Butterflies run amok in my stomach. I've really missed him. I've thought about him non-stop since the minute he left yesterday.

Then our eyes meet. Across a crowded room! Just like they are supposed to meet. He literally takes my breath away. Within seconds he has muscled his way towards me and is picking me up in his beefy arms to swing me round.

'Great speech! I've missed you. You look amazing.'

And he takes my face in his hands. I can tell he likes this new me. This at peace, confident, positive, much better version of myself, me. He kisses the life out of me and when we come up for air, he gives me a wicked look and comes in for another. He really has missed me.

Life is good. Life is like this kiss, full of promise and the unexpected. Although, I'm not sure how professional I am being, snogging in front of clients like this.

Oh My God. My parents!

I swiftly pull out of the embrace and swivel around to the crowd. Most people are busy playing the Psychic Handshake activity to have noticed me breaking rule number four and seven, but I notice too late, my mother making a beeline for me through the crowd. She's got the look of a lion eyeing up a gazelle. Her face has wedding bells and grandchildren written all over it. My dad is scuttling behind and Ava, who is nearby watching my mother approach, is howling with laughter.

Feck, how embarrassing!

I must make absolutely certain that my parents understand that Oliver and I have only just started dating, and not to jump ahead of themselves (I am totally determined to become Mrs Reynolds if it's the last thing I do).

I quickly assure Oliver that my parents will not under *any* circumstances read anything in to the kiss they have just witnessed (my mother will be searching for wedding venues and dresses by the end of the week) and that as parents, they are very chilled and laid back in such situations (my father has always dreamed of having a son, especially one so accomplished who can both help him with his taxes *AND* defend him in a court of law should the need ever arise).

'It's okay. I can handle them,' Oliver says, straightening to his full height.

He's borderline heroic.

· ♥ · ♥ · ♥ · ♥ · ♥ ·

At the end of the evening, the event having been a success and the coach having dropped us all back at the office, Oliver walks with us to the villa and politely answers my mother's intrusive questions. Mothers!

My father gushes like crazy about me and Ava working together and building a business. 'I think you strong, independent, courageous women will do wonderful things together. I'm very proud of you both.'

My mother coughs, 'Me too. Me too. Very proud of you *both.*' She flicks me an embarrassed smile.

And like a gentleman, Oliver declines the invitation of a nightcap, much to my father's relief.

I have a flashback to the last time Oliver came to the villa. Him heaving two unconscious women over the threshold, and me trying to get him to take all of his clothes off and skinny dip in the pool with me.

Me and Ava share a secret look and have to stifle our giggles. Oliver might well be a bit upset with her over his ruined car and the defamation of character. But the truth still remains, that he is a complete and utter fanny magnet.

Then, while the others politely walk ahead to the door, me and Oliver lock lips like teenagers at the gate. He cups my face gently, tipping it to the side so that he can kiss my neck. Shivers run down my entire body with each tantilising touch. He kisses the other side which has me melting into liquid gold before his lips slide softly back to mine.

'I could kiss you all night,' he whispers. I feel exactly the same way. My every molecule is on fire with excitement.

When he finally leaves, because our lips are getting sore, I go into the villa to have hot chocolate and cookies - because my mother still thinks we are twelve. It is a lovely family moment. Our parents are clearly overjoyed.

I'm even in such a good mood that I allow Ava to share my room.

As we change into our pyjamas, I poke Ava gently, 'I'm sorry I've been such a dickhead over the redundancy thing. I'm sure you wouldn't have been able to do much about it.'

'No, I'm the one who is sorry. I've been a complete prick. I never should have been so awful to you at work. I'm mortified at how I went on. I think I was just power-crazed and a bit jealous. Then Karen became like this dictator, and I basically had to do as I was told. She didn't want to be seen doing any of the dirty work, so it was left to me. That's no excuse for how I behaved, especially not to you.'

'Jealous? Jealous of me?' This can't be right, surely?

'Well, you always seem so together and focussed and good at what you do. University degree, good job and Dad always saying how great you are...'

'Only to make up for how much praise Mum heaps on you all of the time.'

'And that's another thing I've always hated. She makes everything into a competition between us and I'm sick of it!'

'Me too,' I sigh. 'Is that why you quit your job?'

We contemplate the weight of what we have just said to each other. All that time wasted not getting on.

'How about we start again, eh? Nelly-Belly?'

'On one condition, ABBA,' I smile back. 'You stop banging on about how you used to manage over TWO HUNDRED fecking people!'

'Don't forget it was across TEN REGIONAL offices though!'

Laughing, we make our way into the kitchen to see Dad working the coffee machine and our mother reorganising the fridge.

'Who keeps asparagus in the salad drawer? It's clearly a vegetable, for which there is a separate drawer. And who doesn't put eggs in the egg tray? I mean that's what it is for, for heaven's sake. And who on earth puts milk lying down? It needs to stand up straight in the front compartment. And who puts ham on the top shelf and chicken below instead of creating a separate meat section... don't get me started on the cheeses! Gordon, look at where they've put the cheeses.'

Ava shoots me a knowing look and has the good grace to look ashamed of herself. We both giggle.

Our father, emotional at the sight of us getting on, disappears behind the Costa Blanca newspaper. It has been far too long since me and my sister laughed together. Far too long.

'So, when are you two coming back home?' my mother questions, instantly killing the mood. 'You can do all of this Life Mentoring stuff from England surely. I'll make both the rooms up. I've already redecorated yours, Nell, ready for you. All neutrals with a splash of Elephant's Breath. You'll love it.'

Ava and I look at each other.

'We'll be staying out here in Spain, Mum. This is our home now, and besides we have a business to run,' I look at Ava and add, 'together.'

'Nonsense the pair of you. You'll both come home and live with us, as usual.'

'Mum, listen...'

'No you listen. You've had your bit fun, now it's time to grow up. You're just being ridiculous. You are both coming home, and that's the end of it.'

My heart plummets. Not this again. A feeling of self-doubt floods through me.

'No, they won't,' barks Dad, putting his foot down from behind the newspaper. 'They are grown women with minds of their own, a business to run and a perfectly good home here in Spain to live in. Leave them to get on with their lives and stop bloody interfering.'

Ava and I watch, as our mother opens her mouth to say something, then shuts it, then opens it again, then shuts it. She takes a good moment to look at each of us in turn. After a hefty silence, a sad realisation sweeps across her face.

'Well, I... if that's what you really want, then I suppose... I suppose I'll just have to let you get on with it.'

Oh my fucking God, did she just agree to do as she was told?

She receives a curt nod from Dad who flicks his paper back up to hide his face. The conversation is closed. Finally! Finally, some balance has been restored. Perhaps now our mother will be more respectful of our decisions and treat us as grown-ups, as equals, and, more importantly, she might leave her controlling ways behind.

'But you must promise to include me in all the wedding preparations, Nell.'

'But we've literally only been on one date.'

'It has to be in England of course, otherwise we'll never hear the end of it. And you couldn't do any better than Longley Hall, I hear they do a marvellous spread and, of course, we'll have to invite all of Mrs Robson's lot from next door. Her daughter eloped you know. It was quite the embarrassment. Wanted only *their* friends at it. I'll not be having that.'

'Mum, you've *just* promised us all that you won't interfere,' Ava reminds her. We exchange perplexed looks as our mother carries on as though neither of us are audible. Dad remains hidden behind the paper. *Really. Are we all just going to let this go?*

'And we'll have it in Springtime. I've always loved a Spring wedding. I look great in a hat, don't I, Gordon? GORDON, don't I? And we'll hire the wedding cars and marquee from... I do hope it doesn't rain. Maybe I should have it in summer, just to be on the safe side, and perhaps indoors. I'll still wear green, then I'm covered for both seasons and all weathers. I suit green, don't I, Gordon? GORDON? Are you even listening?'

Christ alive but she's annoying at times.

Ava leans towards me, 'Fuck. I'm just like Mum, aren't I?'

'Yes, yes you are.' I smile at her. 'Un-*fucking*-bearably so. But don't worry, I know a good life coach who can sort you out.'

Ava gives me a tight hug. 'I love you.'

'Okay, I'm off to bed,' I say, peeling her off me. 'Right after I Google what Ryan says his secret for a happy and lasting relationship is.'

The End

Acknowledgments

So many writer and reader friends helped me get this book to publication. Huge thanks to all of them. I'd like to thank my editor, Nira Begum, for her brilliant support and all the lovely women writers at CWIP. All at Curtis Brown Creative for their support and encouragement during the many, many writing courses that taught me about three-act structures, POVs and how to save a cat.

Last but not least, my awesome and talented writing tribe, beta readers and cheerleaders: Jayne, Jess, Julia, Farrah, Cristal, Amanda, Sid, Nicky, Nichelle, Kim, Keith, Claire, Cara, Joanna, John, Sophie, Wez, Helen, Deb, Genize, Shauna, Mrs B, Mags, Paula, Maria, Shelley, Janine and my sister Philippa who read all the terrible first drafts and encourage me to keep going.

I have enormous respect for anyone who sets out to write a book and gets to the end without wanting to hurl themselves off the nearest cliff. Be nice to writers – we are ALL in varying states of emotional collapse.

About the Author

Jo Lyons spent years working in Turkey as a holiday rep, in the Alpes at a ski resort, in the south of France at a vineyard (trying not to put them out of business) before eventually ending up in Spain as a teacher. She thought she'd put her fairly adequate skills of 'getting on with people' to global good use, but on her way to The Hague, she became terribly distracted by a DJ and motherhood. Twenty of her best, frozen-foreheaded years flew by before she suddenly remembered her previous ambition for world peace and politics... oh yes, and to write a book.

You can sign up to her newsletter and visit her website at

www.jolyonsauthor.com
Twitter: @J0Lyons
Instagram: @Hinnywhowrites

Nice Reviews

"Jo Lyons has written a book and it's hilarious!"
Jenny Colgan, The Summer Skies
"Couldn't put it down!"
"I stayed up half the night to finish it."
"So warm-hearted and uplifting. I loved this book so much."
"Best debut I've read in a long time."

If you have enjoyed reading this novel, please leave me a review on Amazon or on your social media. I love to hear your thoughts and it helps new readers discover my books. Happy Reading!

Benidorm, actually

"Ladies and Gentlemen, we will shortly be arriving in Alicante. Please ensure your big lips and heavy eyebrows are securely fastened, your eyelashes are stowed in the upright position and your leg tattoos are clearly visible for landing."

Connie Cooper's classical music career is at a dead-end. She's singing cheap covers to a sea of bald heads and the nearest she has been to a romantic relationship in years is watching the Bridgerton buttocks scene on a continuous loop. The last thing she needs is a flight to Benidorm to keep up with support band, The Dollz, the flashmob dancing, going out in less than you'd wear on the beach and their obsession with the promiscuous bearded-Nuns next door. The clock is ticking. She's meant to be finding her voice, not finding the brooding good-looks of the music boss irresistibly attractive...

Printed in Great Britain
by Amazon